Trevor Edwards grew up on a council estate in east London in the 1960-70s. After university, he joined the RAF as a Regiment Officer and lost all of his toes to trench foot during a training exercise. He still managed to pass pilot selection and subsequently completed flying training and was posted onto the Jaguar. He left the RAF after 12 years and is currently flying big aircraft for an airline based at Heathrow.

In Memory of

Tom Barrett
Bill Auckland
Mike Auckland
Roger Crowder
Steve Shutt
John Mardon
Simon Burgess
Jack London
Guy Bancroft-Wilson
Mike Sears

All gone too soon.

Trevor Edwards

AVERAGE: A TRAINING DIARY

AUSTIN MACAULEY PUBLISHERS™

LONDON ★ CAMBRIDGE ★ NEW YORK ★ SHARJAH

A CIP catalogue record for this title is available from the British Library.

ISBN 9781528987479 (Paperback)
ISBN 9781528987486 (ePub e-book)

www.austinmacauley.com

First Published (2021)
Austin Macauley Publishers Ltd
25 Canada Square
Canary Wharf
London
E14 5LQ

Why a Diary?

I joined the Royal Air Force in 1985 after finishing university, where I had studied to become a geologist. My initial plan was to do something different for a few years before settling down to a career in geology, and I signed up for a six-year commission in the RAF as a Regiment officer. The Regiment is tasked with defending RAF airfields and its soldiers can best be described as the infantry of the air force. As long as I could remember, I have had an interest in aviation and I thought that the RAF would be sufficiently different and challenging to have six fun years.

During my initial officer training, it became obvious that the best job in the RAF without doubt was that of a pilot. Everyone else was there purely to ensure that the pilots got airborne. I had always thought that becoming a pilot was unachievable for someone like me, but the more I learnt, the more I realised that the difficulties of the selection procedure were very much alleviated by knowing how the system worked.

I am a black man who grew up on a housing estate in southeast London, and I had no idea of how the RAF selected its pilots. I assumed that all fighter pilots were public school educated, quick-witted Caucasian males who were amazing sportsmen and had private incomes. The young men who were destined to start flying training on my initial officers' course did not fit that bill. The more I saw of them, the more I realised that they were no different to me. Normally, getting a transfer out of the RAF Regiment and on to a flying training course was almost impossible. But I was to be lucky, or perhaps unlucky. I will let you decide. Once, initial officer training was completed, I had to endure the RAF Regiment infantry course, which for me was a nightmare from the beginning to end: six months of brutality that culminated in my feet becoming severely frostbitten. The result of spending the majority of a ten-day field exercise, standing in a muddy trench in an army training ground in the north of England during freezing conditions.

At the conclusion of the exercise, I was taken to the nearby military hospital in a lot of pain by a couple of fellow trainees and was immediately admitted with toes that were starting to become gangrenous.

Despite the best efforts of the medical staff, they could not stop the gangrene from spreading and to save the rest of my feet, all 10 of my toes were amputated. At the time, I considered myself very fortunate to get away with such a small loss.

Several extra operations were then needed to apply skin grafts and tidy up the wounds. In a matter of weeks, I found myself at the Service Rehabilitation

Centre at RAF Headley Court, which is just to the south of London. There was no chance of sitting around feeling sorry for oneself at Headley Court. They had me out of crutches and passing the army fitness test in three months. Quite amazing, as some of the medics at the hospital didn't think I would ever walk again.

During my rehabilitation at Headley, I started dating a London girl called Shirley, and was constantly recounting funny and sometimes shocking stories about the characters and situations I had experienced on the RAF Regiment course. Shirley suggested that if I were ever on another RAF course, I should write a diary.

At the time, I didn't imagine there would be any chance of that happening as I was technically disabled, but I met two people at RAF Headley Court who helped me think otherwise. The first was a Tornado wing commander who had ejected from his aircraft and had suffered a bad back injury. I cannot remember his name, but he told me that having no toes would be no detriment to successfully completing flying training. The second was a University Air Squadron pilot called Barry McKenna, who was recovering from almost total paralysis caused by a weird viral infection.

Barry managed to convince his squadron at Bristol University to give me a few hours flying in exchange for some pyrotechnics that I acquired from my RAF Regiment contacts. The flying instructors at Bristol were very generous and I was allowed to have 10 hours instructed flying, at the end of which they wrote me a very good report and sent that to the pilot selection board. Because of that report, I was allowed to take the pilot aptitude tests, and due to my recent flying experience, I passed them with a high score. The only obstacle remaining was the medical department. They were surprisingly little trouble. I had already demonstrated that I could control an aircraft and I had passed the Army fitness test, so as far as they were concerned, I was fit to fly, although strangely, medically unfit to continue employment as an RAF Regiment officer. The end result was a position on a flying training course where this diary starts.

So, this is the tale of my training to become a Royal Air Force fighter pilot. It was a journey I honestly didn't think I had the slightest chance of completing. Tens of thousands apply each year, a few hundred are selected to start the three-year course and of those, only one in five qualifies as a fighter pilot. I thought I would give the course my best effort and try to get solo in an aircraft. This diary is also a record of all the ridiculous things that happen when you put a group of young men through a very stressful three-year professional course.

Elementary

No. 28 Elementary Flying Course,
RAF Swinderby,
Lincolnshire,
1988

Global politics has, of course, a direct effect on how a nation shapes its military capabilities. In 1988, when I took my elementary flying course, Margaret Thatcher had been re-elected as Prime Minister of the UK for the third time, Ronald Reagan was the President of the United States and Mikhail Gorbachev was the leader of the Soviet Union. At that time, the primary role of the RAF was to help defend Europe against potential attack by the Soviet Union. To that end, many RAF squadrons were based in West Germany. The RAF contained 80,000 personnel and was training about 300 pilots a year.

The elementary flying course was four months long and was designed specifically for officers with no, or very little, flying experience. These officers were mostly young men who had joined the RAF straight from school.

Monday 25 April

Day one of flying training and at the beginning of the day, I thought I was back in the RAF regiment. All the members of my course had letters in their rooms when they arrived at RAF Swinderby the previous night. The letters stated that we had to be up and ready for a physical assessment at 6am to be followed by a chat with the station padre at 7am and then report to the squadron at 8am. It sounded like a standard manic RAF regiment morning and I had hoped that flying training would be different.

At the appointed time, we were met on the station sports fields by an angry physical training (PT) corporal. He ran us around the field for an hour while making us do star jumps, squat thrusts and press-ups. He was completely without mercy. There were lots of standard PT instructor's comments, such as 'it's only mind over matter: I don't mind and you don't matter', and everyone was being called Mr in a very condescending tone. As the instructor departed, we were treated to a seemingly endless tirade on how disappointed he was in our performance, how he would expect more from pilot wannabes fresh out of officer training and how we would be seeing a lot more of him during our stay at RAF Swinderby. It could have been day one of regiment training, and I was starting to have flashbacks.

Then there was a mad dash to get showered and changed for an unbelievable meeting with *TWO* padres. They sat us in a circle and made us read passages from the Bible and sing a couple of hymns. The whole thing was more than a little weird. I swear we were very close to holding hands and singing *Kum ba yah*.

It turned out all of this was a practical joke. Thank God! The PT corporal was a senior course member, and the padres were a couple of station officers. Every course gets the same treatment, and I am just glad that it wasn't a standard morning.

There are five guys on my course: Pete Coville, a tall young man who is very keen and has lots of bright ideas (his father is a senior officer and pilot); Tony Shopman, a short, slightly overweight Welsh man who used to be an engineer officer (he is talking too much already); Mark Harris and Adrian – known as Reg – Armeanu, are both young men straight from sixth form, and myself, the 24-year-old ex-infantry officer. As I am the most senior man on the course by a long way, I have been given the position of course leader.

There is only one flying squadron at RAF Swinderby, and a new course starts about every four weeks. The guys on these courses seem a fairly decent bunch, on average only nineteen or twenty years old. Unfortunately, this youthfulness is reflected in their behaviour. It was like a kindergarten in the crew room at times today. I hope this isn't infectious.

I was starting to feel like an old man with all these youngsters about. That was until we met our instructors. They are all in their 40s and 50s. Not quite smelling of pee yet, but the Zimmer frames can't be too far off.

The biggest shock of the day arrived in the shape of the Chipmunk MkT10, the aircraft we are going to be flying. These machines first flew in 1946, their engines are started using shotgun cartridges, they leak oil and fuel and they've got canvas-covered wings. Canvas covered wings! I have spent most of the last year running around in armoured vehicles using some fairly modern equipment, and now I'm going to fly a machine as old as my grandfather, with instructors and technology to match.

The rest of the day was taken up with form filling (in triplicate); getting numerous bits of flying kit; having briefings from various station officers on our non-flying duties and getting to know where everything is on the station. After dinner, I had a quick drink in the bar and then got my head in my books for an hour or so. There is every possibility that I could be airborne tomorrow and I want to have a rough idea of what is going to happen.

The Chipmunk is a two-seat aircraft with a tandem layout of cockpits: the student pilot in the front seat and the instructor in the rear. On our course, pilots wore flying suits, which are one-piece outfits with a zip up the front, a compartment for maps at the knees and a host of useful pockets. The flying kit was completed with a tightly fitting helmet with integral headphone and microphones, and a parachute, which doubled as a seat cushion. Just like the Spitfire pilots in the Second World War.

Tuesday 26 April

Every day on the squadron starts with a meteorological, or met, brief. A student pilot who has completed the meteorological phase of ground school gives each brief. This is similar to the local area forecast given at the end of the television news, but in much more detail. I didn't understand most of it today, however, I guess that is what the met ground school and exams are for. Sooner or later, we will all have to give the met brief.

I spent some time sitting in the Chipmunk and started learning the various drills and procedures. These are called checks, and they have to be memorised. There was no flying today so as well as starting to memorise our checks, we collected the rest of our flying kit.

We also had a standard mile-and-a-half RAF fitness run with a real physical training instructor. This one was respectful and encouraging. He gave us the route to run and set us off. Pete Coville was at the front as he is a bit of a whippet, but he made a wrong turn and like lemmings, we all followed. This diversion added a good distance to the run, and we failed to complete it in the time allowed. We will have to do it again. The boys aren't happy.

I am not sure why, it is only one and a half miles, the wimps.

Our loud Welshman, Shoppo as he likes to be called, is getting noticed already. He managed to annoy the other courses, so the other students pinned him down, strapped his legs together, doused his boots in methylated spirits and burnt his shoelaces. It seems that this is standard procedure when they get fed up with loud children in this kindergarten. Shoppo initially had no idea what the senior guys were going to do and only really started struggling when the matches came out. Our course looked on with more than a little apprehension until it became clear that normally there is no body damage. Methylated spirits evaporates almost as quickly as it burns and the fire is quickly self-extinguished. Nevertheless, you are on fire, and I think I would react a bit more aggressively than Shoppo if anyone tried that with me.

None of my course was due to fly today so we were sent home early. This is called stacking. We were stacked after lunch, so had more time to learn checks and do a bit of the course work.

Each major RAF station has a meteorological office staffed by qualified meteorologists. The students delivering the morning met briefs get all their information from these met men.

Wednesday 27 April

There was no flying for anyone on the station today, but we had a few briefings on our first flights and continued learning our checks. Reg Armeanu and I covered our local maps in Fablon. This is a clear plastic product with one adhesive side, and we use it to make our maps waterproof. It's not easy sticking the maps to the Fablon without leaving big air bubbles. It needs two people and a very steady hand. Anything written on the maps can now be removed with methylated spirits so the maps can be used over and over again. There have been quite a few burnings, mostly in the students' crew room out of sight of the instructors. I think the boys are bored by the lack of flying. Everyone on my course was being sensible and biting their tongues. Except for Shoppo. He is still loud, and will have problems unless he changes his attitude. This evening, a female officer joined us in the bar and we discovered that Shoppo has no idea about women either. I am no expert, but I am not too sure the macho thing he does is the most effective method of getting attention.

Thursday 28 April

Had my first flight today, and I was very uneasy walking out to the aircraft. I was going to fly in an old machine with canvas wings and I still wasn't sure if I would be a half decent pilot or even if I would enjoy it. Flight Lieutenant (Flt Lt) Minards was my instructor. He seems nice enough although he is an older man in his 50s.

We started the aircraft, taxied around the airfield and got airborne. I flew the aircraft myself for a bit and saw the local landmarks. It was amazing being in the air again and seeing the world from above, but I didn't have total faith in my machine. Those canvas wings just don't seem right. I felt a bit unwell, so didn't ask to do any aerobatics. It isn't unusual for new pilots to feel unwell during their initial flights – the motion of the aircraft can take a little while to get used to.

My flight was the first thing this morning in the so-called first wave. There are four waves during the day, two in the morning and two in the afternoon. The flying programme is constructed the night before, so we all have a rough idea of what we will be doing the next day and can get prepared. However, it is dependent on the weather, so the programme changes constantly.

Pete Coville also got airborne and attempted a landing; Shoppo did some aerobatics on his flight and Mark Harris also had his first flight, with the station commander as his instructor. The weather in the afternoon was poor, so I spent some time chatting to Flt Lt Minards, who is going to be my primary instructor. I think we will get on well. He has given me lots of useful tips on learning the checks and how best to approach the course.

Most of the student pilots at Swinderby were Pilot Officers or Flying Officers, the two lowest ranks of officers in the RAF. The instructors were all flight lieutenants or squadron leaders, and as a mark of respect, we addressed them by their ranks. First names were not used when talking to a more senior officer.

Tuesday 3 May

The start of week two and I have spent a lot of the weekend learning checks. Anything we do in the cockpit has a set procedure. Every time we get into the aircraft, each dial, gauge and switch has to be checked, and at the moment this can take some time. Then we carry out the procedure to start the engine, move switches, twist knobs etc., and this also has to be memorised. I haven't even looked at the emergency procedures yet. There is a lot of stuff to commit to memory.

Airborne again this morning, and the flight went very well: I was in control for 40 per cent of the time and had no major problems. For the first time, I was enjoying myself in the air – I think I can do this.

I am feeling like the old man of the course. Mark Harris was describing his weekend, which was along the lines of got drunk, chased women, got drunk, chased women. The boys asked what I got up to in London, which was a bit of DIY, sorting out a mortgage and starting to look for a car. May as well have been talking another language. No one else has got a serious girlfriend, and house buying hasn't even crossed their alcohol and testosterone saturated minds.

Shoppo has a new car, an Audi 100 CD. Everyone agrees it is very nice but far too big. The thing is enormous, with leather seats and lots of gadgets. It's a proper executive car. Not for me, until I'm maybe 40-plus. At the moment, small and fast is the order of the day, and the rest of the boys agree.

Wore a loud red tie to dinner and everyone thought it quite hideous. It is my little way of rebelling. The officers' mess rules state A TIE MUST BE WORN TO DINNER. I have been considering turning up naked in just a tie and maybe some footwear, but I don't think I could get away with it, as there are women in the mess.

The officers' mess provides accommodation for single officers as well as all their meals. It has a bar that is allowed to make only a very small profit, so drinks are very cheap. The mess tends to be the centre of a station officer's social life. It has numerous large lounge rooms that are often adapted for events. Every officer on the station is a member of the mess.

Wednesday 4 May

Our course got together for a check-learning session and it was very productive. With the exception of Pete Coville, the whole course seem more interested in passing the course than collecting prizes, so I hope we have a few more of these learning sessions.

One of the boys on the course four weeks ahead of us is going to be chopped. He has failed three ground school exams. It has made us realise how important it is to put in the work to pass the exams, especially the essential knowledge quiz: there is a pass mark of 100 per cent for that one. To fail flying training by not putting in enough work is just plain silly. One difficulty is that most of ground school is self-study, and we do the exams as we reach that particular phase of flying. Because of that, the exams usually occur on bad weather days. This means that as well as learning all the things we need for a particular series of flights, we have to make sure we are up to speed on the next set of ground school exams as we cannot be too sure when they will be sprung on us.

Pete Coville can be a bit dozy. He is often last into breakfast and to work and has started getting himself noticed by the instructors for all the wrong reasons. I am also beginning to think that Reg Armeanu is the soundest guy on my course.

It is surprising how little military knowledge the guys have. You would think that as aviators, they would read around the subject extensively, but most of them seem to know very little about anything except modern RAF aircraft.

We did our repeat aerobics run today after last week's shambles. I did a good time, so I am feeling quite pleased with myself. Pete was so fast around the course that he could have grown wings.

Thursday 5 May

There was no flying today due to more bad weather. At this stage in our training, we require no rain clouds and a good horizon as all our flying is done visually. If the horizon is obscured for any reason, then we can't fly. Still, I managed to do quite a bit more studying. Two members of the most senior course finished today and went through the student graduation ceremony. This involves being staked out on the grass, having horrible concoctions poured over you and then being hosed down with a fire hose. Some of the more junior courses have had things brewing for weeks for the more 'popular' guys. I hate to think what they will have for Shoppo when he graduates. One of the senior course managed to turn the tables when he was staked out. He somehow wriggled off the stake, got hold of the fire hose and from a lying position, he hosed down his attackers. My course didn't get involved. We just watched and laughed a lot.

Thursday is turning into bad dress night for me. Tonight, it was a yellow bow tie and lime green shirt for dinner. Truly horrible. Not sure what I will do next week.

There was at trip into Nottingham in the evening with Shoppo, Mark Harris and Reg Armeanu. We just hit a few pubs, but I think we will go back as there seem to be loads of nightclubs and the women hunt in packs. Shoppo was being a bit immature with the girls, leering and making stupid comments. It should be interesting to see him trying to hold a conversation with one.

Friday 6 May

A perfect day for flying, but I still didn't get airborne, just did some studying before going back to the mess. I have managed to convince my bank to part with some money for a new car this week, and the old car was heavily loaded for its final trip down to London. I was giving a lift to Pete and two guys from the senior course.

Monday 9 May

Bad weather all day, which is a shame, as I was down to fly twice on the programme.

Hopefully, this will mean I get a few trips the next time we get good weather.

We had our essential knowledge quiz this morning. It was all right, but I am not predicting anything. I will wait for the results.

Shoppo got stopped for speeding last night. We are not surprised this has happened. In that big car of his, he must look like some rich kid to the police. Collected my new car, an Alfa Romeo Sud at the weekend, and I'm very pleased with it. It is a speedy little machine so Shoppo's misfortune has been a timely reminder.

The whole course went into Newark for the first time and had a few drinks in a couple of the pubs. Nothing outstanding, but it looks like a fun town.

Tuesday 10 May

Flew two trips today with no real problems. I was in control for the take-off on the first one and was all over the bloody place. It was surprising how much the torque of the propeller wanted to pull the aircraft off to the side of the runway, and my reactions were far too slow. We were airborne before any sort of terror registered on my consciousness, and there was total silence from the back seat. I assume Flt Lt Minards has seen a lot of this sort of thing. Trying to monitor all the instruments and listen to all the stuff the instructor says is hard, but I think I am getting the hang of it. It is surprising how physically demanding flying is, and I am feeling very tired.

Thursday 12 May

Another bad weather day with no flying for anyone. The old infantry officers' saying that if you don't keep the men occupied, they will get into mischief was true today. The senior courses decided to burn Reg in the large lecture room. However, as they were tying him up Pete tried to help him by running off with the plastic bottle of methylated spirits. It took the senior boys some time to retrieve the bottle, and to stop Reg from crawling away they tied him to a radiator. Eventually, they set alight to his bootlaces but somehow the meth's bottle was left in a position where it also caught alight.

Someone jumped on the bottle to put out the flames, but the bottle burst and poor Reg found himself in the middle of a small inferno, bound hand and foot, strapped to a radiator and totally unable to move. A couple of guys also found their flying suits alight. Two of us were using our hands and feet trying to keep the flames away from Reg as best we could. A lad called John Green from the senior course managed to put out the majority of the flames by upending a table on to them. Thank God, our flying suits are fire resistant. No one was seriously injured, although Reg is not a happy boy.

Needless to say, the carpet has a big burn mark on it, and as luck would have it, next week is the annual station inspection from the air officer commanding flying training. The boss, Squadron Leader (Sqn Ldr) Lovett, is seriously unimpressed. We have all had a bollocking while standing to attention, and 'horseplay' is now banned.

We were eventually stacked at 3pm. I think just to get us off the squadron. Reg and I went to the gym and played a very enjoyable game of badminton for an hour and then did a few weights. I will have to get myself down there more often. My fitness is starting to slide. After dinner, Pete and I went to Nottingham, but we had to go via a nurses' home to pick up one of Pete's local friends and his girlfriend. They brought along another nurse who was all over Pete like a boa constrictor.

Friday 13 May

My first attempt at giving the met brief was this morning. I had already received a brief from the met man, but I still had to create a few slides for the visual display and give an explanation of what the weather would be doing in our local area: what wind speeds and from which direction, how much cloud cover and what type of clouds, would there be rain and at what time that would be expected.

The brief was good, but the weather itself was very poor – yet again no flying. So, we spent the morning watching old aircraft films. The instructors encourage this as it helps improve our aircraft recognition and that is an essential skill on front-line aircraft.

We were stacked at lunchtime and all headed into Lincoln to celebrate Pete's birthday. The boys on the course had bought him a white silk scarf, a frame for his Chipmunk picture and a packet of condoms. The party was somewhat subdued except of course, for Shoppo. He was trying his damnedest to chat up a young female RAF supply officer from Cranwell. Mark Harris got so fed up that I had to give him an early lift back to Swinderby before heading down to London and a quiet weekend with my girlfriend Shirley.

Monday 16 May

Today's weather was beautiful, with no clouds for a change. Only did the one trip with Flt Lt Minards. It was my first complete take-off without any assistance, and what a pile of rubbish it was. I got airborne as I crossed the side of the runway and only just managed to clear another aircraft that was parked there. Fortunately, the rest of the flight went well. No wonder our instructors are such a laid back bunch, if you were at all nervous, I don't think you could survive a sortie with one of us.

The instructors generally only took control when they were demonstrating something, or if a situation started to become dangerous. Despite my reservations, the Chipmunk was a very rugged aircraft. It was hard to break.

Wednesday 18 May

Today we had two exams in the morning and then a presentation on attack helicopters from no. 26 course. It was very good, especially some of the flying scenes we were shown.

My only flight was in the afternoon in very cloudy weather, and we had to climb all the way up to 10,000ft to do the exercise.

John Green finished today and was staked out and hosed down. Good fun as always. This evening, I just had one drink in the bar and then retired to read, learn and absorb. I'm down for two trips tomorrow, including in the first wave after met brief.

Thursday 19 May

What a day, opened up the squadron, did the met brief and then charged straight off for a trip. My flying wasn't too bad, but my rejoin back at the airfield wasn't great. I haven't quite got into my head where exactly I am supposed to be when I make the different radio calls. After landing from that flight, it was a quick debriefed and then straight off again for another. This trip included the dreaded circuits for the first time.

It was all very busy, and I was running out of mental capacity and was unable to remember all of my checks. I'm going to have to do a bit more work on them. I might practise them whilst driving the car, sitting quietly in the crew room isn't realistic enough.

None of the five circuits I flew was very good. My excuse was that the wind was blowing straight across the runway and it was wet. I have got some serious work to do tonight. Another one of the senior course finished today and was hosed down. He was so 'popular' that they painted his face in permanent marker pen, and a specially saved bucket of mouldy jam and other unidentifiable things were poured over him. I can now see why they use the fire hose.

A circuit is best described as an oval aerial racetrack. The runway is the main straight and the first turn allows the climb up to the circuit height. The reciprocal straight is flown at this height and gives time for checks to be completed. The second turn enables a descent back on to the runway. The whole idea is to practise getting airborne and landing. It also helps us to get familiar with all the air traffic radio chatter and with fitting in with the other aircraft that were also flying in the circuit pattern.

Friday 20 May

Today was another good flying day and I was very nervous as I had two circuit trips planned. Didn't leave the squadron all day and only managed an instant meal for lunch. The sortie first thing in the morning was difficult. There were a few bumpy touchdowns, and I totally lost control on one landing and ran on to the grass at the edge of the runway. It shook me up a bit, and the old confidence was knocked. After a good chat with Flt Lt Minards about it over lunch, the afternoon trip was much better. Managed to put together a run of three good circuits and Flt Lt Minards was so impressed he sent me SOLO.

My first-ever solo in any aircraft, and it was incredible! I could not believe that they trusted me to operate an aircraft by myself (last week, I had to work hard to convince the bank that I was trustworthy enough to borrow some money to buy a car). Flt Lt Minards briefed me to repeat what I had been doing in the previous three circuits, fly one circuit and land. He jumped out of the back seat and left me to it. I flew a very good circuit, but was probably a bit too relaxed on landing and had a bit of a wobble on braking, but all in all not too bad. My concentration was to such an extent that the whole thing seemed to be over in no time at all. There were no nerves until afterwards, and then I had the shakes for a good hour.

An amazing feeling, and I didn't stop smiling on the drive down to London. They can chop me now for all I care; at least I got to fly an aircraft by myself.

Monday 23 May

We have been at RAF Swinderby for a month and are now one of the senior courses as a new course started today. I was up at the crack of dawn to act as the belligerent physical training instructor for their morning spoof run. I had the full PTI outfit and a clipboard with everyone's names. I gave them a warm up for 10 minutes that had them all gasping for air, then sent them on a run around the hockey pitches and told them off for slow times and lack of fitness. It seemed quite effective as they all looked totally dejected when they trudged back to the mess for their meeting with the padres. They honestly believed I was a real PTI until they saw me in the crew room later.

I was feeling very tense today, but that seemed to go as soon as I got into the aircraft. I have spent too much of the weekend thinking about circuits. Anyway, the wind was too strong for my experience level, so although the engine was started and we got to the beginning of the runway, I had to taxi the aircraft back to the squadron.

Tuesday 24 May

This morning was clear, if a bit windy, and I flew 30 minutes of circuits with Flt Lt Minards and then 45 minutes solo. Great fun, I was seriously enjoying myself. The circuits weren't all smooth, and the unpredictable winds certainly didn't help, but I am getting better. This afternoon, it was another 30 minutes with Flt Lt Minards, but it got so windy that my solo flight was cancelled. Reg and I played badminton instead and then did a few weights in the gym. It is a good way to relax.

After dinner, a group of us went into Lincoln with the new course. Initially to a very loud and trendy place, but the girls were not a good looking bunch so we headed to a quiet pub. It was late by the time we got back to the mess and then I had to do some work to prepare for a talk I have to give at the morning met brief. Fortunately, I haven't had too many beers.

Wednesday 25 May

Yesterday, the met brief suggested that there would be bad weather today – and that prediction was wrong. We had a great horizon with only a few fluffy clouds and light winds. The flying conditions were perfect. But there were a lot of people in the crew room with hangovers trying to keep a low profile.

I got a telling off from the instructors for eating instant curry noodles for breakfast in the crew room. They genuinely seemed horrified, more by the idea of curry at that hour of the morning than the instant food.

Two dual and two solo trips for me today and they were all in the circuit. More good fun, and I'm continuing to enjoy myself. Shoppo and Reg both managed to get solo, Mark and Pete managed theirs yesterday, so that is the whole course through. It is traditional to buy a barrel of beer and have a bit of a party to celebrate. We are not too sure when we are going to find the time for that. I am exhausted after all of today's flying, added to the effects of the late night yesterday.

Thursday 26 May

The bad weather arrived a day late: no flying. We had another set of exams instead. Reg and I were back in the gym and playing badminton. I'm improving at the game, but still not beating him – the boy is good.

As it was Thursday, it was a polka dot green-and-red kipper tie for dinner in the mess. Stylish!

Friday 27 May

My final set of circuits in the syllabus and today I was: Trevor – The Amazing Ground Loop Man. If you can imagine doing a handbrake turn in a car, well a ground loop is very similar only this one was a 540-degree turn at 80mph. It happened on landing, with Flt Lt Minards in the back seat. He just gave a heavy sigh and took control as we finally came to a halt. I was terrified.

The rest of the circuits weren't too bad, but I wasn't at my best by any means. Missed a couple of radio calls from air traffic and was very glad when the sortie finished. No doubt still recovering from the terror of the ground loop.

Ground loops only happen to aircraft that have tail wheels. Modern machines have a tricycle undercarriage, and there is no danger of their pilots causing a ground loop.

Wednesday 1 June

I flew in the first wave, to be taught practice forced landings (PFLs) in the local area and 45degree turns. The sortie involved lots of flying at lower levels for the PFLs, and I started to feel queasy during the 45-degree turns. This was my excuse for messing up the rejoin to the circuit and trying to land on the wrong runway. Passed the trip, but only just.

We get marked on each sortie we fly with an instructor (known as a dual). The scores are excellent, high average, average, low average or fail. Normally, if you fail, you have to repeat the trip. If you fail again, then you are put on review. They might change your instructor and give you an extra sortie or two if you are lucky. You then get a final attempt to pass the trip.

Fail again and it is bye-bye.

The rest of the day was spent trying to sort out the barrel of beer for our course solo party tomorrow.

Thursday 2 June

I was airborne this morning in the first wave for the sector reconnaissance (recce). This was the first time properly away from the airfield, and away from familiar local landmarks. Managed to fly and navigate the whole thing without any help and was very pleased with my efforts, as was Flt Lt Minards. There was no chance to fly the solo sector recce because of weather, so I spent the rest of the morning with my head in books.

The way the syllabus is constructed means that you are given one or two trips, (also known as sorties), to learn a new skill. These are flown dual with an instructor, and then you get a chance to practise that new skill solo. The teaching trips are very busy, so we have to be very well prepared or risk failing. The solo trips are quite often just called general handling.

We had our course solo barrel in the afternoon, and I managed to drink several pints of it although one was heavily laced with vodka courtesy of Pete Waugh, who is on one of our senior courses. After that, we all headed into Lincoln and unfortunately, Pete Coville volunteered to drive. That was regrettable because he met one of the cooks from the officers' mess. Pete spent the whole evening chatting her up. He even dumped us to go off clubbing with her, so we had to get a taxi back. Not good in my book.

Friday 3 June

The weather started well but got steadily worse throughout the day. My solo flight was cancelled and instead I had a general revision sortie with Flt Lt Minards. Thanks to last night's festivities, I didn't feel well before the flight, and by the time I had flown a few steep turns I was feeling positively ill. Thank God, the instructors can't see you in these machines.

The steep turns were rubbish and the practice forced landings were only just passable. The rest of the day was spent trying to recover and not think about the amount of studying I would have to do this weekend.

We all attended the standard Friday afternoon happy hour in the mess at 5pm, before heading out to the pubs and nightclubs of Lincoln. I danced a lot and even got chatted up, which was very surprising considering how drunk I was. Shoppo didn't last the pace and retired early. No idea how we got home.

Saturday 4 June

Reports from last night say I was so drunk that I couldn't walk and had difficulty standing. My dancing, however, was still good. It seems we stopped on the way home from Lincoln for kebabs, but had to wait 20 minutes while Pete got a special one, which he promptly spilt all over Reg. The guys went to wake up Shoppo in his room when they got back. He has no memory of that event, alcohol induced amnesia I assume. I didn't participate and was last seen heading back to my room clutching a kebab.

My next memory was waking up in my room with all the lights on, an uneaten kebab on the bedside table, head throbbing and stomach heaving. Stayed in bed until the afternoon before headed into Lincoln with Pete Waugh, who seemed totally sober and suffering no ill effects whatsoever. A massive burger and fries managed to sort out the hangover. Saturday evening was spent in a nightclub called Madison's, which was full of girls with big hair and too much make-up. They were just to Shoppo's taste. The music was rubbish and the dance floor very crowded, so most of us left early, minus Shoppo and Pete Waugh.

Monday 6 June

I flew my solo sector recce in the afternoon but was nervous all day until getting airborne. You are supposed to enjoy your sector recce, as it is the first time solo away from the airfield, but I just seemed to work my nuts off flying accurately, navigating and looking out for other aircraft. Flew some circuits when I got back to the airfield and today it was Mr Float Down The Runway And Bounce.

Shoppo is floundering. He failed a trip and hasn't been allowed to go solo again. He is on review, and they have given him a change of instructor and a few more sorties to get his flying up to the standard required. Hopefully, he will be better tomorrow.

Tuesday 7 June

No flying for me today as there was no instructor available. Instead, I had my mid-course interview with Flt Lt Lloyd, the deputy boss. I've got Bs, which I am told is above average. Me, above average, what a laugh! Perfect Pete Coville got Bs and Cs much to everyone's amazement. That's not what he has been telling us. Not so perfect after all.

Shoppo is having real problems with his circuits. He refuses to believe there is anything wrong with them, but the instructors still won't send him solo. Something must be really amiss for that to happen.

Thursday 9 June

We had a visit from a local school this morning. The children were mainly nine and 10-year-olds, small, noisy and excitable. They and the guys enjoyed the visit. It isn't all that surprising, as it was a kindergarten visiting a kindergarten.

We all had to do a bit of gardening in the afternoon, tidying up the areas around the squadron and then Reg and I spent an hour with one of the instructors, learning how to use the navigation computer to plan a route. We need to master it for the next phase of the flying course, but it is going to require a bit more practice before we are proficient. It's Thursday night, and it was a pair of plus fours to dinner. Resplendent!

Monday 13 June

Reg and I did the met brief together. It was a nice clear day, so a simple brief for a change. I had two sorties – a dual and a solo – and had my first experience of aerobatics. A couple of loops to start and they were not as difficult as I thought, and as much fun as the boys have been saying. I don't know why I have waited so long to try them.

Shoppo got chopped today. He failed two flights with different instructors, so went up with the boss, Sqn Ldr Lovett, and didn't produce the goods. He is heading off to be a navigator. No more loud Welshman, and I'm sorry to see him fail. It would have been nice if everyone had got through the course.

Navigator is an old term that doesn't do justice to a modern job. Fast jet navigators are better described as weapon systems operators. You have to be very capable to be a navigator in a fast jet.

Tuesday 14 June

Today's trip was with Flt Lt Hewitt a Central Flying School (CFS) instructor. CFS ensures that we are taught in accordance with the syllabus, and that our progress and ability is correctly reflected in the scores we are given for our sorties. These instructors normally reside at RAF Scampton, that Mecca for flying training, and they venture out every now and again to pass on their wisdom to other instructors and students throughout all the RAF flying training bases. Needless to say, I was very worried to have been chosen to fly with one. It wouldn't be good for the RAF Swinderby instructors or me if I messed up. Thankfully, it went very well. Flt Lt Hewitt seemed very pleased with my efforts, although I did make a few minor errors.

Wednesday 15 June

My first spinning sortie was today. It was quite hairy but not as bad as I thought it would be. You fall out of the sky totally out of control, and have to learn how to recover from that. I am beginning to trust the aircraft a bit more. However, it still worries me on occasions. I'm still not used to the way the engine and propeller stop during some of the vertical manoeuvres and I still can't get my head around the canvas covered wings. That just isn't right. It was a physically demanding sortie today, and I was a very sweaty boy when we landed.

Thursday 16 June

Even more bad weather today, so the course caught up on a few briefings and had a couple of exams. As the course leader, I was given a reprimand on behalf of everyone, which all stemmed from Pete Coville, 'The Kid' as he is now being called. He had his first navigation trip, and it became obvious during the pre-flight briefing that he had not read the appropriate chapters in the study guide, or even asked any of the senior students what needed to be revised. The instructors now think we are all a bunch of lazy so-and-so's who don't read ahead. The Kid can be slow and act brain dead at times.

Shoppo left the station today. He has been told he has a very high aptitude for navigation.

Best of luck to him.

It was Thursday, and dress for dinner was a very nice yellow bow tie and matching waistcoat. The boss happened to be in the mess and was impressed. He said it reflected my officer qualities. I'm not sure if that is a good thing.

Friday 17 June

The boss commented that I wasn't wearing a bow tie at the met brief, very funny man. Flt Lt Minards got his A2 instructor category today. It's a big deal. He is now rated as an above average instructor. The poor man has been in the clutches of the Central Flying School instructors all week.

The morning was taken up with a cross-country run that the whole course had to complete courtesy of the physical education department. Wonderful. Then we flew in the afternoon. On my trip, we had to climb through unbroken cloud cover to be able to do a spinning exercise. It was a good trip, especially since I didn't want to fly. I also learned how to fly a few more aerobatic manoeuvres, and still managed to get off for the weekend an hour early.

Monday 20 June

The weekend was another great few days in London with Shirley. She allows me to talk about the air force on a Friday night and then the rest of the weekend is a non-military zone. It really works well and I am usually much more motivated after a weekend break.

The two flights I had today were a solo general handling followed by solo navigation. Worked hard on both, had a few errors but enjoyed them. My navigation wasn't as good as it could have been. There were a few problems setting the compass. The thing is ancient and has to be constantly reset or it wanders off the correct headings. Still, I managed to find my way back to the airfield.

Flt Lt Minards said that he thinks I will walk in one morning and announce that I was quitting. He is convinced I am not happy about being on the course. The reality is that I just don't like the idea of failing, so I take my time at work very seriously. The semi-permanent scowl on my face also reflects the fact that I think I am in a kindergarten.

Wednesday 22 June

I was acting as the station orderly officer today as well as flying two sorties. The orderly officer salutes the station flag first thing in the morning and again in the evening. He is the main contact for any station problems out of office hours.

The first trip this morning wasn't too bad. I only lost a few feet on my steep turns, but I still have to concentrate to roll out on the correct heading. We flew 10 minutes of low level before heading back to the airfield. The low level was flown at 250 feet and it was absolutely brilliant. I loved every single minute. The second trip was a solo, just general handling out in the local area.

The junior course is now well into their circuit phase, but only one of them is solo. Two are on review. That is not good.

Thursday 23 June

It's my 25th birthday! I finally finished my orderly officer bit by saluting the flag in the morning and then had a trip with Flt Lt Minards. Circuits are getting better, and my general handling was good, but I still feel that I can do much better.

Today was my first flying test on the course, the so-called mid-course check or trip 35. My test instructor was the boss and we flew in the afternoon.

It wasn't the best sortie I have flown by a long way. The general handling was okay, but I got lost for a few minutes before heading back to base. I was then too close to the runway on all of my circuits. On top of all that, it seems I have not been doing a set of checks that are required before returning to base. Flt Lt Minards never bothers with them, and I have been picking up some of his bad habits. Anyway, the trip was a pass, but only with a low average mark. Both Flt Lt Minards and I were expecting high average.

Not a happy Trevor, and I stayed in the bar drowning my sorrows all evening. What a birthday. The call from Shirley and her friend, Jo, was the only nice thing that has happened to me today.

Friday 24 June

It was my turn to give the met brief again this morning, and then I was unleashed on a solo general handling sortie including solo aerobatics for the first time. They were totally brilliant. The Kid Coville failed his trip 35, the poor bugger. By all accounts, he had a disastrous session and is now on review.

The afternoon trip was an introduction to instrument flying, with a new instructor. He is Flt Lt Merrill and is Shoppo's old instructor. He should purge any other bad habits I might have picked up from Flt Lt Minards.

Instrument flying is flying solely with reference to the instruments in the cockpit. The artificial horizon, altimeter (for height), airspeed, compass and vertical speed indicator. You have to be able to work out what the instruments are telling you very, very quickly. There was a Dining In night at the mess tonight. I had no shirt to wear with my mess kit and had to borrow one. The dinner itself was good, but it was followed by some very dull speeches from the non-flying station officers. As the evening wore on, the boys drank more and things livened up. It started getting out of hand when the physical education officer, who has not been popular with the student pilots, was jumped and tied up. The boys were deciding whether to gag him and dump him outside when he had a total sense of humour failure, and started whimpering about the state of his mess kit. I think he heard someone suggest that we should burn him. After that, any chance of officer-like behaviour disintegrated. The student pilots took on the station officers in beer fights, bar fights, drinking competitions and tugs of war. All of this was presided over by the two station wing commanders.

Pete Waugh from my senior course fell on some broken glass, and I dragged him back to his room in a semi-conscious state. It seems my first aid left a lot to be desired. I remember thinking he was bleeding and he was breathing, so he must be all right. Told the rest of the guys in the bar he was fine, but when they checked on Pete later, they found several large cuts on his body, including a massive one through his ear, and the poor guy was still bleeding. They had to take him to the medical centre to get some real first aid.

Dining In nights happened every couple of months to welcome new officers to the station and say goodbye to others who were leaving. It is a very traditional event when smart evening uniform, or the mess kit, is worn. The mess itself becomes the equivalent of a silver-service restaurant with a very good wine selection. At the end of dinner, there is a toast to the Queen and then speeches, hello to this bloke, goodbye to that girl etc., and then the evening stops being 'highbrow'.

Tuesday 29 June

We have had two days of bad weather and three more ground school exams, in one of which I only managed to scrape the pass mark. Today was spent studying like mad for the next set of exams and the rest of the trips in the instrument flying phase. We also had an unplanned general knowledge quiz, which showed us all to have a distinct lack of knowledge of the flying order book, which is our guide to the rules we must follow in the air. It was a timely reminder not to concentrate our studying solely on the ground school exams. The station had a fly by from two Phantom jets in the afternoon. Low, fast, with reheat engaged. Oh yes! We can only dream.

Thursday 30 June

Bad weather all day, so I left a note on the operations desk saying, "Must be fit for instrument flying?"

As a result, had two instrument trips. After all, instrument flying is designed to allow you to fly in bad weather. I am improving, although I did have two good screw-ups. Initially I didn't set the compass correctly, and I keep missing out the checks we need to do every 10 minutes to make sure everything on the aircraft was functioning as it should. My concentration was on the instrument flying to the detriment of everything else.

My instructor doesn't expects great things from me on the instrument flying test at the end of this flying phase. There is also a test for the navigation phase and a final flight test. It is all hard work at the moment, requiring almost total concentration for every airborne minute. It's Thursday night, so it was a nice big blue spotted kipper tie at dinner – straight from the 1970s.

Friday 1 July

The weather improved today, and I made the mistake of thinking I would be on another instrument trip. However, the instructors changed the programme after lunch because of the good weather. Instead of instruments, I had to fly a navigation sortie, but I hadn't looked at any of the navigation procedures for a couple of weeks.

After some very hurried preparation, I found myself in an aircraft taxiing out to the runway, not having much of a clue about what the sortie involved, or even what I did on the last navigation exercise. Luckily, the aircraft developed a fault – we couldn't get the canopy closed – so we had to taxi back. They couldn't get a replacement aircraft for a good half an hour, which was just enough time for me to prepare properly. After that, it was a good trip, and I landed late in the afternoon and whizzed off to London for the weekend.

Monday 4 July

The latest bunch of new guys, no. 30 course, started today, so it was up early to do the physical training instructor bit and run them ragged. They are a very unfit bunch and still looked dazed on the squadron later in the day.

The weather was perfect for instrument flying, so that's what I flew in the morning. After lunch, I was sent on a solo navigation exercise, which didn't go as expected. I was forced way off track avoiding some very big thunderstorms, and after starting to lose sight of the ground due to the low cloud, I called it a day and headed home. There was no way to get around the route using visual navigation techniques, and instrument flying is one of the disciplines we are not allowed to practise by ourselves on this course.

Wednesday 6 July

We have had two good flying days and I have flown five trips. They have all gone well, and the solos are so much fun! Because of all the summer ball work going on, I am not doing very much studying for the exams next week.

The station summer ball is this weekend so every spare moment we have is spent in the mess helping with decorating the function rooms.

Thursday 7 July

The weather is rubbish. No one is airborne except for Flt Lt Minards with his student Flying Officer Trevor Edwards doing instrument flying. I can't complain. Had two sorties and the second was the instrument flying test, for which I managed a good pass.

Two more members of the current senior course finished today and were suitably hosed down, but I was too weary to join in. There was a barbecue for them at the mess in the evening with too much alcohol available.

Friday 8 July

Tired and hung over, but a busy day. A general handling trip with Flt Lt Minards and then the same thing again solo. Great fun. Reg finally passed his trip 35 – and with the best score of the course. We all had a nice early stack for this evening's summer ball.

I picked Shirley up from the local train station and we went into Lincoln for afternoon tea, before heading back to the base and getting ready for the evening. The summer ball was a fairly couth affair, and having a girlfriend around was a very moderating influence. Shirley says she enjoyed herself, which I was very relieved to hear. She is the most unmilitary person I know and I was worried that she wouldn't like the environment.

Monday 11 July

I have been teamed up with Flt Lt Merrill again as Flt Lt Minards is on leave. The weather has been very good and I have flown both general handling and navigation trips. At this rate, I will have finished the course before Flt Lt Minards gets back.

All of no. 29 course are now through their first solo. The last two, Dave Bayliss and Simon White, did theirs today. They are having a solo barrel on Thursday.

One of the junior course had a mad moment in the cockpit this afternoon. The aircraft at RAF Swinderby are normally arranged on the concrete flight line facing the airfield. There are three runways on the base, a main tarmac runway and two smaller grass runways. The Chipmunk is fully capable of taxiing and getting airborne from a grass surface. This particular student had just started his aircraft but was taking his time, so his instructor in the back seat told him to hurry up and get into the air. The comment caused a complete mental breakdown. The poor lad applied full power to the aircraft, accelerated straight across the flight line on to the grass and got airborne. He wasn't on either of the designated grass runways. He hadn't done any of his cockpit checks and he hadn't spoken to anyone in air traffic control. When his instructor pointed out all of these errors, he became totally incapable of flying, and his instructor had to land the aircraft. The consensus is that he won't last long on the course.

Wednesday 13/Thursday 14 July

I am confused and thought Wednesday was Tuesday. What happened to Tuesday I don't know. Anyway, today is Thursday. I know this because I have just had a few pints of no. 29 course's solo barrel, and very nice beer it was too.

No flying today due to bad weather, so we had a ground school exam instead. There is only one more exam and that will be ground school completed.

Reg did the met brief this morning and promised that the bad weather would continue, so we continued drinking after the solo barrel had run out. One of the junior course has devised a concoction called Screaming Yellow Monster, which is very popular.

The boss is very much in favour of having a squadron bad dress evening in the mess next Thursday and I have been told to make it happen.

Friday 15 July

Reg Armeanu is a liar. He had said, "No chance of you flying tomorrow Trev, the weather will be awful." But guess what? The weather was beautiful and I was flying on a general handling trip in the first wave with Flt Lt Merrill. Needless to say, I did not feel well, or fly to my usual standard. I was just glad to finish the trip with a pass. The guys reckon I was green when I got down, and I reckon they were right. The rest of the day was spent praying that I wouldn't have to fly again and hoping for an early stack. Thankfully, God heard me.

Monday 18 July

I was airborne early this morning for a solo general handling flight in the first wave. There were no holes in the cloud to do the general bit of the handling, so I stayed in the circuit for a while before landing. The weather improved a bit later, so I flew the sortie again before lunch.

The Kid passed his instrument flying test on Friday and is getting cocky. I had my final navigation test this afternoon, and it went well. One of the turning points on the route was a microlite site, which I couldn't find. Only during the debrief did I discover that we had over flown it. It was just a field where the microlites sometimes take off and land and I was expecting to see at least a small hangar.

Well, ahead in getting things organised for Thursday's bad dress evening. Showed Reg the wig, jodhpurs and sunglasses that I picked up from Shirley at the weekend.

Tuesday 19 July

Another day at the ranch. Due to fly three times, but only cracked two, and both were general handling. The dual sortie started with a bit of instrument flying revision, which was somewhat unsteady, and then the rest of the sortie was spent on general flying. Couldn't seem to do a decent barrel roll, and that is a first for me. At least the circuits were decent. By the time I had my solo in the afternoon, the weather were such that I couldn't fly any aerobatics, but I managed to practise everything else. Very tired after all of that, and thankfully, I didn't have to fly the last trip.

Wednesday 20 July

My next few sorties will be formation. The first trips are all dual and I am teamed up with Mark for this phase. Half the time, he will be the lead aircraft and I will try to maintain a position a few feet away from him as his instructor manoeuvres, and then we swap positions.

So today, I had my first-ever formation flight, and although I only had my hands on the controls for 15 minutes, I was exhausted. The amount of concentration involved is shocking. Flt Lt Merrill kept telling me to relax my grip on the control column, but I was holding it so hard I got cramp in my hands. Relax – not a chance! There was a big slicer and dicer spinning around at high speed in front of me, and I was feet away from Mark's aircraft and he had the station commander in the back seat as his instructor. It could be worse though; I could have been in the lead aircraft with The Kid just a few feet from my wing.

At this stage of training, we practised formation on the left and right hand sides of the lead aircraft and also in the line-astern position. The lead aircraft smoothly manoeuvres and we had to be capable of remaining in the correct formation position.

Thursday 21 July

Formation again, and it was much better than yesterday. It's still hard work, and I have to concentrate on keeping the correct distance. We have been told that the closer you are, the easier it is, but I don't want to cut Mark's tail off with my propeller.

The Kid and Reg went up on their first formation trips. Mark and I got hold of some black armbands, and saluted them as they taxied out as if we thought we wouldn't see them again. They loved the banter. Reg says that The Kid is very good at formation.

There was solo formation for me in the afternoon. Just two aircraft this time, with Flt Lt Merrill as my formation leader. Really enjoyed it, although it is still hard. Flt Lt Merrill had to ease off on some of the steep turns as I was only just hanging in there.

After landing, it was straight into our final exam for which I was totally unprepared. It was just 10 questions, but I am not confident. If I fail, that's it, no more flying training for me. We had the bad dress evening in the mess, and all the student pilots turned out along with a few of the station officers. There were some very good outfits, but I still think my afro wig and jodhpurs were the best. The boss was very impressed as was the station commander, who had brought his wife along, although she didn't want to get involved. Very wise.

Friday 22 July

I was up with another one of our senior instructors today, for more general handling. My aerobatics were good, and I was probably a bit aggressive on some of the manoeuvres as I could hear him groaning in the back as we passed 4G.

Four times the force of gravity! It wasn't surprising he was groaning. He is an old man after all. I, on the other hand, was enjoying myself thoroughly.

The weather got worse later in the day, so that was it. Only three trips to the end of the course, with one set of exam results to come.

Tuesday 26 July

We received our final exam results today, and I managed to scrape a pass. It is a big weight off my mind.

There were strong winds today, but I was still sent up on my last solo. As far as I was concerned, it was far too windy, and I didn't enjoy it. On my last circuit, I was almost flipped upside down by a big gust of wind. Too scary! The Kid had his solo formation this afternoon, so Mark and I wore kamikaze headbands, as he taxied out. He wasn't amused.

Mark has got an above-average mark for the final navigation test he flew today. Very good news and I am glad, as we had spent most of yesterday going over his navigation.

Thursday 28 July

There was no flying for me today and I had a long chat with Flt Lt Minards about what I can expect on the next flying course. He says I could be very good if I show more determination in the air and accept nothing but perfection. I know what he means, but I honestly don't think I am very good, and I am working very hard just to achieve my current standards. Jules Marshall from one of the junior courses didn't have a good day today. He got lost during a solo navigation trip and ended up over RAF Scampton. That place is full of the Central Flying School demigods and the flying gods called the Red Arrows. He's lucky they didn't send one of their Hawk aircraft up to chase him away. Jules then managed to throw up during aerobatics on his next trip. The instructor classified the trip as Duty Not Carried Out, Student Unserviceable. He won't live that down for a while.

Friday 29 July

Today saw my final dual trip with Flt Lt Minards and neither of us was happy with my efforts. My aerobatics seem to have gone downhill, the circuits weren't great and everything else was just adequate. Still, it was good enough for me to be sent up for my final test with Squadron Leader Winterbottom. He is one of the old, bold, seen-it-and-done-it guys. We did a bit of everything that I have been taught on the course, except for the formation. It all went well, but the aerobatics were rubbish as usual. My circuits, however, impressed him. That was because the wind got up to 35 miles an hour, which is way outside my limits, but I coped without any problems. It was so late that the airfield was closed behind us as we landed. No one else was airborne. The boys had all been stacked an hour earlier and had disappeared for the weekend, which meant I escaped without being hosed down. More relieved than happy about finishing the course, and I headed down to London to celebrate with Shirley.

Thursday 4 August

Reg finished the course on Monday, and Mark and the Kid finally finished today. A great bunch of guys. Everyone has worked hard and we have all achieved above-average grades, which is amazing. We are all advancing to the Basic Flying Training course at RAF Linton-on-Ouse and the mighty Jet Provost aircraft. I can't wait.

That is the end of my elementary flying course and I had achieved 20 hours solo and 45 hours dual flying. My overall grades have been above average and I was assessed as COMPETENT.

Basic

No. 96 Basic Flying Training Course,
RAF Linton-on-Ouse,
Yorkshire,
1988

During the time, I attended the basic flying course the first cracks in the Iron Curtain became evident, and as 1989 unfolded, a wave of revolutions took place across the Eastern Bloc. George Bush senior became the 41st President of the USA, taking office during particularly dramatic times. Meanwhile, NATO remained wary of the Soviet Union and did not reduce any of its capabilities, so life in the RAF continued as normal.

The basic flying training course took almost a year and was designed to produce student pilots who could then be selected for further specialist training. All RAF pilots have to pass this course.

Monday 17 October

The start of a new course at RAF Linton-on-Ouse and I have got a severe morale problem already. Arrived at the base yesterday to find that they didn't have enough rooms in the officers' mess, so I have been stuck in temporary accommodation until next week. This means I will be living out of a suitcase in a room not much bigger than a broom cupboard. The guys on the course look like a good bunch. There are one or two strange ones, but that is to be expected. There are 13 of us:

Adrian Bonwitt
Paul Gerrard
Paul Binns
Peter Coville
Adrian (Reg) Armeanu
Mark Harris
Steve Shell
John Bowland
Bill Owen
Cameron Gair

Andy Pomeroy (Navy)
Ian Reid (Navy)
And, of course, Trevor Edwards

We have been inundated with technical books already. During elementary flying training at RAF Swinderby, we completed our studies in parallel with our flying. Here we have ground school to pass before we start any flying. Judging by the number of books, it looks like it will be quite a bit of work.

Wednesday 19 October

Everything is moving slowly. I feel I have been here weeks already. As well as daily lectures, there is a lot of self-study for this course. We should have physical education included by the end of the week. My morale hasn't improved and that is not helped by the lack of sunlight. Since Sunday, heavy fog has covered this area. On top of that, I am totally fed up with this room. There is no table at which to study, no space in which to unpack – in fact besides a bed, not a lot of anything.

I am slowly getting to know the other guys. Bill Owen tends to talk a bit too much, and our course leader Adrian Bonwitt is a bit serious, but then again, he is the course leader and that is no fun, as I well know.

Overall, the guys are a bit more mature than the bunch at RAF Swinderby. There are several graduates who seem to be ex-University Air Squadron members with quite a few hours of flying behind them. There are also a couple of guys with private flying licences. Everyone has got at least 50 hours flying.

The base is much bigger than RAF Swinderby and is dedicated to training pilots. There are three squadrons, and each has two courses running at any one time. Once, we complete ground school, we are off to no. 3 squadron and we are the 96th course to start here.

There were around 60 student pilots training at RAF Linton-on-Ouse, with 10 per cent expected to fail the course. On average, half of those remaining would qualify for fast jet training.

Thursday 20 October

Hurrah, the fog has started to lift and there is jet noise in the air. The airfield is open for business, and we can at least see the aircraft we will be flying, the Jet Provost Mk3A and Mk5. We start on the Mk3A and, assuming all goes well, move to the Mk5 with its more powerful engine and pressurised cockpit so it can fly higher and faster.

There is so much to learn, and the aircraft are much more complicated than the Chipmunk.

We have all the new jet engine theory and aerodynamics to become familiar with. The Jet Provost has side-by-side seating, not the tandem layout in the Chipmunk, and we sit on ejector seats that can fire you out of the aircraft in an emergency.

It is just nice to be able to see these aircraft in the sky. It should make the next few weeks of exams and study a little more bearable.

Ejector seats are the primary means of escape in an emergency. In the Jet Provost, they have a parachute contained in what looks like a big headrest. You sit on a pack that contains a dinghy, and the seat has connections for your communications and in more advanced versions, your oxygen supplies. When you strap into the seat, you are also strapping on a parachute and connecting yourself to the dinghy pack as well as the seat itself. An ejection is initiated by pulling a large handle between your legs. This fires a series of explosive cartridges that detach the canopy and launch the seat up and out of the aircraft. Modern seats are rocket powered to enable ejections from ground level and at higher speeds.

Monday 24 October

I am still in a hovel that is an excuse for a room, but after kicking up a fuss with the mess management, I think I am close to being moved. We have got a lot of exams in the next few days and I am feeling a bit more motivated this week.

The guys have been winding up Adrian our course leader. Someone sent him an official-looking memo saying that he had to create a course song to enhance team morale. He was half way through writing it before he realised he had been tricked. He didn't find it amusing.

Tuesday 25 October

I have finally been given a room in the mess. Moved in this afternoon and spent the evening sorting my stuff out. Never thought I would long for a desk, but that is the best bit of this room – that and the double bed.

Thursday 27 October

This morning, we had a moral leadership lecture from an old Catholic priest. In fact, an ancient Catholic priest. At one point, he just stopped talking mid-sentence and his chin slowly sank into his chest. We were all wondering if he had died and who was going to do something about it when he burst back into action. When I say that, I mean that he lifted his head up and started talking again. He then asked if anyone enjoyed fighting and to my astonishment, everyone turned and looked at me. They seem to think I am some sort of thug. Not me! I'm a nice guy.

Anyway, the old guy talked at us for an hour or so about God, the military and life. Then we were off for our first proper physical education lesson at RAF Linton-on-Ouse. It was a shock to me, as I had no idea how unfit I had become. A standard military physical training instructor took the lesson. He was merciless. If you were struggling with a particular exercise, then you obviously needed extra attention, and extra attention ultimately led to more pain.

I struggled, received lots of extra attention and consequently suffered a lot of pain. This evening, Reg, Steve Shell and I managed to miss a lecture. We didn't realise there was one scheduled and were in the bar celebrating Steve's 21st birthday. Eventually, most of the rest of the course joined us and the evening became an alcoholic blur.

Monday 31 October

I came up from London last night with my new mountain bike. It is blue and white, with big chunky tyres and 20 gears. They have never seen anything like it in Yorkshire, and it's the most macho on the station by a long way, much to the disgust of Reg. Just a pity I can't ride it very well.

Up early as the duty student, and my first duty of the day was presenting the morning met brief. Shortly after that, I discovered to my horror that there was a maths test, which I knew nothing about and as a consequence had not prepared. Came clean with the instructor, and he just said, "Okay, do it tomorrow."

The guys were very unhappy about that, they expected me to get a serious telling off – and to be honest, so did I. It just shows that honesty pays.

The boys on no. 95 course are six weeks ahead of us and were back from their land survival exercise on the North York Moors today. They didn't have too bad a time as it hardly rained all week. They were just a bunch of very hungry men, which is fairly standard for the exercise.

Stayed in all evening to study for my maths test. The rest of the course went into York.

Tuesday 1 November

It seems I missed a good night out in York last night. Steve Shell has acquired a life-size paper skeleton and it is now the course mascot. It has been named Pilot Officer Bones. Mark Harris has been given the title Moose Hunter after chatting up a large and not particularly attractive local woman. John Bowland set him up by telling her that Mark fancied her. She is coming along to the station open day on Saturday and will be bringing along a whole herd of female mooses. Can't wait.

Thursday 3 November

Steve Shell is getting to be the butt of a lot of jokes at the moment. His girlfriend has had a message from God and is currently a Born Again Christian. Poor Steve. We aren't too sure how that fits in with training to be a steely-eyed fighter pilot.

Pilot Officer Bones was at his desk in ground school this morning, and one of the instructors wanted to know if he had any flying experience, but he wasn't talking.

As if we aren't busy enough, we spent several hours helping with the preparation for the station open day on Saturday. For most of that time, we were unloading a lorry full of tables and chairs.

Friday 4 November

A full day of ground school and studying followed by happy hour in the mess bar. Hurrah! I drank far too much and ended up in a nightclub in York.

Saturday 5 November

When I woke this morning, the question I asked myself was, "Where did this kebab come from?" I had no recollection of buying it.

I was supposed to be selling programmes for the open day, but was in no condition to meet the public. Eventually, I struggled out of bed and managed to con the navy boys into doing the programme bit while I directed traffic. At least I didn't have to talk to anyone, and the navy guys are all in their best uniforms and look very smart. It was a very busy day and the station was packed with people looking at all the aircraft and the flying displays.

When the open day finished, Paul Binns invited the course over to his house. He is married and has a married officer's house on the station. The trouble with Paul is that he can be antisocial, and he didn't seem to want us there even though he had invited us. He even banned Paul Gerrard from going upstairs with his girlfriend 'in case they got up to anything'. Paul Binns had invited one of his neighbours around and he was also a very strange man. He introduced his wife as 'Wife'. John Bowland asked if she had a name and was told no, just 'Wife'. He is off to start the RAF Regiment course in January, and one of his better phrases was that it would be 'a piece of piss'. He is going to have a real shock when he starts.

Anyway, I spent most of the evening chatting to Ali, who is the girlfriend of our naval officer Andy Pomeroy. She is truly beautiful. I tried to convince her to start dating me, but she wouldn't. Not even the promise of mirrors on the ceiling, fur-lined walls and a tiger skin quilt would convince her. Mind you, I would have run a mile if she'd said yes, added to the fact that Shirley wouldn't have been very impressed. Andy said that she wouldn't be interested in me anyway as she had a fetish for sucking toes. I said, "Not a problem, I keep mine in a jar by the bed." He still isn't too sure if I was joking.

Eventually, we got fed up with the cheerfulness at Paul's so we headed back to the mess where a party was in progress. Stayed late, and did some dancing.

Sunday 6 November

I must have been very sociable last night because numerous people who I swear I have never seen or met before have been saying, "Hi, Trevor, how's your head?"

I tried to smile to these comments and not look as ill as I felt. Attempted to do a bit of studying this evening, but my brain wasn't functioning.

Tuesday 8 November

The end of ground school is in sight. We spent the morning at the swimming pool in York doing dinghy drills. I haven't been looking forward to this as my swimming isn't brilliant. The morning started with the swimming test, which I failed, so there will be remedial swimming for me once a week. The Kid will be joining me, as he is of a similar standard.

The dinghy drills began with a backwards jump off a three-metre diving board to simulate landing in the water. We then had to get into the dinghies, which wasn't as easy as it sounds, as they are very small and capsize if you don't get it right.

Back at the base, there was an hour of parachute descent drills. We were taught how to steer a parachute and we learnt the correct technique for landing. Surprisingly, we don't complete a real parachute jump. The risk of injury is too high. It seems that we are too expensive to be exposed to unnecessary danger. Flying training is regarded as dangerous enough.

More lectures this afternoon, including a good one on gyroscopic theory.

The instructor used a spinning bicycle wheel to demonstrate the gyroscopic effect, which made the lecture easier to understand. For the first time, I am beginning to comprehend aerodynamics as well. That is something I would not have thought possible a month ago.

A gyroscope is a spinning device, rotating rapidly around an axis that is free to move and change direction. A spinning top, for example, is a gyroscope. If the top is spinning on a plate, you can tilt the plate but the top will still remain in its original orientation. Gyroscopes are used in some of the flight instruments.

Thursday 10 November

Mark Harris is getting so well-known on his moose hunts in York that he got a round of applause in one pub when he arrived with his latest trophy. God knows what the poor girl thought of the whole affair.

During this morning's lecture, I gave a briefing about jet engine compressor stalls, and explained why an interruption of the smooth airflow into the engine would cause a loss of power, and how to best avoid these engine stalls in the Jet Provost. It went well, so it has been worth spending the majority of the last two nights studying the subject and preparing the briefing.

We had another one of those moral leadership lectures with the old Catholic priest. He really isn't all there. He asked me what my name was more than five times and then wanted to know what 'tribe' I belonged to. Totally confused him by saying I wasn't from a tribe, but from Woolwich in London. He seemed to think that because I am black, I must be from Africa, and ergo I must belong to a tribe. The guys all think it is hilarious. It is the most entertainment they have had in ground school. Won't be bothering going to another moral leadership lecture. They are a waste of time in this day and age anyway. The old boy means well, but he is about 200 years out of touch.

Tuesday 15 November

The days seem to consist of lectures and more lectures, interspersed with occasional physical exercise. The evenings are just as fun-packed: eat, study and sleep. We are due to have our first familiarisation flights in the Jet Provost on Friday, so I have been trying to get my stuff together in readiness.

The whole time we have been in ground school, we have been wearing the standard air force blue uniforms, but flying means green flight suits and I haven't seen mine in months. Also need to put in some work learning checks as the instructors will expect a basic knowledge of them.

Friday 18 November

The whole of no. 96 course was off to the squadron today as we all had our first flights scheduled. I flew with a young instructor, Flt Lt Andy Arundell, and it was great being airborne again. We raced off and were straight into low-level flying before climbing up to a few thousand feet to perform some aerobatics. Everything was strange, as I didn't know my way around the cockpit. Nevertheless, Flt Lt Arundell seemed happy enough over my efforts with the checks. The flight was just the motivation I needed before the next two weeks of exams.

When we landed, I had a message to go and see the chief instructor. He is the wing commander in charge of all the flying training on the base, and he only sees students who have been very, very good or very, very bad. I know I haven't been very, very good, but for the life of me I couldn't think what I had done that's been bad. Well, not anything the chief instructor would know about.

I was a very worried man, as I waited outside his office. But as it happens, it was about my terms of service. Because of the change from the RAF Regiment to aircrew, I could no longer remain on a six-year commission. I was told to sign a 16-year term of service or leave the course. Talk about putting the screws on. There wasn't much of a decision to make, but it would have been nice to have had some options to consider.

As soon as the day was finished, I disappeared down to London to see Shirley for the weekend. A new course starts on Monday so we are no longer going to be the new boys on the station.

Wednesday 30 November

We had the last exam today and that was the end of 10 days of relentless revision, lectures, studying and tests. The military has got this training thing down to a fine art. Among many other challenges, the initial officer training in the RAF exposes you to real hard work. Before my officer training, I would not have believed that you could work for 20 hours a day and do that effectively for several days. It has all been perfect preparation for courses like this one. I have never studied so hard in my life. If I had worked as hard as this at school and university, I would have been a straight-A student without any trouble. The volume of work was huge, with some topics that I found quite difficult. There was no flexibility in the marking either. If you failed, they were likely to kick you off the course.

Flying training is a very expensive business. It cost tens of pounds per hour to put a Chipmunk into the air for a trainee; hundreds for a Jet Provost; thousands for the Hawk fast jet, and tens of thousands for a front-line fighter. A fully qualified fast jet pilot had more than £3m spent on his training. In 1989 money.

Thursday 8 December

During the last week, we have been getting debriefed on our exams. Thankfully, everyone has passed, but there were some close shaves, including my Morse code exam. The tape I had been using for revision was very old and unbeknown to me it had been playing at a slow speed. The actual exam at the correct speed was a bit of a shock and I struggled with the decoding.

We have also started learning the checks and procedures for the Jet Provost and we have been getting more briefings for our week-long survival exercise on the North York Moors. There have been one or two excessive drinking evenings, which isn't surprising after all the exam pressure.

11–16 December

This is our six-day land survival exercise in the wilds of North Yorkshire with no food. You live off the land and are taught escape and evasion. The simulated scenario was that we had ejected over enemy territory. We were going to be taught how to survive and evade detection using only the contents of the ejector seat. Our only clothing was our standard flying suits and cold-weather flying jackets, but we were allowed to wear the sturdier army combat boots, which I was very thankful for. I can't afford to lose any more digits.

Day 1

As with all these exercises, a nice 5am start was the order of the day. It was followed by a long, slow drive in military transport vehicles to the middle of the North York Moors. Only four guys were searched for any prohibited provisions and uncannily they were among the few without any contraband. Cameron Gair had a hip flask of brandy that he had assumed would be found, but he wasn't among the chosen to be searched. I was wearing an old bowler hat from my Regiment days, and they didn't take it away from me.

After being dropped off by the lorries, there was a 10-mile hike over the moors to reach the campsite. We had just enough time before it got dark, to put up our small one-man tents (called bivvies), and then get some sleep. I woke up in the middle of the night to move my bivvy after having a bad dream about being washed away during a rainstorm.

It was my subconscious, bringing up memories of a very nasty night from my RAF Regiment days. Back then, on that wet October night having been on the go for 24 hours, I returned to my bivvy to get some sleep and found a small stream running through the middle of it. My sleeping bag and all my spare clothes were soaking wet. I ended up grabbing a few hours' sleep sitting under a tree with my rifle on my lap. It is amazing what exhaustion will do to you.

Day 2

This was a nice slow day. We had a few demonstrations on how to use a parachute as a sleeping bag and how to use the survival kit in the ejection seat to start a fire and catch fish. I sorted out my bivvy with extra leaves for insulation and put out a couple of fishing lines in the nearby stream. We were all camping within a few hundred metres of each other, so it was quite social. The Kid dropped by and gave me a potato, which was most welcome, and I made a big fire to cook it in. It was my only food for the day.

Day 3

A very busy day. We were told to make three-man bivvies and I was teamed up with Steve Shell and Cameron Gair. We also set up snares and traps for rabbits and birds. Our three-man bivvy was excellent. It was mega comfortable and it even had a door. Cameron was relentless, possessing unlimited energy. As well as his hip flask, he also had some illegal oxo cubes, so we made a drink to go with the small fish I had caught and a turnip from a nearby field. Not a feast by any means, but at least it was a little bit of food. Paul Gerrard, Bill Owen, as well as The Kid and John Bowland came around for short periods, no doubt attracted by the bonfire Cameron created outside our bivvy.

Day 4

The day started with a low-level fly past from a Jet Provost. It was fast and noisy, great! We were taught how to kill, gut and cook a fresh rabbit. The instructors had to buy one, as we hadn't caught a thing in our snares. It's a very messy business, but the roast rabbit was very good. It was the most food we had eaten all week. After that, we broke camp for escape and evasion training, which consisted of five hours crawling around in ditches and along hedgerows avoiding contact with anyone not in our group. At the end of the day, we were allowed to get some sleep in a barn. It was only for three hours but at least it was warm.

Day 5

More escape and evasion training, but we were each on our own. We had all been briefed on various rendezvous points that we had to make throughout the day, but we had to be careful as there were a bunch of guys from the Territorial Army looking for us. That went on all day and all night. I managed to get some sleep in an old hut, although it was freezing. The lack of food and all the walking was starting to add up.

Day 6

The last day and the final exercise was to hide in a wood, putting into practice everything we had been taught during the week. Fortunately, only the instructors, not the army, were looking for us. I found a hollow under a tree and covered myself in dead branches, and wasn't found, but eight of the guys were. From where I was hiding, I could see the instructors looking for them, and the boys being dragged off blindfolded. A whistle signalled the end of the exercise, so the non-found got themselves over to the waiting coaches and everyone was given sandwiches, drinks and chocolate for lunch. I could barely eat a thing as my stomach had shrunk so much. It wasn't until I was back at the base and had showered and put on clean clothes that I realised how badly we all must have smelt. The flying suit and underwear I had worn all week were festering.

The rest of the days up to the Christmas break have been spent learning checks, sorting out the local area maps we have to carry and generally preparing ourselves for flying in the New Year. The Christmas holidays are a bit of a blessing in disguise as we would normally be straight into a full flying programme. At least this way, we have a few weeks to study and get ahead of the game.

1989

Friday 3 January

Christmas was just a bit too good, and I didn't want to come back up here. Had a great skiing holiday with Shirley, and a couple of very social parties in London, which has meant that I have gotten myself totally out of the RAF routine.

The flying programme had me down to go up in the afternoon, but a sortie was added midmorning as Steve Shell reported in sick. At least he bothered to turn up, which is more than can be said for our navy duo, Andy Pomeroy and Ian Reid. For some reason, they thought we started on Wednesday. Ian told Adrian Bonwitt to get lost when Adrian telephoned him. He was convinced it was a practical joke.

Both my flights were with Flt Lt Goodwin, a cheerful New Zealander, and it seems I haven't forgotten everything I was taught on the Chipmunk. We completed just the basic flying handling stuff and although I managed to get all my checks correct, he wanted them completed faster. Totally worn out. It's like being back at the start of the Swinderby course. I have to concentrate on every little thing, as nothing is familiar.

I am also in trouble in the aircrew feeder. This is a small canteen attached to the squadrons, where the pilots can get a quick lunch without having to go all the way back to the mess. The lady who runs it wasn't pulling any punches: she said that one of her female cooks (who fortunately wasn't there) fancied black men, so I should watch out. Great! I can just imagine what she is going to look like, and the image isn't good. It will be a cycle ride back to the mess for lunch for me, at least for a while. I will have to warn Mark Harris to get his hunting gear ready.

Monday 6 January

There has been no more flying all week for me. I have spent the last few days running the squadron operations desk: answering phones, reminding people when they are supposed to go flying and helping the duty instructor keep the flying programme up to date. It is amazing how much can change, with aircraft developing faults and no longer being available. Student pilots reporting in sick or failing trips, and the weather not being good enough for a particular set of exercises. Those are just the things that happen in a normal day. Most importantly, we need to make maximum use of all the aircraft available and give everyone a fair share of flying.

The navy boys eventually turned up on Wednesday, just in time for a visit to the station by a couple of front-line Jaguar aircraft. Their pilots gave us a talk on their capabilities. It was very interesting, but I don't think I could ever fly that machine. I had a good look inside one and it seemed as if someone had just thrown a mass of instruments into the cockpit. There was a big screen in the middle and a head-up display, but the whole thing looked hideously complicated. One of the Jaguar pilots, known as Mewsey, is a good friend of Cameron Gair. They went to the same air cadet squadron in Newcastle. I always thought of Cameron as being a very honest and straight-talking person, but Mewsey is like an extreme version of Cameron. He really does tell it as he sees it, with no allowances for politeness. I like him.

Tuesday 10 January

The last couple of days have been fairly standard. Just one trip per day, and each was with Flt Lt Arundell. All my checks are getting better but he still wants more speed. Both sorties concentrated on the techniques needed to fly circuits in this machine. I flew some aerobatics on today's trip, which was good fun as always. It all happens a bit fast, but then we are going three times as quickly as the Chipmunk. Worryingly, I have had a few headaches. I think my helmet is a bit tight, and I will have to get it adjusted tomorrow. The Kid came down from his trip today looking totally spaced out, while Mark Harris is breezing along and seems to think he doesn't need to work very much. I, on the other hand, am having to work very hard to get any good results.

We have all been issued a student study guide that contains in detail everything the instructor will demonstrate and all the techniques for each and every sortie. I find that I need to have a thorough knowledge of what each trip involves so I can mentally practise any new procedure. That way when I am in the aircraft and the pressure is on, I have a bit more capacity to concentrate on the flying. It is best to prepare at least two trips ahead as you can never tell when the programme will change, and you may end up flying twice in the day.

Wednesday 11 January

I had an argument with Mark Harris this morning about the amount of work that we should be doing for each flight. He seems to think it is all down to natural ability, which is a shame because his natural ability failed him this afternoon and he had a very poor trip. I hope the penny has dropped and he will start to do some work.

Paul Binns called in sick today and was being a bit pathetic with it. Not sure if he was looking for sympathy – there is very little of it around. Flew again with Flt Lt Arundell and had my first experience of the circuit in the Jet Provost. We join at twice the speed of the Chipmunk. Everything was happening so fast that I couldn't keep up at times. Flt Lt Arundell was happy enough. He says my difficulties are quite normal for this stage of the course.

Friday 13 January

Bill Owen had a nightmare trip with the squadron boss, Sqn Ldr Murty. He managed to taxi out in the wrong direction and ended up facing an incoming aircraft. He got a minus mark for taxiing, which is the easiest thing that we do.

The process of getting out to an aircraft was not simple. For instructional trips, we were given a briefing covering exactly what would be taught. The instructor also used this brief to make sure we had read and understood the relevant chapters from the study guide. The briefs could last an hour for the more complicated trips. Student and instructor then headed to the operations desk in the squadron where they got all their flight information. This included which jet you were flying, the latest weather and any airspace restrictions or notices. A final mini brief was completed in front of the duty instructor, to make sure you hadn't forgotten anything before you signed the authorisation sheets to say that legally you were taking an aircraft to complete that specific trip, with all the manoeuvres required. Solo students had to be authorised by their instructor.

Once this was completed, there was a walk to the safety equipment section to don your life jacket, leg restraints, flying gloves and to pick up your helmet before the final stop with the engineers. The guys manning the operations desk had allocated you an aircraft already, so the engineers knew you were coming and they usually had the aircraft's technical log ready for you to check. All that was required now was another signature and off you went to your aircraft to commit aviation.

Tuesday 17 January

The whole of no. 96 course is progressing very well and everyone is in the circuit phase. To stop the congestion that would occur if we all stayed and flew circuits at Linton-on-Ouse we have moved to RAF Dishforth, which is one of our satellite airfields and is only 10 miles away. There isn't much there besides a long runway, an air traffic control tower and a couple of hangars that are seldom in operation. We are the only ones using the place, so it is perfect for us to practise our take-offs, circuits and landings.

I had the pleasure of flying out to Dishforth with Flt Lt Arundell and then completing the rest of my circuit trip. The circuits have gone quite well so far, and they are not nearly as frantic as I expected. I still have to concentrate and think about everything I do, and that is slowing me down. But I assume it will all get easier as I get more familiar with the aircraft. The navy boys, Ian Reid and Andy Pomeroy, flew their first solos today. However, the news that is causing the most excitement is that the pilot crew room at RAF Dishforth is full of porn.

Wednesday 18 January

No flying for me today and we are over at Dishforth again. Reg Armeanu, Adrian Bonwitt and Paul Gerrard all had their first solos. The boys have got a photo of Andy Arundell in the crew room reading a porn magazine. They are going to threaten to show it to his wife, but I'm not sure if bribery is one of the officer qualities we are supposed to be cultivating. Paul Binns is more miserable than usual, and this is encouraging all sorts of bad behaviour to be directed his way. Currently, Bill Owen and Paul Gerrard have convinced him that there is an aerobics run with the physical training instructors on Monday morning. I hope he doesn't turn up for it or he will be ultra-grumpy all next week. I'm just glad that they haven't shown him the porn magazine in the crew room, which contains a woman who looks just like his wife.

Friday 20 January

The Vale of York fog is back, so no flying for the last two days. We haven't left Linton-on-Ouse. Most of the guys have managed to occupy themselves with the usual studying, improving their knowledge of the aircraft systems and emergency checklists, learning new checks for the next phase and trying to improve the speed of the current ones. That all lasted until about lunchtime yesterday and since then, behaviour has slowly deteriorated. Last night, we went out to a strip bar with the student pilots from no. 1 squadron on their belated solo party. The main entertainment was a 'non-natural' blonde who one of the boys managed to chat up between her acts. He did it for a bet and won some money as well as a date with the fake blonde stripper.

Today is Mark Harris's birthday. As he has been a bit cocky over the last couple of weeks, the boys arranged for him to be snatched from the crew room by the combat survival and rescue section. They tied him up and took him up on to the moors where he was dumped.

He was left for only 20 minutes but wasn't amused.

Cameron and I started the evening in no. 1 squadron, drinking the beer they had left over from last night, and then moved on to happy hour in the mess. I tried and failed to persuade Ali to leave Andy Pomeroy (again) and have a vague memory of being in a nightclub with Steve Shell and his brother, Justin, and trying to convince some poor girl that the three of us were all related, as we shared the same father.

Wednesday 24 January

We were back at Dishforth all day again today, and I finally completed my first Jet Provost solo. It didn't seem as big a deal as the first solo in the Chipmunk. The trip itself was no problem, but in the excitement, I forgot to get taxi clearance from air traffic and to switch my taxi lights on. A mixture of nerves and eagerness I suppose. Mark Harris, Cameron Gair and John Bowland all had their first solos as well.

We are getting a bit worried about The Kid. He is finding the course quite tough. I think he is struggling with the speed of the aircraft. Our standard circuit speed is almost the same as the maximum speed of the Chipmunk. Most guys have adapted very well but he hasn't. I hope he can sort it out.

Thursday 26 January

We have been driving over to Dishforth every day but there has been very little flying because of rain and lots of low cloud. Bill Owen and Steve Shell completed their solos in the few breaks in the weather, so that only leaves Pete The Kid Coville.

Monday 30 January

Today was windy so we all headed off to RAF Elvington, which is another of the satellite airfields around Linton-on-Ouse. It is to the south of York and has a massive runway pointing straight into the wind, so just perfect for us today. The only problem with the place is that there is nothing there besides the runway. There isn't even a hangar or any large buildings. It makes Dishforth feel like a modern airfield. Air traffic control lives in what looks like a converted water tower, and we share a hut with the fire section. The engineers are working out of the lorries they drove over.

I was lucky to fly over to the airfield with Flt Lt Tony Barmby, our flight commander. We spent an hour flying around the circuit and amazingly, I got better. As well as enjoying myself, I can now get the aircraft into the air and complete the circuit and land with a fair amount of confidence.

During the next few sorties, the instructors will be steadily adding more complications such as engine problems or simulated low cloud levels. Nice simple circuits will be for our solo flights only. As soon as you get the hang of a technique, it is time to move on to something new. The pressure never stops.

Paul Binns was miserable again today, which prompted Bill to ask if he had much sex at the weekend. Strangely enough, his wife has told John Bowland that she thinks he is a bit unstable at the moment. Couldn't agree more. He is not a happy boy.

Tuesday 14 February

There has been very poor weather for the last week and a half – a mix of high winds and low cloud. We have finished most of the circuit phase, but have been flying every other day instead of the usual twice a day. Still, my checks are now up to scratch and I have read up on the next 10 instructional sorties. I flew with Flt Lt Barmby again today and did my sector recce. This is my first time properly away from the airfield and a chance to look at the local area – and with the aircraft flying at 240kts we were covering a lot of ground. Supposed to fly solo later, but again it was too windy.

Thursday 16 February

Only one sortie today, and that was spinning practice with the boss, Sqn Ldr Murty. We take a perfectly stable aircraft and make it fall out of the sky uncontrollably to show we are capable of recovering from such gross mishandling. The spin is not as quick as the Chipmunk, so I had some spare mental capacity to follow what was going on in more depth. Still not that comfortable with spinning though, as there are too many stories of spins going completely wrong and the pilots ending up on parachutes, or worse.

Friday 17 February

The only scheduled flying today was instrument flying, and I wasn't on the programme. I have been the duty student again this week, having to deal with the trivia that arises. The instructors' crew room decoration was one of those bits of trivia. They had been trying to get it redecorated for a month or so. I had started inquiries and making preparations earlier in the week, which paid dividends today, because as I wasn't flying I could get it done. The painters and decorators managed to get the whole thing finished in the day, and the instructors were most impressed.

The entire course was hanging around the student crew room at 4pm, as they had all finished flying, and I was so sick of them interfering with the decorators that I stacked them at 4.30pm. That was totally my decision, as I later had to explain to Flt Lt Arundell who wanted to know where everyone had gone. Fortunately, he agreed with my decision-making.

The evening happy hour in the mess was a laugh. A member of no. 2 squadron finished the course today and attempted to drink a flaming Drambuie. He failed miserably and succeeded in pouring the flaming liquid down the front of his flying suit. It was a good job that a few of his course were close enough to extinguish the flames quickly.

Sunday 19 February

Shirley has been up to visit me all weekend, and it has been a good change just to spend the weekend up here without drinking too much. We discovered that Bettys Tea Rooms in York is perfect for brunch, and Castle Howard is amazing and has beautiful grounds. Shirley has smartened me up as well. She forced me to buy some new clothes and a quilt for the bed, along with a kettle and mugs for the room. They have really made a difference. I don't know why I have just been making do – not enough time to think about such things I suppose.

Tuesday 21 February

Today was a beautiful day, and I flew two solo trips – but I'm not happy with either of them. Almost got lost on the first one and had to get a position fix from air traffic control, which resulted in a big dent to my pride. The second trip started badly. I activated the engine fire extinguisher during the pre-start checks by mistake. As part of the pre-start procedure, we carry out checks on all the aircraft systems. This can sometimes involve moving or pressing switches or just touching an instrument or switch. I was in a rush and pressed when I should have touched. The result was a bottle of fire extinguisher fired into the engine. The engineers said that it wouldn't damage anything, but it will cause them a lot of extra work as they have to wash the engine and then replace the fire extinguisher. All very embarrassing for me and I had to wait for a replacement aircraft.

On finally getting airborne, I got lost again, although it was only for a few minutes and I didn't need any assistance. As well as all of that, my ability to fly circuits seems to have gone backwards.

Wednesday 22 February

First thing this morning, I delivered a crate of beer to the engineers as penance for my fire extinguisher blunder. Then I was airborne with Flt Lt Barmby on an exercise that included recovering from a vertical position. We had to call it off half way through because my helmet earphones weren't working. The upside of this is that the safety equipment guys have issued me with the latest RAF helmet, the Mark 4. It fits well and is very light compared to the last one. The downside is that at some point in the trip, I managed to trap a nerve in my back. I tried to ignore it, but eventually, I had to give in and went to the doctor to get some pills. I now have two days off work, which is a blessing in disguise as the boys in the student crew room are being merciless about the fire extinguisher incident. Escaped down to London early.

Monday 27 February

After a good weekend away, I was airborne in the first wave with the boss, Sqn Ldr Murty. And I was as sharp as a tree. I'm putting it down to Monday morning blues. The trip was scored as average, which was a bit of a miracle.

Andy Pomeroy, Ian Reid and Steve Shell all failed their spin aeros checks, which is our first flight test. We need to pass it to ensure that we are up to course standard, and that our flying skills are sufficient to enable us to fly aerobatics solo, and be able to get out of a spin if we mishandle any of the manoeuvres. It is also a test of all the various circuits we have been taught. The good news is that the two Pauls, Adrian and Cameron all passed. Three Tornado F3s landed in the afternoon and those of us who weren't flying invited the pilots into the squadron. They were a nice bunch and had to land here as their base at RAF Leeming had closed after one of their colleagues had burst a tyre on landing on the only runway. The F3s are very modern machines compared to the Jaguars we saw earlier, but there is a navigator in the back seat controlling the radar and weapon systems. Their departure made me realise that we have a long way to go in our training to be fast jet pilots. The Tornados put on a bit of a show with a low and fast departure, and the speed they achieved by the end of the runway must have been close to 400 mph.

Wednesday 1 March

Extremely strong winds today but luckily, it was blowing straight down the short runway at Linton-on-Ouse so we have been using that for our circuits.

Because the wind speed is so high, our speed over the ground is a lot less than normal and there is no problem with stopping on the short runway. I prepared for a solo general handling trip, but as I taxied out it was cancelled due to the wind and instead I flew my first jet instrument flight with Flt Lt Arundell. It went well, but I had a severe case of the leans during the descent.

The leans occur when you have no horizon to look at and your senses get confused with all the turns and accelerations. The result can be that your instruments are telling you that you are straight and level, but your body is screaming at you that you are turning or descending or flying on your side. It has caused lots of accidents in the past and will probably continue to do so. I found it very difficult to ignore my senses and believe the instruments. If you don't concentrate, you could get into a lot of trouble very quickly.

The sortie ended with visual circuits, and that was almost as difficult as the instrument flying. The cloud had descended and together with the 30mph wind, the short runway and the number of aircraft flying in the circuit, it was very busy. Thankfully, Flt Lt Arundell only wanted to see a couple of circuits before we landed.

Steve Shell and Andy Pomeroy both passed their spin aeros retests, but The Kid is continuing to have a hard time of it. He destroyed an oxygen hose when he got it trapped against the ejector seat while strapping in and so had to change aircraft. Then he tried to get airborne with the canopy open and no flaps, all with the boss as his instructor. This is not good, and he will be lucky if he passes the course at this rate, assuming that he survives. Attempting to get airborne with no flaps is a good way of getting yourself killed.

Friday 3 March

The weather has been poor for the last few days and there has been very little flying. With all this spare time, a few of us decided to pay a visit to RAF Church Fenton, which is another training base to the south of York. Some of the guys who were at RAF Swinderby with me are training there. Dave Bayliss and Julian Marshall were on good form. Julian is still suffering from airsickness and has even managed to throw up during solo circuits. All credit to him, he is still there and determined to finish the course. Mark Harris, Ian Reid and Bill Owen all passed their spin aeros today.

Tuesday 7 March

There was lots of low cloud and rain again yesterday, and the met man predicted the same again for today. He was wrong. We had crystal-clear skies. I flew my final solo general handling trip before my spin aeros check. Reg and I spent the afternoon testing each other on procedures and techniques, which was very useful. John Bowland and The Kid, who also have their tests soon, joined us for the last hour or so.

Wednesday 8 March

I was airborne in the first wave with Flt Lt Andy Arundell, on my pre-test sortie. It wasn't my best by any stretch of the imagination, but it was good enough. I then had the test almost immediately, with an instructor from no. 1 squadron. It was much better than the morning trip, with just a few silly mistakes such as recovering from one of my manoeuvres at a low height and staying a bit too close to the extended centre line of the main runway at Linton. I hadn't thought about it before, but in retrospect, it is obvious that it makes life hard for air traffic, especially if they have aircraft flying instrument approaches to the airfield. All in all, it was a good pass, which I am pleased with. The Kid passed as well although he admitted it wasn't a great flight. Unfortunately, John Bowland failed his test and he is now on review. We had an emergency announcement mid-afternoon telling us that someone had crashed. It later transpired that it was Bill Owen. He was flying his first solo trip after the spin aeros test when he somehow managed to get himself into an irrecoverable situation, and had to eject. He has been picked up by a rescue helicopter and taken to the military hospital at Catterick – the good old Duchess of Kent Military Hospital, the same place I was initially taken with my bad feet. We have been told that he is all right and just a little bruised, but the boys are shocked.

I phoned Bill's girlfriend, Corinne, to explain to her what had happened. She thought it was a joke until I told her the crash had made the front page of the local evening newspaper as well as the national and local BBC news.

That evening, the whole course headed up in a minibus to see Bill. Paul Binns even brought his wife along, which didn't go down well. Why would Bill want to see Mrs Binns? No one could answer that question, and you would have thought they were best mates the way Mr and Mrs Binns behaved. Anyway, we didn't stay long as Bill looked drained, but he did tell us a great story about trying to get in touch with the base after the ejection. He said the only telephone number he could remember was the one for the officers' mess, so he called that. Flt Lt Ash, one of our instructors, happened to be walking past reception at the time and answered the call. The conversation went along the lines of:

"Officers' mess, Flt Lt Ash speaking."

"Hi, Sir, it's Bill Owen."

"Hi, Bill, what can I do for you?"

"Well! I have just ejected from my aircraft and I'm in a farmhouse south of the village of Malton."

There was a long pause and then lots of expletives.

Flt Lt Ash happened to be the instructor who authorised Bill for his flight. He raced back to the squadron to start the search and rescue process and also to make sure that all the paperwork was correct for the subsequent board of enquiry. This would explain why he was visibly twitching for most of the afternoon.

Bill had managed to get himself into an inverted spin, which we are not taught, as it is not allowed on the Jet Provost. I am amazed that he had the presence of mind to notice that he was passing 5,000 feet and initiate the ejection while upside down, spinning at a high rate and under a lot of negative Gs. I can quite truthfully say that if I were in that situation, I would be dead. I would have been trying to get the aircraft to recover all the way to the ground. Mark is very confident that he wouldn't have got into a spin in the first place. He thinks he is that good.

Thursday 9 March

There was very little flying today, so we took it in turns to drive up to Catterick to see Bill. He is back to more of his usual self and has been entertaining the nurses with tall tales. The latest is that he stayed with the aircraft until he was sure it was clear of a school before ejecting.

He had to walk over a couple of fields with his parachute in one hand and helmet in the other before flagging down two old ladies in a car. He must have looked like something from the Second World War to them, doubly so when he said:

"Excuse me, could you take me to a telephone please, I've just crashed my aircraft." They took him to a nearby farmhouse where he called the officers' mess, and while he waited for the helicopter, he said he tried to convince a very active four-year-old boy not to become a pilot when he grew up.

Weekend 10–12 March

Bill's crash has been playing on my mind, but fortuitously I had a long weekend away with Shirley and five friends at Butlin's holiday camp in Bognor Regis. It proved the best way to forget about the events of the last week. I didn't want to dwell on them, and I didn't want to worry Shirley.

Not sure who decided on Butlin's for a weekend, but it was an inspired choice. Brilliant and totally horrific at the same time, if that is possible. The water park was great, as were a few of the faster roller coaster rides. We sampled all the social activities in the evening, including a concert by Sixties icon Gene Pitney, which was surprisingly good. On the down side, the cuisine consisted of processed food, which was never going to be popular with Shirley as she is a professional chef. She didn't eat a thing, and we had to go to a few of the local pubs for meals. Not that I complained.

I was so tired on Sunday night that I was falling asleep on the drive back up to Linton. Reg said that he was flashing his lights as he passed me on the motorway, but I didn't even notice.

Monday 13 March

Down on the programme for my first navigation flight today, but ended up with an instrument flight instead. I'm sure I still had some alcohol in my system from the weekend, and struggled to believe what the instruments were telling me most of the time.

Wednesday 15 March

Airborne in the first and second waves on my first two solo general handling flights to include aerobatics, and although my flying was fine, they weren't enjoyable. Still, I survived them intact.

One of the senior course forgot to sign out on the authorisation sheets before his flight. The duty instructor told air traffic to allow him to taxi his aircraft to just outside the squadron building, and then he sent the sheets out for him to sign. The whole thing had the look of a 1920s movie set...

"Have my man bring those pesky authorisation sheets out to my aircraft will you."

The Kid had a very bad trip with Flt Lt Tony Barmby. So bad, that he is no longer allowed to fly solo aerobatics and he will have to retake his spin aeros test.

The news from Bill is also not so good. He has suffered some back damage and has to have three weeks' bed rest. He has been moved to the RAF hospital at Ely in Cambridgeshire.

Friday 17 March

I flew my first two medium-level navigation trips today. A dual in the morning and a solo in the afternoon. As always with new skills, it takes a lot of concentration to produce a good outcome and as a result, I am worn out. These trips are flown at a few thousand feet, so you can see quite a distance ahead, but even so flying accurately isn't easy.

The solo took me up into Northumberland, and I had a couple of American F15 fighters show a bit of interest in me. They changed course and headed in my direction and it was very tempting to turn and try to get behind them. I would have been in a lot of trouble if I had been reported – and I don't think they would have taken me seriously anyway. They are 200 times more powerful than my little jet.

In 1989, the American military presence in Europe was huge. There were six big air bases in England and numerous others spread over Western Europe. They outnumbered all the rest of the combined NATO air forces and generally had the best equipment. The F15 was accepted as the best fighter in the world.

Monday 20 March

I managed two trips in glorious conditions today: another dual and a solo. On the dual, I had one of those moments when I needed to engage my brain before opening my mouth. I had to simulate an aircraft fire and call it in on the emergency radio frequency, but total and utter garbage came out of my mouth. Most pilots try to monitor the emergency frequency while flying, so a lot of people have heard my radio call. It was embarrassing.

Cameron Gair has been giving me a hard time about being a Londoner. He is from Newcastle and thinks that there should be a minefield along the M25, along with a permanent combat air patrol and watchtowers to keep the soft southern folk confined below the Watford Gap. I don't think the people I grew up with on my east London council estate would have any problems with a minefield or watchtowers, but I don't want to spoil the illusions of the poor deluded boy.

Wednesday 29 March

We have all had a week off for Easter, and I have spent the majority of it in London with Shirley being very unmilitary.

Back to work today and I spent the morning in the procedures trainer in ground school, getting back up to speed on my checks. Fortunately, I wasn't scheduled to fly until the afternoon, and that was on an instrument flight. Not unexpectedly, it was hard work, but I achieved a good pass.

We have been told that the senior officers on the station are looking for two students from our course to send to helicopter training. They won't necessarily send the worst students as helicopters are tricky machines and need a fair amount of ability to fly. I just hope that my scores are good enough to allow me to stay.

Thursday 30 March

Mark Harris, Adrian Bonwitt, Andy Pomeroy, Cameron Gair and John Bowland all passed their basic instrument flying grading (BIFG) test today. That was despite having the worst controller on the base working on the radar and directing the approaches. She is known as Air Head and even the instructors are a bit wary when she is on duty.

The BIFG test simulates getting airborne into low-level cloud and completing a climb purely on the cockpit instruments, under the direction of air traffic control. Once, at height, you have to demonstrate safe recovery from unusual positions using only the flight instruments. This is to simulate getting disorientated or inadvertently flying into cloud. These positions can be as drastic as the aircraft pointing straight down towards the ground, or upside down. The final part of the test is to demonstrate the following of air traffic control instructions accurately enough to complete a safe descent through a layer of cloud. Once, passed, the students are cleared to fly into clouds solo for the first time, although only with air traffic assistance.

Friday 31 March

I flew my instrument test pre-ride in the morning, and it didn't go as planned. It is obvious that I need more practice at recovery from unusual positions. The rest of the trip was all right, so although it wasn't a fail I will have to fly another. The instructors won't put anyone forward for a test unless they are confident that he will pass. No test for me today and just to rub it in, The Kid and Steve Shell got through their tests today. That leaves only Reg and me to pass.

Monday 3 April

I flew my pre-ride again, with Flt Lt Barmby, and this time it was better, so on to the test. The examiner was another instructor from no. 1 squadron. It was a decent pass, although the air traffic controllers at RAF Church Fenton did their best to mess it up for me with some very poor controlling. Reg failed another pre-ride today. That is his third, so he had better watch out. Bill Owen is back at the station and on good form.

Tuesday 4 April

Today was another hard working day. I flew in the morning with a new instructor, Flt Lt Shaun Errington. He seemed nice enough, a very relaxed man, and he gave me a few very useful pointers during our general handling trip. On landing, it was straight into planning for a high-level navigation trip, which was cancelled. Instead, it was airborne again with Flt Lt Errington on more instrument flying. The test I did yesterday was just a basic level after all.

Reg Armeanu was airborne again on another BIFG pre-ride with Flt Lt Tony Barmby when he had a control restriction. The controls became extremely hard to move when they tried to roll the aircraft. Reg said that Tony Barmby gave him control and then started to tighten the straps of his ejection seat. Reg wasn't impressed with the thought of taking the short route down to the ground. They declared an emergency and landed safely and Reg passed his test in the afternoon.

Another new course has arrived on the station, and they will be joining us on no. 3 squadron when they finish ground school. We won't see them on the squadron for a few weeks.

Wednesday 5 April

The weather was very poor today – cold, low cloud and rain – so no flying for anyone on the station. I am quite glad as I can do with the rest and it has given me time to get ahead with the studying.

Bill Owen had his ejection seat handle and initiation cartridge presented to him by the safety equipment guys. They have mounted them on a wooden plinth, and they look good. What is left of his aircraft is in one of the hangars. The only identifiable bits are the engine and the ejector seat.

Everyone on the course is losing weight although our eating habits haven't changed. I think it is stress. Steve Shell has had a rash on his arm since Christmas and his stress levels have not been helped by the fact that he, John Bowland and The Kid are in the running for the helicopter course.

Monday 10 April

The weather for the last six days has been rubbish, with lots of rain and overcast cloud. There has been no flying and a few of the guys are getting ground-happy. They don't want to get into the air.

Steve Shell managed to get himself arrested for drunk-driving over the weekend, the stupid bugger. He was a marginal fail on the roadside breathalyser, so he was taken to the police station for a blood test and he is still waiting for the results. I hope for his sake they are negative as he will be in a whole load of trouble from the RAF if they aren't.

Spent the morning planning another high-level navigation route, which I still didn't fly. Can't complain though, as I had an introduction to low-level flight instead: 240kts at 250ft, and it is the most thrilling thing I have ever done. I think I will like low-level flying.

There has been a group of young teenage Air Training Corp cadets staying on the station over the last week and a very smart bunch of lads they are. Two of them are black guys, and although I haven't had a chance to chat to them personally, I have nicknamed them the brothers. We were waving to each other madly when I passed them on my ride back to the mess today, much to Cameron's amusement.

BAME

Wednesday 12 April

Up very early this morning to plan for the high-level navigation sortie again, and this time they delayed the take-off until late morning, so I could have stayed in bed. It is supposed to be an easy flight, but I had to work hard. Got around the route and didn't get lost, but there was nothing easy about it. Flew the solo trip on exactly the same route in the afternoon, and it was much easier the second time around. I would even go as far to say that I enjoyed it. As I got strapped into the aircraft for the solo trip, a ground crewman who I had never seen before asked me which air force I flew for and was it the Saudi or Nigerian? I said London, which confused him. Maybe I should have said Woolwich London, but I think that would have blown his mind.

RACISM

When I landed, I spoke to the ground crew chief about it, and he was more than a bit embarrassed. The guy is new, having only just qualified, and the rest of the ground crew are convinced that he is a can short of a six-pack. It isn't the only weird comment he has come out with.

The banter in the crew room today is all about The Kid. He was flying on a solo trip and had a near miss with John Bowland, who was flying dual with Flt Lt Steve Ash. John says he saw another aircraft flash past 20 feet away. It was so close he could hear jet noise from the engine. Steve Ash didn't even see the aircraft, but he said straight away, "I bet that was Coville."

The Kid naturally wasn't concerned. The man has a totally different nervous system to the rest of us. He just said, "Oh! I wasn't that close at all, I've had two or three which have been much closer." Don't mess with The Kid. He is truly dangerous!

Thursday 13 April

The met brief this morning was full of laughter. There were three Central Flying School (CFS) examiners in attendance. They will be flying with instructors and students over the next few days. When the met man walked into the brief, he said, "Good morning, sir, gentlemen and CFS."

That caused much merriment. Most people liked the idea of CFS being a separate subspecies. The fun didn't stop there as the met man suggested that the weather today would be clear, with hardly a cloud in the sky. That brought the house down as outside there was cloud totally obscuring the sky at around 600ft. This he explained was just a quirk due to local conditions that had taken the met team by surprise, and would be gone in a very short while. The low cloud cover stayed around all day, so there was very little flying.

Those met guys should ask someone to get them an office with windows.

I did manage to get a flight in a Jet Provost Mk5. One of the instructors was leading a formation flight for two of the senior course so there was a spare seat in his jet. I spent most of my time in total amazement as we were practically flying aerobatics, with the student pilots keeping exact position on either side of the instructor's aircraft. The three machines may as well have been welded into position their flying was that good. It's a different world from Chipmunk formation.

Steve Shell has been given the clear on his blood test over possible drunk-driving, lucky boy.

Friday 14 April

Most of today was spent preparing all the jokes and high jinks for tonight's Dining In. Someone had got hold of a blow-up doll, rigged it to a canister of helium and hidden the whole thing behind the curtains in the dining room, along with a deflated, chalk-filled weather balloon. There was a lack of no. 1 squadron representation while all this was going on, so many of their napkins were also filled with chalk. As usual, fake wine glasses and a few laughter boxes were scattered about.

My memory starts to get a bit hazy about the evening, but this is what I recall. The normal Dining In night rules applied, and there were no high jinks until after the toast to the Queen at the end of the dinner. I hadn't drunk very much at all at that point, but I do remember then having a few brandies before joining in with the mess rugby against one of the junior courses. At some point, there was a tug of war against the instructors, who were led by the chief instructor. I have no recollection of getting to bed.

Saturday 15 April

I was woken by loud banging on my bedroom door. It was Cameron's Jaguar pilot friend Mewsey who wanted to thank me for a great evening. That was a bit of a worry, as I didn't even know that he was there last night. As I slowly came back to consciousness, the worry increased. My waistcoat and jacket were absent. My shirt had a sleeve missing and had a big burn mark on the back. Most disturbing was the officers' mess ceremonial bell sitting on top of the television.

The carpet in the mess reception has been badly burnt. Someone has obviously tried to burn their course number into it, but only a number 9 can be clearly identified. The other number can't be made out, which means the blame cannot be directed to one particular course. All of the current courses at Linton are in the nineties. John Bowland is a prime suspect. He is a bit of a pyromaniac in his spare time and he is already in trouble as earlier in the evening he set light to one of our instructors, Flt Lt Miriam Williams, and he also tried to ignite the chief naval officer.

The Kid was sent to bed by one of the station officers after being found kissing a picture of the Queen in the main hall. The chief instructor was so impressed with the blow-up doll as it floated across the dining room that he was heard to say it had more airborne time than all of no. 1 squadron this week.

Monday 17 April

The talk on the squadron today is still about Friday night. All the students are going to have to pay for a new carpet in the mess reception. It seems that I also owe an apology to air traffic officer Sue Clark for 'fondling' her during the tug of war. And I might have to write a letter of apology to the station commander after telling him to 'piss off' during the mess rugby. This was the same game in which I got involved in a fight with one of the Royal Navy pilots who is an ex-Royal Marine. I have no recollection of any of this, but the guys reminded me of the eight brandies I drank before I got completely out of hand.

Tuesday 18 April

Flt Lt Andy Arundell is back from a two-week holiday to the West Indies, so I was airborne with him in the morning and again in the afternoon. Both trips were instrument flying, in preparation for the advanced instrument flying grading (AIFG) test tomorrow. Paul Binns passed his AFIG, as did Ian Reid, with an above-average score. The Kid failed his test after thinking that he had flown well. That is always a bad sign. Most students tend to be their own worst critics and it helps to be honest about your weaknesses, otherwise it is hard to eradicate them. The Kid probably just doesn't realise he has any weaknesses. He is wired differently after all.

The AIFG includes a diversion to another airfield with an instrument approach to a runway using air traffic control instructions. You have to demonstrate accurate instrument flying to achieve a pass as you will be cleared to fly in some fairly poor weather conditions while solo.

Wednesday 19 April

I was up at the crack of dawn to do a bit of work for my test today, and it seems that the old RAF Regiment saying of 'Prior Planning and Preparation Prevents Piss Poor Performance' holds true. Passed the AFIG with an above-average mark, even though I was working so hard that at times I couldn't have processed any more information.

Reg Armeanu and Cameron Gair have admitted that they burnt the carpet in the mess last Friday night. The squadron will have to pay, but no one is causing a fuss about it. Even the boss hasn't commented. I think everyone is just pleased that someone owned up. No. 93 course has graduated today, so we are now the senior boys at no. 3 squadron.

Tuesday 25 April

I flew a general handling trip today with Flt Lt Miriam Williams. It was hard work but I got a good result although I inadvertently entered a spin while trying to complete an aerobatic manoeuvre. Miriam found my call of, "Yeah ha! Bill Owen here we go."

Very funny, but in the back of my mind, I thought this could all go very badly and we could end up on parachutes. I did my recovery drills, and we exited the spin pointing vertically down. I was so excited that I pulled too hard and greyed out during the recovery.

At high speed, if you turn quickly the apparent weight of your body increases from 1G, which is your normal body weight. As the G increases, the blood in your body tries to drain towards your feet, and the lack of blood and hence oxygen in your brain causes your vision to become black and white. If you continue to pull to a higher amount of G, you get tunnel vision, which will get progressively narrower until you pass out. A sudden onset of high G can cause instant unconsciousness, which has resulted in many fatal accidents.

There was another crash today. This time it was a Bulldog aircraft from RAF Topcliffe (another of the satellite airfields for Linton-on-Ouse). That airfield and its aircrafts are used by the navy for elementary flying training before students' progress to the Jet Provost here at Linton-on-Ouse.

Rumour has it that a German student on one of his first solo flights flew into cloud. He got himself disorientated, panicked and jumped out of the aircraft. A bit drastic, not sure what's wrong with turning around if you are heading towards a cloud. Anyway, he landed safely in his parachute, but the German government owes Her Majesty one new Bulldog aircraft.

Friday 28 April

I flew my first trip with Flt Lt Ash today. I have been trying to avoid him as he has a fearsome reputation. There were no excuses for me today, as there was 50km visibility, a light breeze and hardly a cloud in the sky. I psyched myself up and blasted airborne in a sleek silver fun ship for some general handling. Enjoyed myself, flew very well and scored my highest ever mark, so much for being wary of Flt Lt Ash. Flew again on a solo in the afternoon, and then disappeared to London for a weekend with Shirley.

Monday 2 May

The course is night flying all this week, so I didn't get back from London until lunchtime. Slept in the afternoon and then went to work at 7pm. It was a very busy night, with two dual trips and one solo. There are no big dramas with night flying, just a bit of mental re-tuning required for the landings, as there aren't the same visual clues. I climbed up to 10,000ft on my solo just to look at the stars. They are quite beautiful without the streetlights dulling them, and it is peaceful up there.

Thursday 5 May

The night flying continues. Flew down to a base in Lincolnshire and did an instrument approach. The air traffic controller sounded like the Grim Reaper as he had an incredibly deep voice and spoke very s-l-o-w-l-y and precisely. It was all a bit eerie.

Escaped down to London early for the weekend and spent most of it building a wooden shed for Shirley's garden. It looks good, even if I say so myself.

Monday 8 May

The squadron was night flying again tonight, but I was due to have the night off, as I finished all my night flying last week. Didn't get to work until midday, and then I found that I was in serious trouble. I was the duty student last Thursday night, and part of my responsibility was to make sure that the crew room was tidy before locking up. I had wanted to escape to London, so had asked Reg to lock up for me. No problem with that, but the assumption that the boys would tidy up after themselves was wrong. They had eaten a take-away curry and left the remains all over the student crew room. It had started to grow fungus over the weekend and our flight commander, Flt Lt Tony Barmby, was not happy. It's my fault for not supervising the primary school children correctly. As a result, I am the duty student again tonight, as well as running the operations desk.

Wednesday 10 May

Our low-level navigation phase has started, and the fun factor has increased as well as the amount of work. We have been told that successful navigation is primarily achieved by accurate planning, so we have been spending a lot of time planning our routes. Flew today with the boss and had a very good trip. It would have been hard not to do well as the visibility was awesome.

The ground school instructors were right. Plan accurately and then just fly the plan. Still, it was hard work flying at exactly 240kts while climbing and descending over the ground to maintain a height of 250ft, as well as keeping on a precise heading. Flew the route solo again in the afternoon, at the height of 500ft, as solo students are not allowed down to 250ft. It still doesn't detract from the sheer enjoyment of going fast at low level.

I am still the duty student, courtesy of last week's night flying shambles. As I was locking up after some extra navigation planning, a glider drifted out of the sky and landed on the grass just outside the squadron. The airfield was closed and air traffic had shut, so it was up to me to deal with the pilot. The poor bloke had been airborne for six hours on some mega cross-country flight and had run out of thermals to keep airborne. It didn't take long to sort him out. Just a few telephone calls to get him picked up and an escort for his transport when it arrived at the station. All in all, a very full day and I am exhausted.

Friday 12 May

Today, I arranged to fly with Pat Voigt, who is one of the young instructors from no. 2 squadron. We had planned a land-away to Farnborough in Hampshire for the weekend. I had been feverishly organising this trip for a while. We flew low level on the way down, and the plan is for another low-level route on the way back on Monday.

I was a bit anxious as the airspace around Farnborough is very congested, and it wouldn't take much of an error in planning or navigation to fly through Heathrow's air traffic zone. That would be very career-limiting for both of us. However, we made it, although I have never landed with such little fuel.

As far as I am concerned, everyone wins on these trips. The boss is happy, as the aircraft has been used productively. I fly two trips from the syllabus and get to experience all the problems associated with operating near the London control zone, and best of all, Pat and I get a long weekend in London without the hassle of the train from York or the A1 motorway. Perfect!

A land-away is a term used to describe any occasion that an aircraft is landed away from its home airfield. It could be just to refuel, to overnight or, as in this case, to spend the whole weekend away.

Monday 15 May

There was a Tube strike in London, and I only just made it back to Farnborough on time. The flight back up was easier than the one on the way down. Pat Voigt is off to Edinburgh tonight on another land-away. By the end of the day, he will have had breakfast in London, lunch in York and dinner in Edinburgh. That's pretty amazing for any job.

Wednesday 17 May

The whole course is getting stressed as we are all very near to our basic handling test, or BHT. This is very important as it ensures that we can progress to the next part of the course for which we fly the more powerful Jet Provost

Mk5. Only students who are selected for fast jet training get to fly it. The boys selected for helicopters and transports continue on the Mk3 and complete separate specialist lead-in courses.

We have just been asked what we would ultimately like to fly, a 'dream sheet'. I have stuck down Harriers and Phantoms. Reg wants to fly the Jaguar, and The Kid has also put down the Phantom. The Kid is still struggling with the basic course, so flying the Phantom really is a dream for him at the moment.

Friday 19 May

I flew my BHT pre-ride in the morning with the station commander and the test itself a bit later with Sqn Ldr Murty. Achieved a good pass and I am relieved and happy. The test consisted of everything we have learnt to date including a short low-level section and I managed not to make any major mistakes.

It was a weird day to be airborne as there was a lot of industrial pollution in the air. On the ground, it looked like an average hazy day, but once airborne, the haze only continued up to around 3000ft and then the air cleared. Climbing out of the haze was like emerging from under water. There was a distinct, yellow boundary between the clear air above and the polluted haze layer. It can't be good breathing that stuff. Air isn't naturally yellow, so it must contain some nasty chemicals.

Adrian had a very scary moment while flying with Flt Lt Miriam Williams. He was using a sideslip technique to lose height on a practice forced landing when the aircraft went into heavy buffet, which is the precursor to a spin. We practise recovering from these situations at several thousand feet because the aircraft can take quite a bit of height to recover. Adrian was only at a few hundred feet, and if they had spun, they would have hit the ground in a couple of seconds with no chance of ejecting. They both seem a bit shaken and spent a long time sitting outside the squadron discussing how they managed to get into the situation, and how to avoid it in the future.

This is the end of the first part of the course, and we are all off for a few weeks holiday. I need a break as the last few weeks have passed at a hectic pace and the pressure has been on. When we return, those of us selected for fast jets will be flying the Jet Provost Mk5 speed machine.

Fast Jet Lead-in

No. 96 Basic Flying Training Course
RAF Linton-on-Ouse,
1989

When I returned to RAF Linton-on-Ouse for the fast jet lead-in course in June 1989, the world was reeling from news of the Tiananmen Square Massacre that had just taken place in China. Official figures of the number of pro-democracy demonstrators killed in Beijing were around 250. According to unofficial estimates, the death toll reached several thousand. Closer to home, the old Soviet Union continued to crumble while in Poland the trade union party.

Solidarity was elected, peacefully taking over from the communist party. Cracks were also forming in the old guard of the RAF: the first female flight crew were selected and were about to start training.

Monday 12 June

I have been away from work for three weeks and oh, it's so good to be back! Joking of course. I drove up last night to discover that the lady who looks after our section of the mess had locked my room. Not that anything would have been stolen, but because she was worried it would have been used by anyone with friends visiting at weekends, especially as it has a double bed. I agree; it would have been like a mini hotel. Anyway, I couldn't get to the keys until the morning so I spent the night in a sleeping bag in John Bowland's room. Needless to say, I was very tired, but because I did quite a lot of work over the holidays, there was no difficulty in passing the Jet Provost Mk5 technical exam that we sat this morning. Still had a few checks to learn for the new machine, although there is very little difference to the Mk3A in the cockpit.

There are no surprises as to who has been selected to continue the fast jet training. Steve Shell is completing a helicopter lead-in course before heading to RAF Shawbury to start flying those machines. The Kid Coville and John Bowland are starting their multi-engine lead-in courses and will continue with the Jet Provost Mk3. It looks as though Bill Owen will join them: he won't be able to fly on an ejection seat for much longer. He has quite a lot of back pain and the doctors are worried that there will be permanent damage to his spine if he has to eject again, so they won't take the chance of sending him to fast jets.

No. 96 course is now the senior course on no. 3 squadron. Our junior course, no. 99, has finished ground school and the survival exercise, and has arrived to start flying on the squadron.

Wednesday 14 June

Flying this morning in the first wave on a general handling sortie with the boss, and after an hour on the ground, airborne again with Flt Lt Errington on an instrument flying trip. I managed a quick sandwich and then was in the air for solo general handling. It was my first solo in the Mk5 and during the trip, I managed to get the machine up to 25,000ft and to 350kts. No doubt about it, this machine is very fast, but I didn't have enough energy to practise many aerobatics.

Two Hawk aircraft from RAF Valley collided and crashed in north Wales this morning. They were flown by student pilots, Simon Tompkins (Tommo) and Mark Seymour from the old no. 91 course here at Linton-on-Ouse. From what we have heard so far, they were completing a turning rejoin to get back into formation with their lead aircraft when they collided. Tommo is dead, but Mark managed to eject safely. I know Mark, as we travelled together down to London a few times, but I didn't know Tommo very well. He was a very good friend of Andy Pomeroy and one of the air traffic control girls. It has been another sobering reminder of the dangers of this job.

We were told at the beginning of the course that there was a one-in-12 chance of being killed in a flying accident during our RAF careers. That is a reflection of the dangerous low-level environment in which most fast jets operate and also of the workloads of the flight crews. That said, there has been a continual improvement in flight safety. Back in 1959 more than 350 aircrew were killed in flying accidents.

Monday 19 June

We are all flying instrument trips at the moment, and getting closer to the instrument rating test, which will clear us to fly instrument approaches in poor weather while solo. It will be the last instrument test on this aircraft. Everyone is busy booking practice diversions to other airfields, as we will have to fly one as part of the test.

Ian Reid managed to fly a whole approach into the civilian airfield at Warton with his undercarriage retracted. He only noticed this after reaching his minimum descent height. His instructor wasn't impressed and Ian says that if he was on a solo land-away, he would have landed with the wheels up. It is a good reminder to the rest of us that civilian airfields do not request a check that our landing gear is down, as they do in the military.

Bill Owen is flying again and is working hard trying to catch up with the rest of the course. He managed to get into another inadvertent spin today, or so he tells us. It doesn't appear to have affected him psychologically – he is still his usual talkative self.

The junior course found a baby bird outside the squadron. They have made it a small cage and are busy giving it bits of food. What is the attraction? I think the creature is just a biohazard myself, but I would not be popular if I voiced that opinion.

Tuesday 20 June

I flew my instrument-rating test pre-trip in the morning and then the test itself at lunchtime with one of the senior instructors from no. 1 squadron. It was a very good trip, so good that I passed with the highest score possible, much to my amazement – and that of everyone else.

It has been very hot over the last few days and today the temperature reached 30°C, and I was being cooked in the cockpit. We still have to wear all the correct layers with our flying suits – long johns and a roll-neck long-sleeved top – because of fire hazards. After all the concentration needed during the test, it was a very sweaty Trevor at the end of the trip. Some people say that this is a glamorous job...

This evening, I took Flt Lt Miriam Williams for a beer in the bar. He has been my instructor for most of my trips leading up to the test today, so the good score is partly due to his instruction.

Wednesday 21 June

Woke up with a very stiff neck and had to cancel today's trips. I was supposed to be flying maximum rate possible turns with the boss. You pull a sustained 4G during the turns on this trip, and your whole body (and head) feels as if it weighs four times more than usual, so there was no way I would survive with a stiff neck. In fact, Cameron Gair blacked out flying these turns. He said it was as if someone flipped a switch and he then woke up about a minute later. If he was manoeuvring at low level when that happened, he would not have survived. Scary stuff.

Took advantage of the free afternoon to visit air traffic control. I wanted to have a chat about the few mishaps that occurred yesterday. Ian Reid was almost sent to the wrong airfield on his instrument test and Reg spent 25 minutes being directed around the skies to get to RAF Leeming, which is only 15 miles away. They weren't on form over in air traffic control and I didn't get any constructive answers to my questions. It must be the heat.

Thursday 22 June

We have the annual summer ball tomorrow night, so after a general handling flight this morning the rest of the day was spent in the officers' mess helping to prepare for the party. Every department on the station has been given rooms to decorate and the overall theme is the Wild West. All the rooms are looking grand and a lot of effort has been put into decorations. The mess bar has been transformed into a saloon with a swing door entrance, unadorned tables and chairs, sawdust on the floor, subdued lighting and an old piano in the corner.

Friday 23 June

Happy Birthday to me! The lady who runs the reception at the mess rang the squadron crew room and sang me happy birthday. It made my day. Didn't get the day off though. I was airborne flying low-level navigation with Miriam Williams, and it was not easy. My speed control was poor throughout the trip. Constant adjustment is required as the aircraft climbs and descends over terrain and I have not mastered this. I don't normally criticise instructors, but I'm not sure about Miriam Williams's techniques. His demonstrations are not very clear and I am beginning to think he isn't very good at low-level. Instrument flying is obviously more his thing. That doesn't help me, as I have got to achieve at least an average standard of low-level flying to pass this course.

The baby bird is starting to get airborne around the crew room. It is a much faster learner than the rest of us, and it doesn't even have a flying instructor.

I picked Shirley up from the railway station after work and the entire course headed over to the house of one of the instructors for cocktails before the summer ball started. It was a fun-filled evening without getting totally out of hand. Shirley and I did not manage the 5am champagne breakfast, although more than a few people did.

Saturday 24 June

It seems that one of the guys from no. 98 course, known as Mac, chatted up the – young and slightly drunk daughter – of one of the squadron leaders at the ball last night. The inebriated young lady was persuaded to accompany Mac to his room in the mess. On hearing of this, the squadron leader immediately went to find his daughter. He eventually found Mac's room and knocked on the door, only to have it opened by a young man wearing just a condom. Mac thought one of the boys from his course would be at the door. Unsurprisingly, the squadron leader was not laughing. Mac, it seems, has not got a very good reputation on the station. He has a series of mishaps behind him and most people think that this will be the final nail in his coffin.

Tuesday 27 June

Mac is on his way out of the air force. He has been told to be off the station by tomorrow. I don't know the bloke, but somehow he has managed to upset most of his fellow students and all the people in authority that he has come into contact with. No one is trying to defend him and no one is sad to see him go, not even his fellow course members.

The baby bird was out of its cage again today. It is getting bigger but is still a bit unstable. It was standing on one leg cleaning itself when it overbalanced and fell off its perch. It also caused a lot of amusement by shitting on the shoulder of one of the junior course. They will insist on playing with the creature. Once, it is more stable in its flight, they intend to release it into the wilds of Yorkshire.

Thursday 29 June

I was airborne early today, on a navigation exercise that included my first-ever target. We are taught how to overfly (and later on bomb) a specific target from low level. It is a core skill of any ground attack pilot. We plan these target runs on large-scale Ordnance Survey maps, which are very similar to the ones that hill walkers use. I am told that once we become more proficient, we can expect targets as difficult as telephone boxes. At the speeds we fly, the target runs are only about a minute long. The trick to a successful run is to pick a big initial point that you can easily find, and make sure you are nicely lined up on the correct heading before the start of the target run as it is all over very quickly.

Flew the trip again solo in the afternoon and then escaped to London for a long weekend. Shirley is taking me to the Royal Opera House to see The Marriage of Figaro. She is still trying to smooth out my rough edges.

Low-level target runs are planned on a larger scale map than that used for general navigation. This is to enable smaller targets to be accurately attacked. The target runs are started from an initial point, which is normally a large and easily seen feature such as a big rock outcrop, a distinctive bend in a river or a wide road intersection. An accurate track and time from the initial point to the target is drawn on to the maps to enable the target to be found. The attack has to be flown at the correct heading and speed otherwise the planning is useless.

Weekend 1–2 July

I don't normally write about what happens at the weekend, but this is an exception. Shirley had entered and won a cooking competition for which the first prize was a weekend at a Michelin-star hotel in the New Forest. I had never been to such a place, and didn't realise how affluent the clientele would be, until we drove through a car park that was full of Rollers, Jags, Mercs and BMWs. We didn't use the valet parking as we were in Shirley's Mini Metro, and it would have been too embarrassing.

The place was amazing and the staff incredibly attentive. Men were required to wear a jacket for dinner and the manager didn't bat an eyelid when I said that I hadn't packed one.

He just took me to an office and gave me a choice of three sizes.

The food was unlike anything I have tasted before. Even Shirley was impressed and that doesn't happen very often. She did insist that I choose the wine at every meal though, and my meagre knowledge was tested severely as the wine list was a small book. I didn't have the nerve to order one of their £500 bottles. Shirley asked for a picnic instead of lunch on Saturday and I almost had to get help in carrying the basket to the car. Bone china and crystal glasses in a picnic hamper! They should market the idea. The whole weekend was fantastic and we would love to go back. I will just have to start saving.

Tuesday 4 July

RAF Linton-on-Ouse was almost like a front-line operational station today. We had F4 Phantoms, Harriers, American A-10s and a couple of German Alpha Jets in the circuit at various times.

The helicopter road show from RAF Shawbury was also at the station. They were demonstrating the merits of a career flying the whirly birds. Went along to see what they were about and left convinced not to go down that route if I could help it. Helicopter pilots have a very good chance of ending up carrying a rifle and living in holes in the ground for long periods while working with the army. I have already had a taste of that and I don't want to do it again.

Thursday 6 July

Today was my first formation trip on the Jet Provost. Flew with Flt Lt Andy Arundell as part of a three-aircraft formation, along with Reg Armeanu and his instructor on the other wing of our leader. It was hard work but not as scary as formation in the Chipmunk – there is no propeller spinning in front of the aircraft. Reg seemed to be coping very well on the other wing.

Cameron Gair has been stuck in bed for the last two days with acute food poisoning. The consensus is that he got it from the sandwich toaster in the crew room. The toaster gets very grubby as there are only a few guys who bother to clean it. Personally, I never use it.

Monday 10 July

Formation, formation and formation: that's all I did today. Flew in the line astern position this morning and got up to high angles of bank on some of the turns. It was a bit much for me this early in the phase but I was coping quite well by the afternoon. I was flying with the boss by then, and he was more than happy with my progress. Reg on the other wing had no problems at all.

The same cannot be said for Paul Binns or Binnzy, as he is now being called. He is finding all this a bit difficult, which is a first for him. He has been breezing through the course so far. He hasn't been helped by the fact that Paul Gerrard is the other member of his formation and as always he is very good.

Wednesday 12 July

Flew in the lead aircraft of a formation with Mark Harris on one wing and Paul Binns on the other. It was good to see how other guys were coping. They are no better than me, which is reassuring. I never think I am any good and I tend to say so. Other people will have you believe they are breezing through the course with their natural ability.

Andy Pomeroy is having serious doubts about whether he wants to continue with this career. He has been badly affected by Tommo's death and Bill's ejection. He says it is constantly on his mind that he might die, and it is a struggle

Nerves

to keep motivated. The idea of dying has not been bothering me too much. I am more worried by the thought of failing the course. Mark Harris, on the other hand, is convinced he is indestructible and will live forever. I just think that any fatalities will happen to the other guy.

Thursday 13 July

I had to take Cameron over to the station doctor this morning as he had split his knee open on a door while rushing to the toilet last night. The doc has sent him up to the military hospital at Catterick.

On getting back to the squadron, there was a flying programme change, and I was surprised by a very short notice general handling and instrument flying revision trip with the boss. It was a bit scrappy, but I managed to remember most of what I have been taught and put in a good performance.

We landed to hear the news that Cameron is in an isolation ward at the hospital because of his sickness. They suspect it is salmonella poisoning. Reg and I took a few bits and pieces up to him in the evening. He didn't look well, but then he hasn't been eating much for the past week. He was more concerned about his mum, as she was in a very stressed state – but not because of his illness.

She had been walking along the platform of the main railway station in Newcastle with her little dog when she tripped and fell over a loose paving slab. Unfortunately, as she fell, she kicked her adored dog over the edge of the platform. Regrettably, the dog was on a short choke chain and she didn't let go of the chain. By the time she got back on her feet, the dog had died. Basically, she had hung her dog. The incident sounded like a comedy sketch to us, but Cameron says that she was distraught. Reg and I were glad Cameron had told us the story before we saw his mum later in the evening. She insisted on recounting the whole event and if we hadn't heard it all before, I don't know if we would have been able to keep straight faces.

Friday 14 July

Until today, we have been getting airborne as individual aircraft and then joining up in formation, but this morning, I had my first formation take-off and landing. I was very aware of how close I was to the lead aircraft, so there was total concentration and more than a little bit of adrenaline flowing around my body. We were also taught turning rejoins today, and that is the same manoeuvre that killed Tommo last month.

The turning rejoin wasn't difficult but as with everything we are taught, if you don't obey the rules, it can be deadly. Although I have been cleared solo for turning rejoins, I am more worried about my formation take-offs and landings. During these, my hands are moving all over the cockpit raising and lowering gear and flaps as well as staying in formation. That seems to be far more hazardous.

Tuesday 18 July

Just solo flying for me today. General handling with a bit of instrument flying in the morning, followed by a solo formation flight in the afternoon.

Binnzy was also flying solo with my formation in the afternoon. He is still struggling with this phase of the course. Mind you, I scared myself during one of the formation changes. I glanced down at my instruments for a second and when I looked up the formation leader, with Paul on his wing, was turning towards me. The closure rate was huge, but I managed to fly below both of their aircraft. My heart was trying to break out of my chest for a few seconds.

near miss

Reg and I drove up to Catterick in the evening to see Cameron. He is improving and has started to eat properly again. He still looks stick thin though, and his knee is totally wrecked.

Friday 21 July

I flew a good trip with 'Sir' George Broadbent, the most senior instructor on the base. He is known as 'Sir' because of his vast experience and the fact that he treats instructors and students alike with utmost respect. He was actually impressed by some of my aerobatics, and that does not happen very often. They are normally described as being 'unsubtle'. I don't do subtle very well.

The squadron had hired a party boat on the River Ouse for an evening drinks event today. I picked Shirley up from the station and we had a fun evening on the river. There was a lot of banter, which was helped by all the cocktails and a very good jazz band. Most of the banter was centred on Binnzy's body odour and his unhappy demeanour; whether Reg or Mark put in the least amount of work on the course and, surprisingly, if I am a thinly disguised hooligan. Isn't it just great to hear what people think about you? It's not as if I have been in any fights. Well, none for a while at least. Shirley didn't defend me at all, but that wasn't a surprise as compared to her, I am a Neanderthal.

A perfect evening was spoilt by the behaviour of Miriam Williams. Not sure if it was just the alcohol or if he was fed up about something, but he was extremely childish and irritating. Normally, I consider the general behaviour of the guys on the course to be akin to that of primary school pupils but Miriam, one of our flying instructors, was just as bad. I managed to lock him in the toilets for half an hour and that gave everyone a bit of relief. But unfortunately, he was worse when he got out, and the result was that he was thrown into the river as we docked. Oh, dear! Cue one very wet, pathetic looking flying instructor with a split lip, a broken tooth and a total sense of humour failure. He got very little sympathy. Even Shirley said he deserved it.

Monday 24 July

A scorching day and it didn't start well. Miriam has been in casualty having his tooth fixed after Friday night, and the boss is all of a sudden very annoyed about the whole affair. We are all feeling a bit hard done by as he didn't say or do anything on Friday night although he witnessed the events as they occurred. We can only assume that there is a bit of squadron or station politics involved.

The upshot of this is that the whole course has been punished and we all now have to stay on the base over the next weekend and report to the station duty officer every four hours. The decision has gone down like a lead balloon. Reg is so annoyed he is considering an application to the airlines.

I had a formation trip with Miriam today and that didn't go well either. I am rapidly losing all respect for him in the air. He demonstrated a turning rejoin that was appalling and then tried to cover up his ineptitude by giving me a hard time over a couple of minor mistakes. It was a real struggle not to argue with him during the debrief.

I try never to argue during a debrief, as the instructor has usually made up his mind about how well you have flown, and they are usually correct. Arguing just annoys them and might even get you a bad reputation. Students with bad reputations tend not to pass the course. I will ask our flight commander, Flt Lt Tony Barmby, for an instructor change but it will have to wait a few days, as he is not in the best of moods either.

Binnzy had a hydraulic problem on his solo formation, which required him to declare an emergency and get back on the ground. Flt Lt Barmby is unhappy about the way he handled the emergency. Binnzy completed his drills from memory and; at no stage did he get out his flight reference cards to check the procedures. This is not what we have been taught to do in these situations. I can understand his actions though. The emergency could have very easily developed into the failure of some of the flight controls or even the loss of the aircraft, and he just wanted to get back on to the ground as fast as he could. The good thing is that I can't see any of the rest of us making the same error again, since we all learn from each other's mistakes.

Tuesday 25 July

Flt Lt Barmby has restored some of our faith in the RAF. He does not agree with the boss about punishing everyone next weekend and has invited the course to a barbecue at his house on Saturday evening. Miriam is not invited, which is a good thing. Paul Gerrard also had an unhappy formation trip with him today. I have had enough of him and have asked Tony Barmby for an instructor change. He was expecting it and has allocated me Flt Lt Steve

Ash for the navigation detachment next week, which will be based at RAF Kemble down in Gloucestershire. The goal of the detachment is to give us experience of navigation in unfamiliar terrain and of coping with a strange airfield and new procedures. It is also supposed to be fun.

The Kid, much to everyone's delight, has passed his multi-engine lead-in course and is a very happy boy. He will be off to RAF Finningley in South Yorkshire to fly the Jetstream and will then go on to one of the transport aircraft. He will have his wings and be a qualified RAF pilot before me, that's for sure.

Thursday 27 July

There was more formation flying for me today, with the highlight of the morning being an 11-minute tail chase. The boss was leading the formation and he was going for it during the tail chase. Loops, barrel rolls and lots of high-G turns. From the ground, it must have looked as if there were three aircraft in a dogfight.

Flt Lt Barmby says that one of the aims of the tail chase is to get students used to working out their position in relation to another aircraft and not to the ground. In fighter aircraft, the ideal position to shoot down an enemy with guns or short-range missiles is a few hundred yards behind them – in other words, the position in which we fly the tail chase.

It is an amazing amount of fun, although I was exhausted after the mammoth session this morning. It's surprising how much physical effort is involved and how little you notice that effort, what with all the concentration.

This afternoon, I went up to Catterick to see Cameron and he is looking much better. The nurses said he could get some fresh air, so we went to one of the teashops in nearby Richmond.

In a tail chase, you follow the leader, which sounds simple enough but the trick is to try to fly through the same area of sky he has flown through. It is easiest to think of it as a roller coaster where you are in a separate car to your leader. You have to follow the same track because if you just point at your leader, you will rapidly decrease your separation distance, become out of position and even overtake him. A three-second delay before following any manoeuvre seemed to work in the Jet Provost.

Friday 28 July

There wasn't much flying today as it was no. 95 course's graduation. The station was full of their relatives and friends, and the boys were in full dress uniform. The graduating course had organised for a number of fast jets to fly over the airfield. The four Jaguars on a simulated airfield attack were by far the best. We knew they were coming as they had given us a precise time. But there was no sign of them until exactly the appointed second. The first aircraft appeared from behind the hangars at high speed and low height and then screamed over the control tower. The noise and the lack of warning were very impressive. As the aircraft disappeared into the distance, the next arrived from a totally different direction with the same effect. It is very hard to believe that we will ever be capable of flying machines like that. Theoretically, there is only another year and a half of training to go.

As everyone was staying at the station due to our punishment, there was a good turnout for the graduation party. It all got very hazy: I do remember drinking quite a few White Russians, whatever they are.

Saturday 29 July

I don't know why I put my body through this. Yet again, I wake up feeling like death. We all managed to make it to Tony Barmby's for lunch, and it was just what we needed. Some very good food in between the body relapses.

Sunday 30 July

We were off to our navigation detachment today, and Ian Reid drove a mini-bus with seven of us down to our accommodation at an old RAF supply base 10 miles from RAF Kemble. Kemble is another of those bases with just a runway and a few hangars. We were carrying the kit for all the boys who are flying down in the jets tomorrow, so it took a while to get everything unloaded and into their rooms. Ian then managed to get lost driving us over to Kemble to drop off our planning and operations equipment. He then got lost again getting over to Cirencester for food. How he is going to navigate while moving at five miles a minute I dread to think.

Monday 31 July

A 6am start to meet the engineers at Kemble and help them unload the rest of the planning and operations equipment. By the time we finished, the jets had arrived and before I knew what was happening I was airborne with Flt Lt Steve Ash on my first trip.

I managed to find my low-level entry point and then everything went downhill. Firstly, I misidentified a couple of features and ended up flying down the wrong valley. I had to use so much of my spare capacity dealing with that error that I missed the initial point on my target run, which meant I never saw the target. I then proceeded to get hopelessly lost. To compound it all, when I carried out the lost procedure on the radio and asked London military air traffic control for a position fix, they told me I was 10 miles west of Hereford, so I set off on a heading of west to find the city. It was only a couple of minutes before I realised I was going in totally the wrong direction. Should have been heading east, but travelling at 300mph we were now 20 miles west of Hereford. Eventually, I did sort it out and found my way back to Kemble, having completed only about five minutes of a 45-minute navigation route. Flt Lt Ash, as expected, was very thorough in the debrief but, as he said, at least I got most of the major mistakes out of the way in one trip.

Not surprisingly, we went up and repeated the trip in the afternoon. It was much better the second time. Found all of the turning points and flew directly over the target, but it wasn't enjoyable. I just hope the rest of the week improves.

Reg Armeanu was on a solo in the afternoon and his target was his parent's house. They were in their garden when he roared overhead, and his mum told him afterwards that she couldn't believe that he flew such a fast machine.

Tuesday 1 August

A really hard day at work today, up early flying solo, followed by a trip with Flt Lt Ash, and then solo again repeating the same route. To complicate matters, there was a royal helicopter flight leaving Gatcombe Park, which disrupted flying. Gatcombe is only a few miles away and Princess Anne lives there. For security reasons, we are not allowed any take-offs or landings within 30 minutes of a royal flight.

When work was over, a group of us headed to a water park in Swindon for an hour of fun on the slides. It was a great way to de-stress and it was the only break I had all day. After dinner, Adrian Bonwitt and I had to head back to Kemble to get our planning completed for tomorrow's early navigation trips.

Wednesday 2 August

Another 6am start, and typically the weather was very poor in the west of England where I had planned to fly. So, after a frantic hour of re-planning, I took off with Steve Ash on a high-to-low-level trip over to the east of England. We dropped into low level near Cambridge and then came back across the middle of the country. The plan included two targets but shortly after the first, I calculated that we didn't have enough fuel to complete the low level route, so we climbed up to a few thousand feet and headed directly back to Kemble.

High-speed, low-level flying uses fuel very quickly, so we were constantly calculating how much fuel we needed to make it back to base in a straight line at a more economical speed. Once, this 'chicken fuel' state was reached, it was the end of the low-level fun. Fuel is a constant worry as the Jet Provost does not carry very much and the engines are of such an old design they use it at a tremendous rate.

The weather improved in the afternoon, so I flew the western route I had previously prepared. It was a solo flight and the first time I had flown a high-to-low level by myself into unfamiliar terrain, but it all worked out.

Everyone is getting two or three trips a day even though some of the weather conditions have been a bit marginal. Miriam Williams really isn't any good at navigation and even the other instructors are starting to make fun of him.

Dinner was a curry in Cirencester and then back for more planning.

Thursday 3 August

I am getting used to these early starts, with another one today. Flying with Flt Lt Ash again, and we got airborne on a land-away to RAF Shawbury near Shrewsbury. The trip out there was good, but I had to have my wits about me whilst joining the Shawbury circuit. Shawbury is a helicopter base and there was lots of unfamiliar radio chatter as well as slow moving helicopters getting in the way.

We landed, got fuel and were soon airborne again. This time on a high-to-low, dropping into low level in north Devon. The intention had been to fly low level all the way back to Kemble, but we hit a large bird just after my first target run. The bird collided with the leading edge of the right wing with a big bang, and we could see a large dent and a small crack in the wing.

I declared an emergency on the radio and diverted to the naval air station at Yeovil. It was good doing all the emergency procedures that we have learnt over the last few months in a real situation: a low-speed handling check to make sure the aircraft would still fly at landing speeds, followed by a precautionary forced landing circuit in case the engine was damaged. Amazingly, I managed to remember all the drills and didn't get too excited. We had to spend the afternoon with the navy, until some of our engineers could get down to us and carry out a temporary repair on the wing.

I am seriously going to get a small Union Jack flag sown on to my flying suit. I am getting fed up of being asked which country I am from. It happened again today at Yeovil with a navy lieutenant commander. He wasn't being nasty, just an ignorant w**ker.

Friday 4 August

Another standard Kemble early start. My last trip from the base and it was an unseen low-level navigation into Wales with Flt Lt Steve Ash. It is classified as unseen because I did not plan the route and was only given the maps during the brief before flying. No problems getting around the route and a good performance, even though I missed one of the targets.

Ah, well! It was my last trip so who cares.

The guys taking the last four jets back to Linton-on-Ouse flew a very good formation fly-past of the air traffic control tower before they left. It was a diamond formation and it looked inch perfect.

I wasn't lucky enough to be selected to fly back, so had to help pack up the vans and minibus for the drive up the M5 motorway. Then headed straight back down to London on the train for the weekend.

Monday 7 August

Spent this morning planning and the afternoon flying a solo land-away to RAF Cranwell. Cranwell is also a Jet Provost training base and is in Lincolnshire so the terrain is totally different from the hills of Wales. You are lucky to find a hill in Lincolnshire. Thinking about it, they do have one, and they built a cathedral on top of it.

I got there and had a coffee with an old school friend, Ian Cameron. He has just qualified as an A1 flying instructor. An amazing achievement, as there cannot be more than half a dozen A1 instructors in the entire air force. He was always one of the clever ones at school.

Tuesday 8 August

Airborne in the first wave with 'Sir' George Broadbent, and the trip was free navigation, which was demanding. I was given a low-level chart of North Yorkshire and the Lake District with 12 points marked on it. As we got airborne. Sir George said, "Take me to point number five."

And so it went on. On each occasion, I had to estimate how long it would take to fly to the point, estimate a heading and work out any corrections for wind and then make sure I had enough fuel to get there. Mental gymnastics at a height of 250ft and a speed of 300kts! Still, I managed to get to all the selected points, and even pulled out of low level before getting to the last one as we were running out of fuel. Spent the rest of the day planning for my final navigation test, which should be the next trip.

Mark Harris was his normal cocky self. He hadn't bothered to do any planning and borrowed Reg's maps for his solo land-away. One of these days, he is going to get caught out. Andy Pomeroy scraped a pass on his final navigation test with an instructor from no. 1 squadron.

Ian Reid also managed a good pass – Not too sure who his examiner was.

Adrian Bonwitt is more than a little hacked off as someone ran over his pushbike in a car. The front wheel is bent in half and the frame is buckled, so the bike is beyond repair. There have been no confessions. The guilty party could be anyone on the base.

Wednesday 9 August

What a day. The weather wasn't great, and I planned a route into the area with predicted good weather, but didn't get to fly.

Paul Gerrard and Binnzy both achieved good passes on their final navigation tests, but Reg got a technical fail after messing up a low-level abort manoeuvre.

Andy Pomeroy has had his pass reversed and has been told that he has to re-fly his test. That has not gone down well, and yet again, he is seriously thinking of quitting the military and heading for the airlines.

Everyone is feeling the pressure at the moment. We are all working flat out, with maybe the exception of Mark Harris. Every sortie demands a great deal of preparation and concentration and we are getting a little frayed at the edges. Yesterday, Ian Reid was physically sick before his final navigation test. No one is surprised, but the important thing was that he still managed to produce the goods.

Thursday 10 August

The met man promised good weather to the north, so I planned my final navigation test route up to Scotland. Unsurprisingly, with our met man, the weather in Scotland turned out to be dreadful so yet again my trip was cancelled.

There is lots of trouble brewing over Andy Pomeroy and his navigation test. He has told his test instructor exactly what he thinks of him. It's not the sort of thing that students are supposed to confront instructors about. The instructor initially thought Andy had scraped a pass, but as he wrote the report for the trip, he realised that he couldn't pass him. Anyway, Andy has been told that he doesn't have to fly the whole thing again, which is good as the test is planned as a land-away to a different base with more navigation on the way back. There are just too many things that can go badly wrong during all of that. Andy just has to fly a local navigation route to make sure his technique is correct.

Monday 14 August

My final navigation test at long last. There was good weather all over the country, and I flew down to Bedford with one of the station senior instructors. I managed to get there and back without any disasters and achieved an above-average pass. I was so busy that the day just seemed to disappear.

Any Pomeroy did his local sortie and passed (again), and Mark Harris and Reg passed as well. Adrian failed, and his instructor was the same man who had passed then failed Andy Pomeroy. He is not winning any popularity contests at the moment.

Wednesday 16 August

I flew three trips today and am completely worn out. It started with a solo general handling trip in the morning followed by a dual formation and then a solo formation with me hanging on to the wing of Flt Lt Andy Arundell.

Adrian passed his navigation test and is happy again, so to celebrate a group of us went out for a quick Diet Coke. Conversation centred around the 'mechanically perfect' car that Mark tells us he has bought; Reg being seriously worried about being sent to transports, and the fact that Bill Owen still hasn't stopped bullshitting.

Friday 18 August

I have flown 12 trips this week, which have all been good and at this rate, the course will be completed in a few days. I did have to ask for my third trip today to be cancelled. I was supposed to have flown it with Sir George. I had just landed from my second trip, which was a solo, to find that I had not removed the safety pins of the ejector seat. That is a schoolboy error, which would have meant that the seat would not have fired if I had tried to eject during an emergency. I put it down to fatigue and Sir George agreed with me. He cancelled our dual flight and then sent me off for an early weekend.

Monday 21 August

I've had a nice relaxed weekend but I am still feeling a bit dull. Off on a solo general handling in the first wave and when I landed, I was told to ring the duty instructor. That is usually a prelude to a reprimand but for the life of me, I couldn't think what I had done wrong.

It turned out it was just Flt Lt Miriam Williams full of the joys of summer having been on holiday, and wanting to tell me that I wasn't 'punchy enough' walking back from the aircraft. That's no problem! From now on it is going to be head up and swagger, but it would help if I wasn't feeling constantly tired.

Andy Pomeroy had his final handling test with the chief instructor today and I managed to find a tape of the music from the 1964 film 633 Squadron to play, as they walked out to their aircraft. I like to think it helped: Andy passed with a very good score.

Tuesday 22 August

My final handling test was today. I had an early morning pre-ride with Miriam Williams and then the test with a squadron leader who is one of the standards squadron instructors. It was a typical Trevor Edwards solid performance earning a high-average pass. Just glad to have completed the course, and I should be heading for RAF Valley and the Hawk in the next couple of months. Mark Harris passed as well so we both had a few too many beers in the bar in celebration.

Friday 25 August

I have just spent two days partying like a mad person and today I crawled to the squadron to fly down to Farnborough with Pat Voigt. I'm not sure how he got the authority from his boss, but he kindly invited me along as he had a spare seat. There were no great navigational skills used this time, just a fairly straight line down the country. It was just as well as my body was punishing me for all the abuse it has suffered in the last two days. Had to use 100 per cent oxygen to clear my head more than once.

Tuesday 29 August

The weekend was the August Bank Holiday and Shirley had a big party for the Notting Hill Carnival, so yet again I was flying in a less than ideal physical state. Pat Voigt did most of the work on this morning's flight up from Farnborough.

Adrian and Paul Gerrard passed their final handling tests on Friday but Reg failed his. He is getting extremely worried about not being selected for fast jets.

Friday 1 September

I have been Trev The Problem Man all week. I've listened to people's problems, assisted with paperwork problems and even helped out with some duty student problems. I am totally familiar with the last one, having done more than my fair share on the operations desk thanks to the night flying incident of the crew room curry in May. Reg finally passed his test, and he is the last of the course to finish, so that is everyone through basic flying training.

Binnzy announced today that he would not be inviting his parents to the graduation party.

Why he feels the need to share that with the rest of us, I don't know. Bill has described Binnzy as a blue whale. He is moving calmly through the ocean, but has five miles of wake turbulence behind him. I tend to agree.

Monday 4 September

For some reason, I have been selected as one of the competitors for the course aerobatics trophy. I don't consider myself to be particularly good at aerobatics and this was confirmed as I was walking out to the aircraft with Flt Lt Tony Barmby. We passed one of the standard squadron instructors who said, "Oh no! Aerobatics with Trev!"

To which Flt Lt Barmby replied, "I'm just going to eliminate him from the competition."

I didn't disappoint them. Flt Lt Barmby described my aerobatics as 'agricultural', which is better than his description of the efforts of Mark Harris. He said that those were (and I quote verbatim) 'crap'.

That had all of us in stitches, although Mark was not impressed.

The rest of the week was spent completing various bits of paperwork and getting sorted for graduation on Friday. The best news of the week is that all the Jet Provost Mk5 student pilots are going to RAF Valley for fast jet training.

Friday 8 September

Today was another typically overcast Yorkshire day and in a way this was fitting for our last day at Linton-on-Ouse – so much of our time here has been spent under grey clouds. I collected Shirley from the station and we went straight to the instructors' crew room for coffee and biscuits. The planned flying display was severely reduced because of the weather. The Jaguars cancelled, as did the Hawk aerobatic display, but we did get a very good formation fly past by Linton's own Jet Provosts, an airfield attack by some Hawks and a Tornado F3 flying some very low overshoots in the circuit. The mums and dads were suitably impressed.

Graduation lunch was followed by speeches and then the presentation of prizes. Amazingly, I won the instrument flying prize. Binnzy won the best flying prize and Paul Gerard the best overall prize. Adrian Bonwitt won the aerobatics prize. Unfortunately, our course photo does not include Bill Owen or Cameron Gair, which is a shame, as they have always been a big part of the course even though Bill is now completing his flying on another squadron. For a change, the evening was a sedate affair – the presence of so many mums, dads and girlfriends I suppose.

Saturday 9 September

Shirley and I packed up the car and said our goodbyes, then headed south. We stopped off to see Cameron, who is now in the RAF hospital at Ely, and took him some adult reading material and some food. He looks much better than the last time I saw him, and the doctors are saying it should be fine for him to continue flying training although they aren't too sure if he will get clearance for ejector seats.

That was the end of basic flying training and I had 40 hours solo and 65 hours dual flying in the Jet Provost. My flying scores have been above average and my assessment was PROFICIENT.

Adventure Training

Washington DC,
Virginia and West Virginia,
USA,
1989

Every course gets the chance to organise a leadership and adventure training expedition.

No. 96 course has planned an expedition of white water rafting and canoeing in the USA. When I say no. 96 course, I actually mean Adrian Bonwitt. He has pretty much organised the whole thing by himself, which is no mean feat as there is a prodigious amount of paperwork involved.

Unfortunately, because of training commitments, only the guys being posted to RAF Valley have the time off to participate. So, the team is Adrian Bonwitt, Paul Binns, Paul Gerrard, Mark Harris, Reg Armeanu, Ian Reid, Andy Pomeroy and myself. Our staff members are Tony Barmby, Miriam Williams and Sergeant Alex McKenna from the physical education department.

The plan was to fly out on the daily VC10 transport to Washington DC, hire minivans from the airport and camping equipment from a navy base nearby and then spend two days white water rafting on the Gauley River in the Blue Ridge Mountains of West Virginia. This was to be followed by three days canoeing on the Shenandoah River and a day visiting a few of the tourist sites in Washington before heading home.

Day 1

As with all plans, reality has refused to cooperate. We arrived at RAF Brize Norton in good time to catch the flight, only to find that there was an hour delay due to a technical problem with the aircraft. The VC10 is an old machine. So old that it is no longer used by any of the international airlines. The RAF possesses the only flying examples, and half of them have been converted to tanker aircraft. Like any old machine, they have a habit of breaking down. We eventually got into the air but were told a few hours into the flight that we would be landing in Gander, Newfoundland, to refuel. The headwinds across the Atlantic were so strong that the poor old VC10 couldn't get to Washington non-stop.

We arrived at Washington three hours late. Under normal circumstances, this would not have been a problem, but it was Friday evening and the US navy closes its outdoor equipment section at 5pm sharp – and doesn't reopen it until Monday morning. We arrived at 5.30pm. So, no camping equipment.

As white water rafting was only available over the weekend and we had already booked our guide, we decided to continue on to the rafting site and worry about accommodation later. I wasn't disappointed as I have developed an aversion to camping – even if it is in the beautiful wilds of the USA.

Our hire vehicles were two luxury vans. I mean that to British officers they seemed like luxury. They were turbocharged, with automatic gearboxes, power steering, cruise control and air conditioning. My little Alpha Romeo Sud has none of these.

As one of the four people over 25 years old, I was designated as a driver for one of the vans. I was in the lead vehicle, with Adrian in the front seat as my navigator. Adrian and I had visited the US before, but most of the other guys hadn't and they had no idea of the scale of the place. We quickly decided it was best that we didn't tell them the drive to Summersville would be about eight hours, the equivalent of driving from London to Inverness.

"Are we there yet?"

"How much further is it?"

Questions started after about three hours, to which Adrian would reply, "Oh! Not much further, we are almost there." It was just like taking primary school children on holiday. Fortunately, as it had been such a long day most of the guys simply fell asleep. We finally arrived in Summersville in the early hours of the morning, found a campsite and slept in the vans.

Day 2

Our van rest was short lived as we had an appointment to meet our river guide at the dam over the Gauley River at 7.30am. We used the ablutions at the campsite, had breakfast in the adjoining motel and got to the dam nice and early, as expected of military men. The Gauley River downstream of the dam has a mix of canyons with some very good rapids and stretches of calmer water. A 25-mile stretch is part of a national park, and we would be floating down a section of this in our rubber rafts. To make the white water rafting more exciting, this weekend was one of the few when they open up the sluices on the dam to create what I can only describe as a raging torrent.

We collected our wetsuits, helmets and lifejackets and met our guide, Steve. He was 20 years old and a wildlife and recreation student who was guiding the white water rafts as a summer job. He informed us that we would be on the Lower Gauley today, the 'easy one' in his words. There was a bit of a bus ride to get down to the start, and we had five minutes of instruction on paddling and controlling the raft. All very simple: left or right; forward or back; all forward or back, and 'Oh Shit'. The 'Oh Shit' call meant get to the bottom of the raft and hang on.

The first set of rapids was very benign, so Steve made us float through them individually in our life vests. The whole white water thing is a bit mad, and I can't say that I was very keen but Mark Harris loved it. There were some big rapids and very fast flowing sections and we survived the day without anyone getting thrown out of the raft.

On the bus journey back to Summersville, Paul Gerrard and Paul Binns got chatting to a couple of ladies from another raft and managed to get everyone invited to a dance in town. I think they were enthralled by the Pauls' charming British accents and the trainee fighter pilots stories.

The dance was very good. The boys drank far too much but for a change, they didn't get totally out of hand. The two Pauls continued chatting up the ladies from the bus, one of whom was heard to say to Paul Binns that she thought English men were very polite. How anyone could imagine Paul Binns as polite, I don't know, although being drunk does seem to improve his personality. I also heard the same lady telling Paul that her husband didn't understand her, just before the two of them went outside to discuss her problems.

I made the almost fatal error of being polite and smiling at a very big girl who I recognised from the reception at the motel. This was obviously taken as some sort of signal and I had to spend the rest of the night avoiding her. Most of us slept in the vans again.

Day 3

The morning found everyone hung over, including Tony Barmby and Miriam Williams. Reg looked like death warmed up. We couldn't raft the Upper Gauley, as there was a technical fault in the dam and there was too much water in the river. So, we were back on the bus with about six other raft teams and we headed down to another section of the Lower Gauley.

There were some seriously big people on the bus. I'm not sure what folks in the US are eating, but they produce some badly overweight people. That said, they were having fun and were going for it on the river. The Gauley was roaring, and we got flipped over on the fifth rapid. Steve didn't even have time to say 'Oh Shit'. Suddenly, everyone was tossed into the river. I was sitting next to Steve at the back of the raft and time seemed to slow down as I became airborne. I felt that I was watching the guys below me in slow motion hitting the water one at a time. We all had to cope with the rest of that rapid individually and then rescue the raft in the next section of calm water.

In this section of the river, there were names for most of the rapids. The one where we came to grief was called Guide's Revenge. Other good names were Masher, Gate of Heaven and Pure Screaming Hell.

Ian Reid and Paul Gerrard were thrown out at Gate of Heaven, and poor old Reg chose to float through one of the lesser rapids by himself since he did not feel well. It seemed to work as he had a much better colour about him when he got back into the raft. The river calmed down considerably after Pure Screaming Hell, and we had a bit of a water fight with some of the heavyweights we had met on the morning bus. They had thrown their guide into the river and decided that Steve was going to be next. No way. We fought and we won. They were left swimming in the river along with me, but I was the only one from the raft HMS Pilot to have been thrown out.

We said our goodbyes to Steve, handed back all our kit and set off in the vans for the Shenandoah. Just a five-hour drive this time, and because we have saved so much money by sleeping in the vans Tony Barmby has given us permission to spend some of it. We have booked into a motel, which is much cheaper than renting camping equipment for three days.

Day 4

One of the motel staff has taken a shine to Miriam and is calling him Honey. None of the rest of us has been accorded this privilege. I just wonder how long it will last once she gets to know him.

After breakfast, we headed down to the canoe equipment shop; to be told that they weren't keen on letting us on to the river as it was at a very high level and fast flowing. The lady at the counter was very concerned that we might fall out of a canoe and go over one of the rapids. We politely pointed out that we were British fighter pilots, that we would have no problem in dealing with the river and that we had spent the last few days battling the Gauley River and level-five rapids. She eventually relented; we got our two-man canoes and have had a very calm day floating serenely down the Shenandoah. The one rapid turned out to be a very tame affair and even Mark Harris managed to stay in his canoe.

We ate on the way back to the motel, as the town didn't have much to offer in the way of food and drink. In fact, it was completely dry. Since no alcohol could be bought in the town limits, we had to drive 10 miles to get a few crates of beer for the evenings. The main evening entertainment in the town seemed to be cruising. The local youngsters got into their cars and drove up and down the high street.

Ian Reid was first to notice this form of recreation. He was outside chatting to Adrian and happened to notice two very pretty girls drive by. Then 10 minutes later, they went by in the opposite direction, and then 10 minutes after that, they went past again. So, he and Adrian got into one of the vans and followed them. Word spread and soon we were all in the vans cruising. Miriam was driving one of them and made the big mistake of stopping in the main turning point at one end of town. A boy who looked all of five years old told him:

"You can't park there, mother****er."

We had to move; the kid looked deadly serious.

Strangely, cruising has proved a lot of fun and we have managed to get chatting to some of the locals.

Day 5

The morning greeted us with rain and it didn't stop all day. We still got on to the river and managed a 20-mile paddle. Everyone was cold and wet by the end of the day and with the weather forecast suggesting more of the same over the next 24 hours, I feel I have had enough of canoes.

In the evening, we decided to forego cruising and headed to Harrisonburg. This was a university town only 45 minutes away. We had a much more festive evening, even though Miriam Williams was doing his social hand grenade trick again.

Day 6

By popular vote, canoeing in the rain was cancelled and we headed to Washington a day early. On the way, we stopped at the Luray Caverns. A very impressive set of limestone caves. In one of the biggest, there was a pool of water that was so still it gave an almost perfect reflection. Looking into it was like gazing into a deep, sheer-sided pit. It was hard to believe you were seeing a reflection of the roof.

First stop in Washington was the Pentagon where we managed to get an exclusive 'military' tour. A very impressive building, but we had just a few too many statistics from the tour guide. The US senior officers were a much friendlier bunch than their UK counterparts. I can't imagine a tour of the Ministry of Defence happening any time soon, even the non-restricted parts of that building.

We managed to get rooms in the officers' quarters of Fort Myer and then headed into Georgetown – a historic neighbourhood that offered reasonable nightlife.

Day 7

Our final day started at the National Air and Space Museum. What an amazing place – everything that an aviation enthusiast would ever want to see, all under one roof. That was followed by a quick tour of the FBI building and an evening in the officers' club at Fort Myer that started slowly but somehow ended with memory loss.

Day 8

The trip home was uneventful. The VC10 departed on time with eleven slightly weary and hung over men on board.

Advanced Flying Training

No. 2 Training Squadron
RAF Valley,
Anglesey,
North Wales,
1989–90

As I started my training at RAF Valley, the fall of the Berlin Wall was beginning – leading to the reunification of Germany less than a year later. In the Baltic States, civil resistance against Soviet rule was taking effect. And in South Africa, negotiations for the release of Nelson Mandela, after 27 years in prison, were under way. Peace seemed to be breaking out all over the world. Advanced flying training was a six-month course, flying the Hawk aircraft. All fast jet pilots in the RAF complete this course and graduates are deemed qualified RAF pilots, and are hence awarded their wings.

Monday 6 November

After the best part of a month off work, today I was back to reality and RAF flying training. I drove up from London last night and on reaching, Anglesey it was dark, blowing a gale, with horizontal rain. On the course are:
Adrian Bonwitt
Paul Binns
Reg Armeanu
Steve Williamson
Ian Gibson
Gary Sawyer
Roger Colquhoun
Major Mahmud Almahoun
Steve Williamson was at Linton-on-Ouse on an earlier course to mine and has been waiting a couple of months for this course. Ian Gibson and Gary Sawyer are from the training base at RAF Cranwell. Major Mahmud Almahoun is a helicopter pilot from the Brunei Defence Force, and Roger Colquhoun is a navy pilot converting from the Lynx helicopter. We have been launched full tilt into lectures.

RAF Valley airfield is on the island of Anglesey in north west Wales. It is very different to the other 1930s-built bases that I was stationed on. The officers' mess is a large angular three-storey building that is a mile away from the airfield.

As well as being the base for UK fast jet pilot training, there are also search and rescue helicopters stationed there, and fighter aircraft use the base when firing air-to-air missiles on the weapons ranges in the Cardigan Bay. The student pilots fly the BAC Hawk a high performance advanced training aircraft.

Tuesday 7 November

The routine for the next six weeks of ground school will be lectures, simulator exercises and fitness training. Everyone has found the fitness training difficult after all the time off. Reg was a very wheezy boy after the two-mile run today, and he struggled in the parachute, dinghy drills and the swimming test at the local pool this morning. We have been told that next week there will be more parachute drills over the sea, and we can expect to be dragged behind the search-and-rescue boat to simulate being dragged by our parachutes in high wind conditions. I can't wait.

Friday 10 November

Our first exams already, but I have been working hard and knew my stuff, so no problems. We had our first visit to the simulators today, and I'm very impressed with them. There is no motion, but all the instruments behave just as they would in the aircraft. It will make learning all the checks and procedures much easier.

Monday 13 November

I spent the weekend on Anglesey visiting a few of the local haunts with Roger Colquhoun. A group of us had a very alcoholic curry on Saturday night, which unfortunately meant that yesterday was a bit of a washout. I had intended to study for the combat search-and-rescue exam today but hey, how hard could it be?

The answer was very hard, especially if you have no idea as to what the questions are asking.

Tuesday 14 November

Sea drills today. We had to put on immersion suits, and we made an early start. It was a very foggy morning so there was no helicopter to winch us out of the sea, but the water was calm so the drills were easy. We were thrown off the boat with a dinghy pack and then had to inflate the dinghy, get into the thing and wait to be rescued. Unfortunately, my immersion suit leaked, so I was soaking within minutes and freezing cold shortly after that.

Immersion suits are similar to dry diving suits, with tight seals around the wrists and neck. They are worn over any flight clothes and require special internal G-pants. Immersion suits are designed to keep the pilot dry and warm if he has to eject over the sea. Without immersion suits, survival in the winter water temperatures around the UK would be measured in minutes. The suits are uncomfortable, they cause you to become very sweaty and they don't look great.

I had my first simulator session after lunch and discovered that the aircraft is very twitchy in roll. The flying controls are powered by hydraulics, which means that most of the time you can fly the aircraft with little effort, and I think I am over-controlling. I also discovered that my simulator instructor is only in the job because he failed his Bulldog instrument flying test. The instrument test we all completed on the Jet Provost is harder than that, and I am starting to wonder if I should try to get another instructor.

We received the results from our first set of exams today, and they were as expected. There were lots of errors in my combat survival-and-rescue exam but amazingly Roger had more. We are allowed only 12 errors for the whole of ground school. I now have three, but Roger has eight already. He is the boy, go navy!

Adrian and I were giving Reg a hard time today. Reg never admits to being wrong. When he is shown as being in error, he says it's because he has been persecuted, or it's the weather, or someone else's fault and so on.

Thursday 16 November

We have just been told that we have to redo our sea drills because we didn't get winched up in a helicopter. Why we bothered in the first place, I don't know.

Today was fun and games with our general duties training. We were getting re-qualified on the standard aircrew pistol and the use of the chemical warfare equipment. Our ex-RAF Cranwell pilots, Ian Gibson (Gibbo) and Gary Sawyer turned up in full camouflage kit complete with boots and puttees. They looked like idiots! Who the hell wears puttees these days? I didn't think anyone still had the things. The rest of us were in our flying suits as expected.

Puttees are gaiters covering the lower leg and they look like attire that has escaped from the 1930s.

I struggled to remember all my weapon training from Regiment days, and my shooting wasn't very good. I was never very good with pistols – a belt-fed machine gun was my weapon of choice. The drills in the gas chamber simulated chemical warfare conditions. They didn't go well as my gas mask had a leak and I had several breaths of the CS (or tear) gas that they use. Very nasty stuff.

Monday 20 November

Spent the weekend in London. Adrian and I got the train together. It was all very relaxed and I needed that break as we were back to work with a vengeance this morning: lectures followed by more exams, which went well.

The two ex-Cranwell guys are girlie swots and a little bit arrogant with it. They have spent the whole weekend studying.

I had my first assessed simulator flight today and it was good, but I just wish the instructor would let me get on with it. He kept on interrupting and trying to tell me what to do, which was more of a distraction than a help.

We had our G-pants fitted today, and that was a bit of a laugh. Everyone is making fun of Reg as his G-pants make him look pregnant. Something to do with the little potbelly he has developed.

Mark Harris and Paul Gerrard started their course today. They haven't changed. Mark should still be in a kindergarten and Paul is still a know-it-all.

Under G, blood is forced towards the lower body and legs. G-pants are worn over the flying suit or under an immersion suit. They consist of multiple pouches that inflate, squeezing the waist, thighs and calves and so restricting the flow of blood into the legs. More blood is thus retained in the upper body and head, and this enables the pilot to remain functional at much higher Gs. G-pants are connected via the ejector seat to an air supply so they can be inflated under high Gs. They are very defining. Only fighter pilots have G-pants.

Wednesday 22 November

Binnzy has decided that Gibbo is arrogant, and no one disagrees with him, including Gibbo, which says it all.

We all had more exams this morning, followed by another simulator session for me at lunchtime. In the simulator, I learnt not to rush into emergency checklists. 'Sit on your hands and take your time', was how it was explained and it seems to work. Adrian and I headed back to the simulator at the end of the day and did some very useful work. It certainly helped my confidence.

I ran into an old friend called Johnny May in the mess. We were both on the same initial officer training course. That was before he started his flying training and I went to the RAF Regiment. He told me that he had just been sacked from an F4 Phantom squadron after flying the machine for 10 months. I couldn't believe it, 10 months! He was combat-ready, had flown live interceptions against Russian bombers over the North Sea, and they still sacked him.

Johnny had fallen foul of station and Ministry of Defence politics. There had been a lot of flying mistakes on his station and one of the senior officers at the MOD had said that the next person to f**k up would be sacked. Unfortunately, that was Johnny. Despite all of that, Jonny was his usual cheerful self and was staying at Valley and getting a few Hawk flights while they decided what to do with him.

He has only recently got married, and the stag party sounded like a heavy-duty affair. They went to France and participated in events that I cannot mention. On the ferry journey back home, Johnny was stripped naked, and he was subsequently seen sprinting through customs shouting, "I have nothing to declare."

I almost wished I'd been there.

Weekend

It was a full house down at Shirley's in London. Cameron Gair, who was very ill during our basic flying course at Linton-on-Ouse, came to stay for the weekend. Adrian, his girlfriend, Verity, and his sister, Caroline, were around on Saturday night.

Cameron is looking much better although he is still very thin. He was an eating machine all weekend and seemed to remain sober the whole time, although he always had a drink in his hand. How does he do that? Verity let slip that Adrian is the proud owner of a poodle, which is kept at his parent's house. I'm not sure if it is acceptable for a fighter pilot to be in possession of a poodle, but Cameron was in no doubt. He was merciless with the poodle jokes until Caroline started spilling more dirt on Adrian. It seems he was also a holiday donkey derby winner from 1974 to1976. Oh the perils of introducing your girlfriend and sister to your so-called friends.

Monday 27 November

Reg was trying to kill himself on the drive back to Valley last night. He has a new car. A nice, sensible Nissan Micra, but he drives it like a sports car. Paul Binns made the mistake of overtaking Reg on the main road to Anglesey. This caused Reg to display all his competitive tendencies. He overtook Paul on a blind bend and was not seen again for the rest of the hour-long drive to the base. Binnzy is still in disbelief. He didn't realise that no one messes with Reg Armeanu, even if he drives a Nissan Micra.

We were all taken over to see the station dentist after lunch, to make sure any fillings we had were good enough to survive high altitude flying and all the high-G manoeuvres. The dentist was about to retire from the air force and, I quote, "Didn't give a monkey's."

He did say that if we heard the word 'cavity' while he was checking us to start to panic. No one heard that word, except for Reg. He had the cavity filled and subsequently dribbled his way through the afternoon's lectures.

Friday 30 November

Another fun-filled week of lectures, exams and simulator flights completed. The doctors have told Cameron Gair that his spine is fusing together as a side effect of his illness. It doesn't look as if he will ever be able to fly on an ejector seat. It's a real shame, as he was doing well on the course at Linton.

There were three training squadrons at RAF Valley, and my course was part of no. 2 squadron. The training followed the same pattern as at Linton-on-Ouse. We learnt very few new skills – mostly following the same techniques but in a much more capable and much faster machine. Each squadron had around eight instructors and although we were assigned a primary instructor, we flew with any of the instructors on the station.

Monday 4 December

I managed to get airborne today: my first flight in the Hawk T1. My main impression was FAST. Everything was fast. As it was just a familiarisation flight, I only got to take the controls in the air. The flight was 30 minutes and it was over far too quickly, it felt like 10 minutes. It is a great machine.

As I was on the squadron for the day, I took the opportunity to get all my maps sorted. There isn't such a thing as a local area map. The Hawk has the range to fly the entire length of the country.

Binnzy was bantering with Gibbo in the planning room. He is of the opinion that all students at Cambridge University are issued with a bucketful of arrogance at the start of their degrees. Gibbo immediately replied that arrogance was issued in parcels every time they passed an end of year exam. There was no reply to that and I suppose that is why Gibbo went to Cambridge and Binnzy didn't.

Monday 11 December

Today was my first instructional Hawk flight. All the simulator work proved to be good preparation as it went well, although I did start to feel ill towards the end of the hour. I have had this before during my first flights on the Chipmunk at RAF Swinderby, so I am confident that I will quickly get used to this machine. Without doubt, some of the queasiness could be the left over effects of a very social weekend in London.

Mark Harris didn't have a very good simulator session this morning. Firstly, it took two hours to complete, which is twice as long as normal, and secondly, it was with the failed Bulldog instructor. Mark was having difficulty interpreting one of the instruments, and the instructor commented that it was just the sort of difficulty that he had on his Bulldog course. He also said that Mark reminded him of a younger version of himself. Mark is very unhappy with that comparison, although Reg and I think it is very funny.

The Hawk is still used by the RAF as its primary fast jet trainer and is also flown by the Red Arrows aerobatics team. It has tandem seating, with the instructor behind the student. Both pilots sit on Martin-Baker zero zero rocketassisted ejector seats (zero zero means that they can operate safely with zero forward speed from zero height, or ground level). The aircraft is highly manoeuvrable and is stressed to +9G although normal limit is +7.5G/-4G. It is very fast and can exceed the speed of sound in a shallow dive. In 1989, RAF Valley Hawks were painted in the same colours as the Jet Provost: red and white.

Friday 15 December

The weather has been rubbish all week, which has meant very little flying on the station. One of the senior courses managed to find some decent weather, but they had to go all the way up to Stornoway in the Outer Hebrides.

Today however, I did manage to get airborne for a general handling trip. Although the instructor was happy, I wasn't. I am still trying to get to grips with how the aircraft handles. In most circumstances, it requires a delicate touch and Mr Ham-fisted Edwards is not currently supplying that.

Tuesday 19 December

The last two days have been very busy: two flights each day and a simulator ride as well. I am working at my maximum capacity. The flights are taking it out of me physically and mentally. The sheer speed of the Hawk requires a bit of getting used to. The constant G forces in turns and the associated G-pants inflations are much more physically tiring than I would have believed. Everything is more serious, including the students. It is hard work, but it is good to leave behind some of the primary school behaviour from Linton-on-Ouse.

1990

Tuesday 9 January

We are back from a two-week Christmas break and straight into action. I spent yesterday morning re-learning checks and the afternoon re-learning how to fly a circuit in a Hawk. Today has been manic. The course had a brief on spinning and practised forced landings first thing in the morning, and this was followed by my pre-solo trip with Flt Lt Stu Atha as my instructor.

I honestly think my circuits were the worst I have flown, and they weren't assisted by the constant chat coming from the back seat. I prefer a quiet cockpit when I am working hard.

Stu was happy enough to authorise me for my solo flight.

Solo in the Hawk is very grown up. Instead of one circuit and then landing, it consists of once around the island of Anglesey and then two or three circuits. There is a tale of a solo student who missed the Menai Strait, which is the most southern point of the island of Anglesey. He then continued along the Welsh coast and was eventually contacted by air traffic who asked him exactly which island he intended to fly around. They were of the opinion that it was the whole of the UK. He was probably enjoying himself too much. Solo was no big event, it was just another hurdle out of the way.

Wednesday 10 January

I can't seem to get rid of the headache I have had since returning after the Christmas break. It's not helped by the work rate around here, which isn't slacking. I had my first two instrument flying flights today, and both were all right, but I was feeling as sick as a dog after the second.

Had dinner with Andy Pomeroy and Ian Reid this evening. They are already half way through their course, having started a few weeks ahead. The navy boys told a good story about a pilot on an American aircraft carrier who strapped into his aircraft, took his ejector seat pins out and was then promptly catapulted from the carrier. He hadn't even started his engines. I have been in the RAF for more than five years, and today I have been promoted from flying officer to flight lieutenant. This is the same rank as most of my instructors. The pay rise has been most welcome.

All officers join the RAF as pilot officers and are then promoted to flying officers after a period that varies depending on your entrance qualifications. After three years, the next promotion is to flight lieutenant. This is the last automatic promotion. The next ranks are squadron leader (Sqn Ldr), wing commander (Wg Cmdr) and then group captain (Gp Capt). These positions are gained on experience, ability and merit.

Friday 12 January

The weather today wasn't that good, but I was launched anyway on a trip with Stu Atha. It was a nightmare before even getting off the ground. I walked out and started strapping into the wrong aircraft. Eventually, I got to the correct machine, and managed to do my checks totally out of sequence. I then tried to take off without any clearance. The trip had to improve after that – and fortunately, it did.

I was being taught spinning and forced landings. Spinning is wild and wacky, and forced landings are only attempted if you can get to an airfield and a runway. If there is no chance of that happening, you eject and land with the parachute.

Monday 15 January

I was supposed to have two solo flights today, but there was no chance of that. The weather was totally unsuitable. I didn't check the programme for changes and didn't notice that I had a simulator session until Reg pointed it out five minutes before it was due to start. The simulator was a practice of short notice diversions, which was ironic considering how much notice I had before it started.

Steve Shell, from my Linton course, and Dave Bayliss, from my time at Swinderby, have flown in with their Gazelle helicopters for a night stop. They are both on the same course at RAF Shawbury. Note to self: keep out of the bar when they are around, they drink too much.

Tuesday 16 January

It's windy and cloudy again, so instrument flying was the order for the day and for me that meant a practice diversion to Warton in Lancashire. The first jet that I strapped into was unserviceable and the second had a partial radio failure just as I was completing the diversion. I couldn't talk to air traffic on the normal frequencies and air traffic control at Valley were so busy they couldn't spare the time or personnel to talk to me on the secondary frequency. They instructed me to fly around in circles for half an hour to keep me out of the way, and then ignored all my requests until I had to declare an emergency as I was running out of fuel.

Friday 19 January

Maximum rate turns, or 'turning and burning' as Adrian calls it, was the order of the day. These are sustained 6G turns, and they are physically demanding. The G-pants are pounding the lower body and even keeping your head upright is difficult, as it weighs six times more than normal. It was great fun, and one of the first trips I have enjoyed on this course. As usual, the weather consisted of wind, rain and patchy clouds all the way up to 20,000ft.

A maximum rate turn puts into practice the ability to turn the aircraft at its highest rate. This depends on the aircraft's speed and height, and is aerodynamically just before the aircraft loses lift and falls out of the sky. Bizarrely, it means that although you have to use a lot of muscle power to pull the jet around the turn, you need a delicate touch as the difference between a maximum rate turn and falling out of the sky is small. In a dogfight, most of a pilot's manoeuvres will be in this small margin.

Tuesday 24 January

Night flying in the Hawk – yeah ha, what fun! I say night but it is more like late afternoon flying. It is dark so early up here. Two trips, all done and dusted by 2200 hrs.

Gibbo was getting constant attention from the instructors this evening for all the wrong reasons. He forgot his torch, which is not good on a night flight. Then he was caught creating some vile odours in the crew room – the result of a curry and beer on Monday night. Finally, he was late for his briefing on his second flight. It is nice to know that the superior Cambridge graduate has faults just like the rest of us.

Wednesday 25 January

A late start today after night flying and, surprise surprise, the air outside is moving past at 25mph. There is little flying, but lots of good banter in the crew room from Steve Williamson. He spent the morning imitating Binnzy. "I hate this, I hate that. I hate the RAF. My rank means nothing." I love banter.

Flew with Stu Atha again in the afternoon, practising general handling with maximum rate turns. I am beginning to like these. The wind made the circuit a fun place to be.

There is a big group going out clubbing in the local town of Bangor tonight, but I think I will give it a miss. I'm far too tired.

Thursday 26 January

There were 100 mph winds over the island today, so no flying on the station. They can't even open the hangar doors in these conditions. We had a brief on low-level Tornado GR1 tactics from our ex-Tornado instructors Dave Lord and Simon Tranter. Flt Lt Dave Lord told a very funny story about being thrown off the weapons ranges in Sardinia after dropping a practice bomb a bit too close to the range warden's hut. He says he then tried to sneak back on to the range using a different call sign but was found out.

It was an early finish, so the course gave 20 minutes' notice and headed over to Flt Lt Simon Tranter's house, and he did very well to provide food and beer in such a short time. We subsequently discovered it was really his wife who was doing all the providing.

Monday 30 January

There's been a hurricane all weekend and it is still mega windy, so again no flying today. Reg Armeanu has had some dreadful news. His dad has been shot and killed while on a business trip to Tanzania. Reg has gone home. He is very upset, and worried about his mum. The squadron has given him as much time off as he wants, and I don't think we will see him for a while. I hope it doesn't affect him too much in the long term. It is hard enough to pass this course without any extra problems.

Tuesday 31 January

The wind has finally died down enough to allow us to get airborne. I had an instrument flying trip and flew a practice diversion to the Isle of Man. It was a bit scrappy after the layoff we have just had, but was a good pass.

Adrian survived another accident today. At 200 feet above the ground, as he was coming in to land, he struck a goose. The bird went down the engine and caused so much damage that the engine failed. Fortunately, he had just enough energy to glide to the runway. If the incident had happened a few seconds earlier, he would have had to eject. As always with Adrian, he is very cool about the incident.

Steve Williamson has been chosen to represent the squadron at a formal dinner at the station commander's house. He received his official written invitation this morning, and it had the RSVP bit crossed out. He thinks that means he has no choice and will be going. Oh the joys of military life.

Monday 5 February

The wind has not abated over the last five days, and there has been very little flying on the station. I had a letter from The Kid, Peter Coville, who has almost finished his multi-engine course and has just come back from a land-away to Berlin. They will be telling him what aircraft he will fly operationally next week. The Kid will be the first member from the old no. 96 course to get his wings.

Tuesday 6 February

I am sick. I woke up this morning with a head cold and a bad sore throat, so I took myself down to the doctor and am now off flying until Thursday.

Thursday 8 February

This is typical. I am sick and grounded and the boys are flying. Roger, Adrian and Steve have all passed their instrument rating tests while I have been laying around feeling sorry for myself. This is the first big test on the Hawk and they now move on to the low-level and formation flying phases of the course. That is where the fun really starts.

Anyway, I wasn't feeling any better today, so I have been signed off until Monday. As a result, I am escaping from Anglesey and heading to London to see Shirley for a long weekend.

Monday 12 February

Another hectic weekend. One of these days, I will have a restful one. There was a party on Saturday and I met a woman I decided to call Millie Tant. She had a social conscience, loved trees and flowers and could not understand why I wanted to be in the military and fly aeroplanes. It certainly made for an interesting evening.

I am now fully fit and had hoped to be eased back into work. Not a chance! An hour in the simulator closely followed by a general handling trip and then I was running the operations desk in the afternoon. That is more work than I have done in two weeks and on top of that, they have programmed me for my instrument-rating test tomorrow. That should be fun as the wind is still very sporty.

Reg was back at work again today and showed no signs of the stress he must have been under for the last two weeks. He has got some catching up to do.

Tuesday 13 February

I flew first thing in the morning on my instrument test pre-ride, and I didn't fly well. That is not surprising, as I haven't done any instrument flying in a while. Nevertheless, I passed the trip with an average score but I'm not pleased with my results. The wind was back with a vengeance in the afternoon, so that scuppered any more flights.

Wednesday 14 February

The weather was still quite poor, but I managed to get airborne on my test in the morning and had a better trip than yesterday. A good pass and a big relief to get another hurdle out of the way.

The pass of the test had caused me to relax a bit too much, and I was totally unprepared for the short notice high-level manoeuvring exercise that appeared on the programme. Luckily, it didn't require much preparation. There was so much cloud around that I had to demonstrate my newly qualified skill as a Hawk instrument rated pilot to get back on to the ground.

I had to walk past no. 1 squadron on the way back to the mess, and I think they have all got mad cow disease down there. There was a lot of mooing coming from their crew room. They are a mad lot on that squadron.

Thursday 15 February

Today was the first good weather day we have had in a very long time, so there was a lot of solo flying taking place. I flew two solo flights. The first one in the morning was okay, mainly just getting back into the groove of flying without an instructor looking over my shoulder. The afternoon flight was interesting. Half way through my aerobatics, I got an AC1, AC2 and GEN caption on my central warning panel, along with a lot of red lights and warning bells in my headphones. I reset the GEN, which cleared the AC problem, then I noticed that I also had a HYD2 fault. I reset that as well, but by now, I wasn't very happy with my machine, so I spoke to the duty instructor on the radio and headed back to Valley.

The engineers couldn't find anything wrong with the aircraft, and they think I might have touched the relight button during my aerobatics, which would have caused similar symptoms. The relight button is at knee height, so I'm not sure how it could have happened, but I was scared rigid for a few moments when the warnings went off.

Any faults with the major systems on the aircraft are displayed on the central warning panel. GEN is the generator attached to the engine and produces electrical power in the form of two alternating current supplies called AC1 and AC2. HYD refers to the hydraulics, which are used to move the aircraft controls and are also powered by a pump attached to the engine. There are two hydraulic systems.

Friday 16 February

Today was another crystal clear day, and I was again airborne on another solo flight. Took the jet up to 37,000ft and from there, I could see the whole of Ireland, Wales and a good part of England. The Hawk is an amazing machine. It seemed to take no time at all to get up there.

I flew only the once as there was a course graduation in the afternoon with the associated flypasts: Hawks, GR1 Tornados and F4 Phantoms, which were all suitably loud and impressive.

Shirley was up for the weekend, and my old university friend, Gary Fisher, and his girlfriend, Sue, were also over for the graduation party.

The theme of the party was gangsters and tarts. I was dressed in a dinner jacket, cravat and wrap-around sunglasses and clutched a water pistol loaded with tequila. Gary Fisher quickly got the hang of the bar chits system that we use in the mess instead of cash. My bar bill will be a bit larger this month. I am ashamed to say that Shirley and I were at the bar when it opened and still there when it closed.

The rest of the weekend was very quiet, mostly just recovering from the excesses of Friday night. It was good having Shirley, Gary and Sue staying as we managed to get out and about on Anglesey and I finally saw some of the nicer parts of the island. Up to now, I haven't been very impressed by the place, but it does have some very beautiful beaches. If only it were warmer and not as windy.

Tuesday 20 February

Another wet, windy and overcast day in Wales. I got airborne this morning on a dual sortie. The weather was appalling and the only place we could fly aerobatics was in a small gap in the clouds near the coastal town of Conwy. My instructor decided to show me his aerobatics routine, and it was very aggressive. At one point, I was kissing my knees in an unexpected 7G turn. That will teach me not to look down at my kneeboard in the middle of aerobatics.

Back at the squadron, I was walking along the corridor, and I heard someone behind me say, "Trevor?"

And without turning around I replied, "Yeah! Who speaks?"

I looked back to find it was Air Commodore Chris Coville, who is the officer in charge of all RAF flying training. He is the man who has the ultimate say as to whether you pass or fail – and happens to be the father of Pete, The Kid, Coville. There was much apologising on my part. Chris Coville is a bit of a legend in the fighter world. He has flown the Lightning, F4 Phantoms and the F3 Tornado and rumour has it he can still teach the younger guys a thing or two when it comes to air combat.

This evening, in the bar, there was a great story from one of the Scottish University air squadrons. A new boss had just arrived and the students were taking him out for a curry. Thinking it would be great to play a joke on him, they pre-arranged payment with the restaurant and told the waiters they would be faking a runner with the apparent intention of leaving the new boss to pay the bill.

That was all good in theory, but when runner was called the boss was the third man out of the door. He had been in the air force for a while and having seen this sort of thing before was fully aware that the last man out is normally the one who has to pay. Those students are going to have to work much harder to catch their boss out.

Thursday 22 February

I flew a dual and a solo yesterday, and the same again today. The weather still consists of strong winds and showers, but I am getting quite used to that now. Ian Reid, who resides on no. 1 squadron, had a near miss with another Hawk at low level today. His instructor was flying at the time, but Ian had to take control as they were on a collision course. The instructor only saw the other aircraft when they passed above it a few seconds later. Ian still hasn't worked out who was flying the other aircraft. No one on the station has reported a near miss, and it was definitely a red-and-white Valley Hawk. Maybe the other pilot just didn't see them.

Friday 23 February

I had my mid-course flying progress test today. The pre-ride wasn't my best, but the test itself with the station commander was much better. The 'Staish' gave me a thorough workout: maximum rate turns and aerobatics at medium and high levels, spinning, a couple of stalls followed by an assortment of simulated emergencies; then an instrument recovery back to Valley for circuits and practice forced landings. I was exhausted by the time we landed, but the results were good.

Weekend

For a change, a nice quiet weekend with very little alcohol involved: got the train down to London, stayed in and did very little. This Sunday evening, Adrian was involved in an accident on the motorway on his drive back up to Valley from Bournemouth. Reg happened to be driving past and recognised Adrian's wrecked car, so he turned around at the next junction and went back. That was very lucky for Adrian as his car was undriveable and he had started to wonder how he was going to get to Valley.

Tuesday 27 February

There were howling gales and rain all yesterday, and today there is more of the same. So much so that a couple of towns in north Wales have been flooded. I have spent the last two days in the navigation planning room re-learning target runs and getting my maps and routes sorted for the first few navigation trips.

I had my mid-course interview today with the boss, Squadron Leader Brockley, and everything is on track. We have all had an instructor change, which is normal at this stage in the course. Up until now, I have flown most of my instructional trips with Flt Lt John Adams, but now I have been assigned Flt Lt Stu Atha. The reality is that we fly with whoever is available. At this stage in our training, there is much benefit in absorbing experience from as many different instructors as we can. Everyone on the course is doing well although Reg still has a bit of catching up to do.

When Roger Colquhoun was asked who his new instructor was, he replied that he was going to 'self-teach' from now on. Navy guys – they don't lack confidence.

Wednesday 28 February

Amazingly today, there was no wind, but we had low cloud and rain instead. The only good weather in the country was in Scotland, so that is where I ended up.

I flew a land-away to Inverness for my first formation trip in a Hawk. It was also my first-ever visit to Scotland. My instructor was Flt Lt Steve Hunt, and I was in formation with Adrian, who was flying with the boss.

Adrian and I were thrown in at the deep end. In the trips to and from Inverness, we covered all the formation positions that we had learnt on the Jet Provost as well as a few new ones. As there were only the two aircraft, we each had to take turns in leading and that was great, as it gave me a chance to relax and also to see what Adrian's formation flying was like. Flight time up to Inverness was one hour, and we didn't get back to Valley until the late afternoon. Adrian and I were both very weary men.

Thursday 1 March

More formation today, again paired up with Adrian, who seemed to be struggling at times. He didn't think his flying was that bad, but during the debrief the boss disagreed and wouldn't clear him for solo. Adrian wasn't happy with the decision.

Roger has spent a good hour in the navigation planning room today writing a monthly report for himself. It was very funny and typical of Roger, but I can't see it making its way into his official training file. According to Roger, he should be flying Sea Harriers already.

Friday 2 March

Good weather for a change. I sat in the back seat of the formation lead for Adrian's solo check, which was good. We were both solo in the afternoon, flying formation on either side of the boss. Great fun and he made us earn our money. I worked so hard that I was a sweaty mess by the time we landed. Escaped down to London on the train as soon as I could.

Monday 5 March

The chat in the crew room this morning was about a certain individual, who will remain nameless, and his treatment of his girlfriend. The nameless one was part of a new course that had recently started, and he had invited his girlfriend over from York for the weekend. The poor girl crashed her car on the way over on Friday night, so to comfort her he took her straight to bed and then told her he didn't want to date her any more. He then got her another room in the mess and went to the bar to start drinking with the boys. She was semi hysterical at this point, so he took pity on her, and they spent the night together. In the morning, however, he told her that nothing had changed and sent her back to York. She crashed her car again on the way back home, and now the nameless one says he feels a bit guilty, as her dad has died and her brother recently committed suicide. What a bastard! The girl must be close to suicide herself by now.

Tuesday 6 March

This morning, there was much merriment in the student crew room. Someone has managed to get hold of Roger Colquhoun's training file. We are all having a good laugh about some of the comments the instructors have been using to describe him: gash, overconfident, shambles, a strong whiff of bull…and other such expressions.

The instructors have got him nailed. Roger doesn't disagree with any of these descriptions. He worried me a bit this morning by telling me that his girlfriend, Helen (who is gorgeous), has been having dreams about me. I was feeling totally flattered until I thought that her dreams might well be nightmares. Helen is a very capable girl, but needs to be in order to keep control of Roger.

It has been a day of minor emergencies. Bill Auckland, a student over on no. 3 squadron, had a microphone failure during take-off on a solo trip, and he was back on the ground in three minutes. His instructors decided that was good enough to mark the trip as successfully completed. It was his last solo before his progress check, and he was hoping to practise everything he had been taught before his test. They are playing hard rules over on no. 3 squadron.

Reg had an engine surge at high level and spent 10 minutes worrying about engine failure before he was back on the ground.

Gary Sawyer had one of his electrical generators fail during another solo flight.

There were another two dual trips for me today. They were both formation, and I am worn-out.

Wednesday 7 March

No flying today but lots of banter in the navigation planning room. Adrian managed to spend most of the morning trying to decide the best way to attack a target, and was more than a bit upset to find that he had come to the same conclusion as Reg, who had taken five minutes to think this through.

Roger was trying to tell the junior course that they didn't need to spend very much time preparing elaborate maps for their instrument diversions. They were listening to him attentively until it was pointed out that Roger passed his instrument-rating test with an average mark, whereas Adrian, who had put the work in and was immaculately prepared, had passed with an exceptional score. That was the end of the discussion and a good lesson for the junior course.

Thursday 8 March

The boys on no. 1 squadron were night flying yesterday and were up to mischief. They had chosen a 'quiet' frequency among themselves and were playing silly buggers.

"I want my mummy, it's dark."

"I've turned out all my lights."

"I can see you."

"No, you can't."

And such was relayed on the radio.

Unfortunately, for them the frequency they had chosen was also the one used by Dublin military. The Irish controllers kept dropping subtle hints on the radio to say that it was their frequency, but only John Green was sharp enough to spot the accent in all the conversations taking place. Luckily, the Irish controllers have taken it as a big joke.

Roger was in the crew room this afternoon trying to find an instructor to go flying with when the deputy chief instructor walked in.

"Hello sir! Would you like to go and fly with me?"

"Sure, Roger, what's the trip?"

"Formation, sir."

"Oh! I think I've got a headache."

Much merriment all around. Roger's reputation is starting to spread.

I flew twice on the final two close formation trips in the syllabus. They were both solo and I think I have got the hang of close formation in the Hawk.

Tuesday 13 March

My last few trips have been mainly navigation, and today has been no exception. I had a dual high to low with Lieutenant Jack London. Jack is the only navy instructor on the station and is an experienced Sea Harrier pilot. We flew high level to Devon and then low level all the way back, with two simulated targets to attack and a simulated bird strike emergency to deal with. I was working at full capacity for the entire 90 minutes.

Brian Kelly from the course about to graduate has today been told that he will be a creamy. He was so shocked that he couldn't talk for 10 minutes. He just kept opening his mouth and then closing it again. The rest of his course was totally merciless in making fun of him. As Roger says, wait until a man is down and then kick him.

A creamy is a pilot who has passed the fast jet-flying course at Valley and has then been sent to become a flying instructor as his first job. It is not popular as most pilots want to get to the front line and fly the machines they have dreamed about, not remain in the training system. Only above-average pilots with mature attitudes are selected to become creamies.

Thursday 15 March

I have had a nightmare day. I failed a trip, and it was my worst flight in a Hawk. I just couldn't do anything right, and it was only a general handling trip. Binnzy had a similar day and says he is worn out and needs a rest. I agreed with him and planned to get to bed early. That plan was scuppered by Roger who persuaded me to stay in the bar for most of the evening chatting to a University Air Squadron girl who is due to get a Hawk flight tomorrow.

Friday 16 March

I spent the morning worrying about re-flying my general handling trip, which was scheduled at lunchtime. When I got airborne, the trip was much better than yesterday. It was a good pass, so they immediately launched me again solo and it was very late before I landed – on a Friday afternoon as well. I was so happy to have survived the day I didn't care. The University Air Squadron girl flew twice, on a formation trip followed by a low-level navigation trip. She was sitting in the crew room saying that she couldn't believe how physically exhausting it was. Lots of G will do that to the fittest of people.

Mark Harris had an interesting experience today. He was on a formation trip and had to fly a snake climb. As he cleared the clouds after the climb, he saw a red-and-white Hawk in what he thought was the correct position. He called visual on the radio and slipped into formation, just as his 'Leader' started an aerobatics sequence. Mark had managed to join up with a solo student who hadn't even noticed him on the wing. He didn't stay in formation long as instructors don't usually start formation manoeuvring with a high-G loop.

Normally, two aircraft will carry out a formation take-off and can then climb above any clouds in close formation. This is one of the benefits of formation flying. However, if a pilot is not qualified to carry out a formation take-off, another option is to carry out a snake climb. The two aircraft follow the exact same flight path in the climb with a 30-second separation. They can then join in close formation once above any clouds.

Tuesday 20 March

I spent most of the morning helping with a trip for a director of British Rail who was flying with the station commander. The bloke looked totally out of his depth as they taxied out, but he had a great time.

I then sat in the back seat with the boss as he led a formation trip for Major Mahmud Almahoun. It was the Major's first solo formation flight, and he was hanging on very well. One of the young Brunei student pilots on our junior course was explaining why he goes down to Exeter at weekends. It seems that the young girls there wear short skirts and that drives him wild. He also hates the pop singer Jason Donovan, and I won't put into print what he wants to do to Kylie. I think that it is also a short skirt thing. He is only 20 years old after all.

A student from no. 1 squadron blacked out his instructor today while recovering from an unusual position during an instrument flying trip. He was flying using his standby instruments when the standby artificial horizon started to fail, so he snapped the aircraft back to straight and level but pulled 8G completing the manoeuvre. That resulted in one unconscious instructor. It took the instructor a few minutes to regain consciousness and a few more to work out where he was.

Thursday 21 March

Two navigation trips today. A solo high-to-low around Scotland in the morning and dual high-to-low with a land-away in Edinburgh in the afternoon. The morning flight was good, but the afternoon was another matter. The high bit was no trouble, but I was only at low level for about five minutes before I became lost. I subsequently discovered that this was caused by a mistake I had made during the planning of the route.

My instructor, Lieutenant Jack London, was just sitting in the back laughing. I managed to 'find myself', but then promptly got lost again, and the net result was 30 minutes at low level, charging around Scotland in random directions not finding any of my targets. At least I managed to find Edinburgh.

Three other Valley Hawks were also on navigation land-aways in Edinburgh: Gibbo with Flt Lt Steve Hunt, Adrian with Flt Lt Stu Atha and Roger with Flt Lt John Armstrong. Jack London was very gracious in his debrief of my trip. As it was an error in planning, and I had used all the correct techniques when I got lost, he was happy to pass the trip. He agreed that we would have a good night out and as long as we 'looked after' each other on the trip back to Valley in the morning, I would receive another pass. Great! I didn't manage to drink my body weight in beer but I must have got close.

Friday 22 March

It took three telephone calls to wake me at the hotel this morning, and I couldn't face breakfast. The transport was due to leave at 7.45am, however, the two navy boys, Jack London and Roger were missing. They were last seen heading off to a party with a bunch of university students. That was not good. In fact, it was very bad for me as I now had to fly back with Roger's instructor, the only man to get to bed early, Flt Lt John Armstrong. Getting airborne, he was all business as usual, and there was no way I was going to mention the deal I had struck with Jack. I just put my oxygen flow to 100 per cent, concentrated very hard and managed a pass even with the hangover.

It turned out that our navy pilots had woken up on the floor of a student flat on the other side of Edinburgh and had struggled to find a taxi to get back to the hotel. Back at Valley, the four student pilots and three instructors who were still suffering the after effects of last night were quietly dropped from the flying programme for the rest of the day.

Monday 26 March

I have had a very quiet weekend as my body was still saturated with alcohol from Thursday night. I was glad I was well rested as today I was in the squadron for 11 hours. Flew another high-to-low trip into Scotland and didn't get lost this time. Then had an hour in the simulator and spent the rest of the day in navigation planning routes for tomorrow. The Major had an unexpected radio call from London military air traffic while airborne today. He was returning at high level from a solo navigation trip and was enjoying the views so much he wasn't aware that he had passed Valley and was heading across the Irish Sea into Irish airspace. London military finally managed to speak to him on the radio and turn him back. Just imagine the newspaper headlines – Mad Brunei Major Defects to Ireland.

Tuesday 27 March

Another 11-hour day 'in the office': a solo high-to-low but heading south into Devon this time, followed by a dual general handling and instrument flying with Flt Lt Stu Atha. There were no problems on either of the trips and the rest of the time on the squadron was again, spent planning.

There is a good story from Linton-on-Ouse circulating at the moment. The boys on no. 100 course were on their navigation detachment to Inverness and had headed into town for the evening, as the met man had predicted poor weather the next day. Never believe a met man. The weather the following day was glorious and so off they went flying, although a few student pilots had rather large hangovers. In the middle of the day, their squadron received word that a Jet Provost had flown through the air traffic zone around Aberdeen International Airport. Questions were asked, but there were denials all round. A few weeks later, after looking at the recordings of the air traffic radar for that day, they found the trace of a solo student who got airborne, dropped to low level, then pulled up almost immediately. He then spent 30 minutes flying zigzags at 7,000 feet before going directly through Aberdeen's airspace to get back to Inverness. Busted! I won't put his chances of completing the course as very high.

Wednesday 28 March

Today was more navigation: a high-to-low into East Anglia in the morning, followed by my final navigation test in the afternoon.

The morning flight was with Flt Lt Dave Lord, who we are all convinced is a bit mad. The weather was only marginally suitable and I wasn't entirely happy about being at low level, but Dave seemed to think it was perfect. We spotted a GR1 Tornado about 20 minutes into the low-level section and, laughing hysterically, Dave took control and was on its tail in seconds. When he finally gave me back control, I had to work hard to get back on to my planned route, as we were miles off track. I was thumbing my way along my map with one hand and flying with the other for quite some time. Not the approved technique at all. The final navigation test was easy compared to that. It was a good pass and was flown with one of the station's senior instructors.

Thursday 29 March

Today I did very little for a change and enjoyed it. Steve Williamson, Gibbo and Binnzy returned from their navigation land-away to Prestwick, which is the Scottish airfield where British Airways is currently training cadet pilots. One of the cadets was an ex-navy officer who had received a court martial and been dismissed from the service. He had incorrectly set the running depth of a practice torpedo to eight feet instead of 48 feet. Unfortunately for him, the torpedo was fired at a brand new German frigate and punctured the side of the vessel and flooded several compartments.

Roger has managed to get tomorrow off to go down to London. He was spinning the line that his parents live in Africa and he needed a day for a reunion with them. I tried to reason that as my great, great, grandparents also used to live in Africa then I should have the day off as well. The boss just looked at me and said, "What's your name? Roots?" I took that as a no.

Tuesday 3 April

Andy Pomeroy has had a near miss with the Mad Major. Not the fault of either of them as they were both under radar control at the time, but Andy saw the shadow of the Major's aircraft as it passed overhead even though he was flying in thick cloud.

Binnzy is not happy at the moment. He had a sneaky look at his training file last night and saw a few of the comments the instructors have written about him. The one I like the most was from Flt Lt Dave Lord: "A noisy union man who should keep his opinions to himself."

Brilliant! I have no intention of looking at my training file. I will be happy enough to pass the course. Anything else is a bonus.

Friday 6 April

The last few days have been very slow and I have only flown a few times. Andy Pomeroy and his course graduated today and there were the usual fly pasts, and festivities in the mess. I am having an attack of apathy at the moment. We have a week off for Easter soon, and I am unlikely to get more than a couple of trips for the whole of the next week. Just want to get on and finish the course. There are only 10 more trips to go.

Tuesday 19 April

I'm back from the week-long Easter break, refreshed and ready. Today, I got a taste of low-level tactical formation and it is as much fun as everyone has predicted.

Up to this point, all the formation we flew was of the close variety where you are only a few feet away from your leader and have to keep that position when he manoeuvres. It demands a lot of concentration and is very inflexible as all your attention is fixed on the lead aircraft.

The basic tactical formation has two aircraft flying parallel to each other but separated by 500 yards to 1500 yards. This allows both pilots to navigate and look out of the cockpit for any baddies. There is a lot of fun in the turns, as some mental gymnastics is required to work out the geometry and remain in position.

Saturday 21 April

There was a Dining In night at the mess last night, but for a change, I wasn't too badly behaved, although for some reason I did spend a fortune phoning my old university friend Louise who is living in Los Angeles. No idea what I had to say to her that was so important.

Today, Pete Lightbody from our junior course drove Roger, Steve and myself to lunch at Dave Lord's house. Pete skilfully managed to drive the whole way with a crate of beer on the bonnet of the car. We had bought flowers for Mrs Lord and water pistols for his two small kids. That turned out not to have been the smartest move as the children both fired at us constantly during the afternoon. The little girl limited her aim to around knee level, but there was no such joy from the little boy – he is as mad as his dad. By early evening, we had decamped to the pub, with Dave leaving his house saying that he was just stepping out for a single pint. We were all still there at midnight.

Monday 23 April

Flt Lt Dave Lord has been in trouble with his wife. When he got home on Saturday night, he crawled up the stairs to his bedroom to find her still awake and waiting for him.

"Hello dear, I'm home."

To which she replied, "Bastard."

Then he said, "I haven't been drinking, honest. I've been on Coke."

And promptly got, "Liar."

He said he was up early with the kids, cooking breakfast by way of penance.

Dave was also telling some great stories of his time flying the Buccaneer. The Bucc is a maritime attack aircraft and he had some good tales of dumping fuel over Soviet warships.

On one occasion, he had an engine failure while getting airborne from here at RAF Valley. They landed safely after the emergency and later in the crew room one of the student pilots, who had watched the events unfold, told him that it was obvious he was in trouble as one of his engines did not go into reheat. Dave said he had fun explaining to the young lad that the Buccaneer has no reheat and the flames he saw were the result of the engine being on fire.

Steve Williamson is not a favourite of Binnzy at the moment. It seems on Friday night he told Mrs Binns that she is shaped like a Dutch windmill. She wasn't amused, but they do say that the truth hurts.

Superb weather all day, and I flew twice – a dual and a solo, both of them tactical formation trips. It is much easier being in close formation and not having to work at navigation and lookout as we do in tactical formation.

Wednesday 25 April

I got airborne this morning on what was supposed to be my last solo flight on the course. As I climbed away from the base, the air conditioning system started to sound as though it was about to explode, so I turned around and headed back. As it happened, that was a lucky event. An unforecasted sea fog had started to roll in over the base. It wasn't too bad when I landed, but shortly after that, visibility dropped down to 200 metres and the boys who were airborne had to divert and land at other airfields. There was a Bulldog pilot from RAF Topcliffe in the crew room who was on the phone sorting out his departure with air traffic. When he sat down to make the call the outside, visibility was 5 km and when he finished, it was 200 metres. It all happened that quickly.

Friday 27 April

Today was very busy and my last day of course flying at RAF Valley. I was airborne in the first wave for my test pre-ride, followed by the final handling test at lunchtime with the chief instructor, Wing Commander Thorpe. It followed the usual format, a bit of low-level navigation with a target, general handling including my agricultural aerobatics, an instrument approach and then I finished off with circuits. It was an hour-long flight resulting in a very good pass. Next!

Considering I had just passed and qualified as a fast jet pilot in the Royal Air Force, I felt very underwhelmed; just relieved to be through and a bit tired. Drove down to London, and Shirley made sure we celebrated by taking me out to a very good restaurant in Kensington.

Monday 30 April

The course isn't due to graduate for another three weeks, so I have been given a week's leave. Which is great, as I have been told that I am now due to start my next course on 63 squadron at the Tactical Weapons Unit, RAF Chivenor, north Devon, on the Monday after our graduation.

The sting in the tail to the week's leave is that I have to attend a memorial service on Friday at the RAF memorial at Runnymede just outside Windsor. I've tried everything to get out of it but to no avail.

Andy Pomeroy starts his course at RAF Brawdy today, and Roger has been pencilled in to start at Chivenor next week. The navy obviously doesn't believe in leave.

Friday 4 May

I drove to Runnymede for the service and in retrospect, I was very glad I was selected to go. I had no idea how many airmen were killed during the Second World War. The Runnymede memorial is solely for Commonwealth airmen and women who were lost and have no grave. There are more than 20,000 names engraved on its walls. Attending the service was a very humbling and sobering experience.

Wednesday 16 May

I am back from leave and have missed lots of action. Last week, a Phantom landed and burst a tyre. Air traffic control transmitted on the radio that they were on fire, so the navigator promptly ejected. The pilot calmly shut everything down and climbed out.

The next day, one of the Brunei students got airborne, had a control restriction and ejected. He landed safely in his parachute on the runway and the aircraft exploded spectacularly on some wasteland just outside the airfield.

Today we had a big course night out, accompanied by Cameron Gair and Flt Lt Miriam Williams who were over from Linton-on-Ouse. Gibbo was selected to say grace before dinner and came out with what we think was one of his old Cambridge prayers.

"The Lord be praised and my belly be raised one inch above the table, for I'll be damned if I'm not crammed as much as I am able."

That pretty much set the tone for the rest of the evening. Miriam, to no one's surprise, was not well received by the fast jet instructors. Roger managed to fall asleep standing up, and someone got hold of a wheelchair for our most senior instructor.

Thursday 17 May

I didn't see much of the morning, and in the afternoon we had rehearsals for the graduation ceremony. It was a total shambles, which was unsurprising considering the physical state of most of the participants. God help us tomorrow.

Friday 18 May

The Big Day: wings presentation. It went very well, and we received our Royal Air Force Pilot Wings from the main man himself, Air Commodore Chris Coville. The flying display was hampered by the weather and we only had some of the Valley Hawks airborne for the display.

I couldn't stop looking at the shiny new wings on my uniform. It is still hard to believe that they are real.

The graduation party was as excessive as expected, although Shirley and I were very restrained. She has started to realise that this wasn't the end of my training and she was not happy about that. I can't say I blame her. I spend as much time with her as I can, but the courses are so intensive they don't leave much spare time. That is the danger of having a girlfriend who is totally non-military, but I won't have it any other way.

Ian Gibson and I would start our next course at RAF Chivenor on Monday 21 May. Reg Armeanu received his wings but wasn't selected for further fast jet training and eventually became a VC10 transport pilot. Major Almahoun successfully completed the course and returned to Brunei, although his air force never acquired the Hawk or any other fast jets. (He already had pilot wings.) The rest of the course started their tactical weapons course at RAF Brawdy in June.

Shirley and I drove out of Anglesey late the next day and it was dark, blowing a gale and the rain was horizontal. Exactly the same conditions when I arrived six months ago.

That was the end of the advanced flying training course. I now had 25 hours solo and 55 hours dual on the Hawk. For most of the course, my trips have been scored as above average and overall I have been assessed as PROFICIENT.

Chipmunks RAF Swinderby

Left to right; Ian Reid(navy), Reg Armeanu, John Bowland, Steve Shell, Pete Coville, Paul Gerrard, Trev Edwards, Paul Binns, Andy Pomeroy(navy). Standing on aircraft; Mark Harris, Adrian Bonwitt.

Hawk over North Wales

With Dave Lord at my graduation

Me and my Jag

Oops at RAF Lossiemouth

p144

Tactical Weapons School

63 Squadron
RAF Chivenor,
Barnstaple,
Devon,
1990

During my time at RAF Chivenor, the old Soviet Union was continuing to splinter, meanwhile East and West Germany were officially reunited. But while The Cold War appeared to be ending, elsewhere notions of world peace evaporated with the Iraqi invasion of Kuwait in August 1990.

Two Hawks squadrons (63 and 151) were based at Chivenor as well as a detachment of search-and-rescue helicopters. Chivenor was part of RAF Strike Command, and both squadrons had a secondary war role along with their primary training tasks. The Chivenor Hawks were painted in camouflage grey and were fitted with simple gun sights for weapon aiming. The Hawks could carry bombs, air-to-air missiles and a gun.

The tactical weapons course is an intensive four months during which qualified pilots are taught how to fight the Hawk aircraft. It is another compulsory course on the journey to becoming a fighter pilot.

Monday 21 May

I drove here from London on Saturday with Shirley, and we had a very relaxed weekend exploring north Devon. The base is small compared to Valley, and it is very modern. The officers' mess is only a few years old, and I have been given a room with an en-suite bathroom. I didn't know such things existed in the RAF. We even have telephones in the rooms, which is the height of luxury. The other boys on the course are:
Ian Gibson
Andy Offer
Bill Auckland
Dave Waters John Letton

Ian Gibson was on my course at Valley. Andy Offer is a creamy instructor from Linton-on-Ouse and Bill Auckland was on no. 3 squadron at Valley. Dave Waters and John Letton are converting to fast jets after flying other aircraft. We have all joined 63 squadron for the duration – and judging by today's events that won't be very long.

The squadron runs only two courses at a time, and today they chopped a third student from our senior course. He was getting fixated on targets during attacks and was pulling out of his dives very late. The instructors say he would have killed himself if he had been allowed to progress. There are now only two pilots left on that course, an Arab student and a creamy. This is not going to be easy.

Tuesday 22 May

We were straight into full work mode today: an essential knowledge quiz in the morning and then two simulator trips in the afternoon to get back up to speed. Flying starts tomorrow – and as we have already seen they don't take prisoners here.

Wednesday 23 May

Dinghy drills in the local pool in the morning were followed by a familiarisation trip, which was just a quick once around the local flying area with an instructor pointing out the salient landmarks.

Bill Auckland managed to fly twice and is due to have his instrument-rating test tomorrow. It is all coming thick and fast. I am going to have to stick to soft drinks in the evenings and not go out during the week, or I will be struggling.

The instructor in charge of our course is Flt Lt Martin Whitehead, but everyone calls him Snapper. He is an ex-Jaguar pilot and is currently a member of the British bobsleigh team. To say that he is larger than life would be an understatement, but most of the instructors have that in common.

Thursday 24 May

It was another early start today: into the simulator first thing, followed by a dual trip and then my instrument-rating test. I didn't fly very well at all and failed the trip, so I will be flying the test again tomorrow. Can't believe that I'm in trouble already, and the course is only four days old.

Friday 25 May

I had my re-test first thing this morning and thankfully, it went well, so I was launched on a solo which was great fun. Flew down to Cornwall and over the top of a friend's parents' house, and then a bit of low level on the way back. As I am now a qualified air force pilot, for the first time, I can fly down to 250 feet while solo. It was just nice to be in an aircraft without the stress of having an instructor analysing my every move.

Tuesday 29 May

It's been raining cats and dogs all day, so instead of a nice slow day on the squadron, we had briefs for the next two phases of the course and lectures on

Soviet missile systems and main battle tanks. I enjoyed that, but we all got a telling off for not being well prepared. There is no sitting down drinking coffee and chatting at this place, and there aren't enough hours in the day for the amount of work we have to get through.

Wednesday 30 May

The boss of 63 squadron is Sqn Ldr Guy Bancroft-Wilson, and he is a former Red Arrows pilot. This morning, I flew a close formation refresher trip, and the boss was leading. He seemed to think he was back in the Red Arrows. After take-off, we were straight into steep turns and his roll rates were the fastest I have ever experienced. I didn't hack it, so I have to fly the trip again. Not sure how many times they allow retakes, but at this rate, I will be lucky to survive two weeks.

Thursday 31 May

I had my formation trip again this morning with two Sqn Ldr instructors who are referred to by their initials, PADS and RBS. They are both old-school fighter pilots. PADS is ex-Lightnings and Phantoms, and RBS is ex-Jaguar. They both have reputations of being unflappable, and they were good to me this morning. PADS was flying the lead aircraft, and RBS was my instructor. The roll rates were much more gentlemanly and I had no difficulty in keeping position, so the trip was a good pass, and I was launched on a solo formation. PADS flew the lead aircraft again and gradually increased the difficulty until we were flying barrel rolls. I coped, although the first time I noticed that the horizon was upside down did result in a big wobble in my formation position.

Bill Auckland had problems on his formation today as well, although he did manage to pass his trip. He said that when they lined up on the runway, it was as if someone had let a goat out of a cage and he had to catch it. He could get close to the animal, but he never got it under control.

This evening, we had a squadron social event at a local pub and I decided to drive – and so not to consume any alcohol. I needed to have a clear head for the morning as I am struggling enough at the moment. As we left, I was stopped and breathalysed by a policeman who was waiting outside the pub. One of the instructors who I am sure was not sober, fell down a pothole before getting into his car, but PC Plod was too busy telling me all about the dangers of drinking and driving to notice.

Monday 4 June

I stayed at the station for the weekend and got some work done. This morning, we had several briefings from Snapper and then I flew on a trip that taught the use of the gun sight and how to track targets with it. They call it simple cine, but it is far from simple. Anyway, I was good enough to fly again solo in the afternoon.

The gun sight on the Hawk is generated in a small device on top of the instrument panel and projected on to a piece of glass directly in the line of sight of the front-seat pilot. The sight can be configured for air or ground targets. The aircraft has to be flown with a fair degree of precision as the sight is only calibrated for accurate gunnery and bombing at a set distance to the target.

Friday 8 June

The weather has been poor all week with lots of low clouds, but that hasn't stopped the flying. I have been kept ticking over with one trip a day, and today was no exception. A low-level tactical formation trip which I really enjoyed, although the 4G turns at low level will take a bit of getting used to. Any descent in the turn and you are likely to be a smoking hole in the ground.

A course from Valley landed this afternoon on a land-away trip, and it sounded as though they had a hard time getting through the weather. I can sympathise, but Valley seems like a long time ago and a bit of a holiday camp in comparison to this place.

There were so many high-G manoeuvres on this course that the average student's collar size grew by two inches. In a 4G turn, your head weighs four times as much but you still have to be able to turn it and look out the cockpit, sometimes even over your shoulder. The neck muscles respond to this punishment by getting bigger.

Thursday 14 June

This morning was the advanced gun sight tracking teach. They call this one 'cine impossible', and it is impossible. You have a target aircraft that is manoeuvring hard, but in a set pattern. You would think that tracking it would be relatively straightforward; however, it is fiendishly difficult. The target aircraft is in the middle of the gun sight for only fractions of a second before its manoeuvres take it elsewhere. Even if you know the sequence of manoeuvres, as I did, it is extremely challenging. Nevertheless, I passed the trip and have my solo tomorrow. I had another low-level trip in the afternoon with another ex-Jaguar instructor. Yet again, my flying was dreadful. As Bill would say, the goat was out and running. I just couldn't get settled in the low-level environment and was getting flustered which made the situation worse. I got myself into such a mess that I wasn't using even basic navigation techniques. Fortunately, the air conditioning system failed after 20 minutes, and we had to head back to base. My instructor kindly recorded the trip as not completed due to an aircraft fault, so I get to fly it again with no jeopardy. I will have to get my finger out; there have been too many poor trips.

Friday 15 June

The senior course over on 151 squadron finished today and got their postings to front-line aircraft. One pilot was sent to fly the Jaguar and the rest will be flying the two variants of the Tornado.

I was scheduled to fly three times but fortunately only managed to get airborne twice, which was enough. Both flights were solo attempts at cine impossible. As the instructor said during the debriefs, my technique was great but my tracking was lacking.

Weekend 16 June

Peter Lightbody, from the junior course at Valley, was visiting the base for the weekend and as always with Pete, there suddenly seemed to be women and alcohol in abundance. Friday night ended in a nurses' party in Barnstable, and most of Saturday was spent in The Thatch pub in the village of Croyde. This pub has become the local for the pilots on the course. Fortunately, Pete had to leave early on Sunday, so I could dry out and do some work.

Tuesday 19 June

The station doctor had received my medical file and insisted that I visit her. For some reason, she wasn't happy about me flying without any toes, and she also wanted to place a zone restriction on my flying category. This would mean that I couldn't deploy to any cold countries in the future.

The woman was just bored by having to look after a station full of healthy, fit young people, and I was an interesting case for her to play with. I managed to persuade her that I had no issues with cold weather and if ever deployed to Norway, would make sure that my footwear was adequate. The whole thing was a distraction that I could have done without. Flew twice, a low-level trip, which was tough, and an air test with PADS. I was just his passenger, but it was very interesting to see the aircraft flown beyond the normal limits. His flying is so smooth it's incredible.

Dave Waters is in trouble. He is struggling with leading the two-ship tactical formations we fly at low level. Those trips are next.

The low-level tactical formation we used is called 'battle'. We were given an introduction to it at RAF Valley. Pairs of aircraft fly parallel to each other separated by up to one and a half miles to enable mutual cover. In this formation, they can easily check each other's six o'clock position and spot any attacking aircraft. The formation leader has the responsibility of navigation and time keeping as well as keeping a good look out. As an additional complication, we were given specific times to attack some of the targets.

Our low-level planning had set times to achieve at each turning point, so a speed adjustment had to be made if the formation is early or late. The Hawk is only equipped with a stopwatch to aid this calculation.

Wednesday 20 June

Oh, yes! Leading battle formations at low level is a nightmare. The goat was out and running, and I didn't get close to it for the whole hour of the flight today. No idea what was going on for the majority of the trip, and I have to repeat it again tomorrow. This is becoming a recurring theme. Not good.

Thursday 21 June

There was lousy weather at low level throughout Wales, which meant there was no formation for me today. Instead, I had my first air combat manoeuvring (ACM) trip. We had to fly over to Norfolk to get to the good weather, but I have found something I am good at. I had no difficulty in thinking in three dimensions, understood what I was being taught and most of all, enjoyed it. I might have a chance of passing this course.

Air combat manoeuvring is a formal name for the classic fighter vs fighter dogfight as seen in many an old war movie. During this phase of the course, we started with simulated gun-armed aircraft to ensure the basic concepts were well understood. We then moved on to simulated missile-armed aircraft and eventually two aircraft and one targets.

For this phase, you need to think in three dimensions as the 'enemy' could be several thousand feet below or above your aircraft. Your aim is to manoeuvre yourself into range for a guns kill or within parameters for the heat-seeking missile to get a lock-on and start automatically tracking. The best position for both of these is directly behind the enemy aircraft – in other words, in its six o'clock.

Air combat is physically tough because much of the time is spent in high-G turns, and although the pilots don't fire anything at each other they all want to 'kill' the opponents. Having a colleague getting into your own six o'clock is surprisingly stressful. Every time it happened to me, I could just imagine the bullets heading in my direction. Any claimed 'kills' were checked with the aid of the gun sight camera.

Friday 22 June

The weather looked appalling on the ground in north Devon this morning, but in the air, it was much better. My flying was much improved as well. I completed the low-level battle lead trip without getting lost, and managed to keep the goat under control. A much happier Trevor.

The second trip of the day was another air combat manoeuvring trip. This time, defensive manoeuvring and another decent trip. I really like this air combat stuff.

Shirley was up for the weekend, and we went to the station's summer ball on Saturday night.

Weekend 23 June

The summer ball was a very small affair compared to the others I have experienced, but that didn't detract from the fun of the evening. Shirley and I managed to pace ourselves and we lasted until breakfast, which is a first.

Sunday was a very slow day, so I took Shirley into one of the hangars to show her the aircraft. She wasn't very impressed by any of it, not even the great big gun pod or any of the missiles attached to a couple of the machines. She was more impressed by The Thatch pub and the scenery down on the coast, but then again Devon in the summer is a different world from Anglesey in the winter.

Tuesday 24 June

There was a station alert early this morning, and I was still in bed as we had been night flying. There were lots of people running around in camouflage outfits and most of the instructors got airborne in aircraft with practice missiles under the wings. I had no idea what was happening. There is no role for trainee fighter pilots in war games, so we were told to stay out of the way.

The alert finished before lunch, and I incorrectly assumed that I could have the afternoon off as I was scheduled to have another night flying trip. No such luck. I was off on an air combat manoeuvring trip with the squadron's newest pilot, Dave Cullen, as my instructor. Dave is an ex-Harrier pilot, in fact the only ex-Harrier pilot we have on the squadron. They call him The Machine, and I can see why. He is very, very good. We pulled lots of Gs and fought and beat the other aircraft. Great fun, but I was very weary by the time we landed. Fortunately, I had dropped off the programme for night flying.

The alert was simulating an attack on the station by a formation of enemy aircraft that had dropped several bombs, with ensuing casualties and damage. Alerts like this were a regular occurrence during the Cold War especially at the front-line stations in Germany. They would have several every year, with some lasting days.

Monday 2 July

The weather was glorious, but there was no flying for any of the students at RAF Chivenor as the instructors have been having their annual bombing and gunning competition. I tried to get a trip in a back seat, but I have been told that none of the instructors wants to show students any bad habits or give away any tricks.

There was a sweepstake on the winner, and I initially put down Dave Cullen until it was pointed out that he hasn't been flying the Hawk for very long. So using that logic, I have gone for PADS.

Tuesday 3 July

An instructor nicknamed Gonzo won the guns and bombs competition. No one bet on him, so he gets to keep all of the sweepstake money.

Airborne first thing today on a solo low-level formation with an instructor as my wingman. He had an air cadet in his back seat. I had no problems, as the visibility was so great that it would have been hard to get lost. The poor air cadet was a bit worse for wear though. He struggled to cope with all the Gs in the turns. The instructor couldn't decrease the amount he used as that would, put him out of position and create problems for me. The lad just had to endure, which he did without complaint.

I landed from that trip and had to go into a rapid plan for another low-level trip. The weather has been so good that the boss has decided we should get as much of the low-level flying completed as we can.

Two of the first-ever female University Air Squadron pilots turned up today for a two-week stay. They are Ann and Helen and both are good-looking girls. The testosterone levels in the crew room have dramatically increased. I am trying not to get distracted.

Wednesday 4 July

It was a good job that we got the low-level trips in yesterday as today the clouds were from 100 feet up to 25,000 feet all over the country. It was crystal clear above that, so perfect weather for air combat. This morning's trip was a two vs one teach. These trips are wild and involved much more talking to your wingman than usual. There are also whole new sets of phrases to learn and use.

My second trip was a one vs one with me solo against PADS, the Air Combat King – brilliant! We fought for almost 45 minutes, but at no time did I get my gun sight on to his aircraft. The man is too good.

I felt very light headed on the recovery back to the base and I think it was due to all the G. Just keeping my head up at 7G is difficult.

Thursday 5 July

It was windy as hell today and in the morning, there was no flying. We spent our time having weapons briefs, specifically on the 1000lb bomb, and the Sidewinder, which is a heat-seeking air-to-air missile. The Hawk can carry both these weapons.

I didn't expect to fly, but in the afternoon, I went up on a solo air combat one vs one trip against Dave Cullen. It was great fun as always, and I managed to get on his tail and stay there for a few seconds. He would have been toast in a real fight.

Friday 6 July

Flying air combat again this morning. Another one vs one and again it was fun – but exhausting. I was finding it a struggle to look over my shoulder in some of the high-G turns. It is physically tough and my neck muscles still aren't used to it yet. I managed to get a guns 'kill' during one of the engagements, but on another I was so focused on the fight I lost awareness of my position and flew through the base height with the aircraft pointing towards the ground and accelerating.

Base height is normally several thousand feet above the ground and is chosen as a safety buffer to teach awareness of height during combat. In a real fight, the base height would be ground level and errors in height awareness would be fatal.

Happy hour in the evening was a very vocal affair. Most of the members of 63 squadron were in attendance and for a change so were most of 151 squadron. Squadron rivalries were at a peak. I have a vague memory of drinking flaming Drambuie and having an altercation with Ian Walton from 151 squadron. There is an even shoddier memory of a party in Barnstable, which I think might have involved some nurses.

Saturday 7 July

It seems happy hour last night was far worse than I first thought. I have a massive hangover and my flying suit is shredded, although I have no idea how or why. Rumour has it that I spent most of the evening antagonising 151 squadron, not helped by RBS who, unbeknown to me, was adding fuel to the fire by making sure that my glass was topped up at all times. The party in Barnstable was at the nurses' accommodation, which was fortunate as poor old Dave Waters had hurt his leg during happy hour and was limping so badly that one of the girls insisted he went to casualty. He was convinced he had just sprained it, but they discovered it was broken. Dave also has to see the station commander on Monday morning, something to do with being disrespectful during happy hour.

I was the station duty officer today so had a nice quiet day recovering from my hangover. The only incident I had to deal with was a suspected stolen car near the base in the early hours of Sunday morning.

Monday 9 July

Today was my first day on the weapons ranges, and my first flying an armed aircraft. The 30mm cannon is mounted in a big pod under the fuselage and contains several hundred rounds of ammunition. Today, I was taught how to strafe, (firing the gun at ground targets,) and flew two trips with the boss. Although my range procedures were good and I was using the correct techniques, I didn't manage any hits. I was cleared solo, but still managed no hits and, as expected the rest of the boys are starting to take notice and are being their usual sympathetic selves.

Dave Waters is out of action for six weeks with his broken leg. The good news is that the station commander has put his talkative behaviour in the bar as alcohol induced and is taking no further action. Dave is going to be joining our junior course when he gets back to fitness.

The main weapons range we used was at Pembrey on the south Wales coast. This had a variety of targets, mainly consisting of 20-metre bullseyes painted on to the ground for bombing and five-metre square vertical panels for strafing, along with systems to score the results. Only small practice bombs were dropped on the range. They were the size of a two-litre plastic bottle, and four were carried under each wing in a streamlined dispenser. They had similar ballistics to real bombs and exploded with a big flash and a small bang. All Chivenor Hawks had gun sight cameras so that weapons release or guns attacks could be analysed and debriefed.

Tuesday 10 July

I had three trips again today. Two solo strafes in the morning and a dual bombing in the afternoon. The morning trips were frustrating. No hits: nil points. This has been the source of much amusement on the squadron. The debriefs of my films showed that I was using the correct techniques and getting close to the target, but that is no comfort.

The bombing trip in the afternoon was dual. It went very well and I got some good scores. In fact, it went so well that I had dropped all my bombs and had some spare time and fuel. My instructor, Richie Thomas, decided to use the time to re-teach my strafe. It was a bit of a revelation. All this time I have been firing slightly out of range, and I haven't been making enough allowance for the wind. The re-teach resulted in a score of 21 hits out of the 50 bullets fired. That should stop all the banter I have been receiving in the crew room.

Wednesday 11 July

Another glorious day, and more range work for me. Just the two trips and they were both bombing. No sweat for a change, with some very good scores for my bombs.

Andy Offer has been getting very flustered about a rumour that he might be sent to fly the Buccaneer. He is by far the best pilot on the course, but the boss is saying they might need a qualified instructor on the Buccaneer, and Andy fits the bill. He doesn't want to go up to northern Scotland to fly the Buccaneer and would prefer the Harrier or the Jaguar, both stationed on nice southern airfields. His wife, Amanda, is not keen on the north of Scotland either.

It was Bill Auckland's 21st birthday today, and the two University Air Squadron girls, Ann and Helen, bought him a cake and organised a party for him. Those girls are good value. They have been flying in quite a few back seats and have worked hard on the ground helping out whenever they can. They still refused Bill's suggestion of birthday sex…although Bill wouldn't have made such a suggestion if they didn't have a sense of humour.

Pilots are usually selected to fly aircraft that best suits their abilities. The Harrier and the Jaguar are single-seat aircraft, but the Tornado, Phantom and Buccaneer have navigators in a second seat behind the pilot. In an ideal world, the top pilots would fly the single-seat aircraft; however, they go where they are needed.

Thursday 12 July

The met brief this morning was fun. The met man started by thanking Richie Thomas for taking him flying and making him feel ill. He then extended a general invitation to anyone to spend an hour in the met office with him at any time. An hour looking at synoptic charts and trying to guess the weather – I don't think he will get any takers.

The weather was scorching again, not a cloud in the sky. I was airborne solo bombing in the morning and just wasn't in the groove. The bombs were all over the place and one missed the target by 100ft. Luckily, there was a problem with the gun camera, and there was no film for the instructors to debrief. We can't pass a solo weapons sortie without having a film to debrief, so I got to fly the trip again in the afternoon. That was much better. All my bombs were within 20ft, and although I had a stoppage on the gun after just one short burst, I got one hit with five rounds and that was recorded as 20 percent accuracy. Happy days! Bill is trying to convince Ann and Helen that he needs one of them for a sex check sortie. He has explained that it is nothing personal. He says that he has been solo for far too long and therefore needs a dual check. It is great banter. The girls are impressed, and he could even get lucky.

Monday 16 July

Today was another hard-working day with three trips. A dual-level bombing teach and then two solo trips. I hardly seemed to spend any time on the ground. Our junior course started today, and there are several guys from my old junior course at Valley, including Pete Lightbody, but I was far too busy to chat to them.

Tuesday 17 July

There was low fog over the airfield in the early morning, but that soon burned away to leave another clear day. As soon as it cleared, I was up on a dual trip being taught air defence and one vs one with John Letton in the other aircraft. We both flew another air defence sortie in the afternoon.

Gibbo was the man on the range today. He had a strafe score of 32 hits with 50 rounds and a set of very good bombs as well. Not even the instructors get scores like that very often. Pat Voigt, who is one of the creamy instructors from Linton-on-Ouse, landed this afternoon on a land-away. His Jet Provost Mk5 looks a bit pathetic next to the Hawks. It is amazing to think that just a year ago, I was flying those machines and struggling my way through basic formation.

The air defence phase of the course was an introduction to what the big air defence fighters do in the real world. Soviet long-range bombers often flew down the North Sea to test the air defences of the UK. Air defence fighters would be scrambled and directed by ground radars to a position where their onboard radar could detect these bombers. They could then shoot them down with long range missiles or get close to visually identify them. As we did not have onboard radar, we were directed until we were able to visually identify a target. The ground radar operators were known as fighter controllers. In the more advanced trips, two aircraft were directed on to one target.

Wednesday 18 July

The morning started with a brief on air-to-air gunnery which looks as though it will be a difficult skill to master. I then had a mid-course general handling trip with RBS that I didn't expect. Partly due to this lack of preparation, I did not fly to the required standard, which means I will be flying the trip again.

The banter in the crew room in the afternoon centred on our instructor, Dave Cullen, and a student navigator, Simon Cleaver, getting lost at low level. A sharp ex-Harrier pilot and a navigator getting lost in 30km of visibility! To add to the fun, the other aircraft in their formation (their wingman) was Sqn Ldr Thurley who is going to be the next leader of the Red Arrows. He is an old hand at Chivenor and says he was always aware of his position. 'Following out of idle curiosity' was the phrase he used.

Thursday 19 July

The weather was still amazing, with huge visibility. I could see the Channel from 20,000ft over the Severn Estuary. Up on another air defence trip flying against John Letton. We were taking turns acting as the target until the fight merged, that is when you are both within visual range, and then the fight became a standard one vs one. For the first time, we were using simulated heat-seeking missiles as well as guns. The missiles make the fight much easier, although I have never had any trouble fighting John. He is useless at air combat. I flew my general handling retake with a Squadron Leader who normally works in station operations. It wasn't the best I have flown, but it was a pass and that is all I care about at this stage.

Paul Stone, one of the navy pilots on the junior course, has decided that the simulator should be renamed the humiliator after he had a particularly difficult session. Even some of the instructors are agreeing with him. The instructors also have to complete monthly emergency exercises in the simulator, and I get the feeling that they enjoy it as much as we do.

Roger Colquhoun over on 151 squadron was due to be leading a pair of aircraft on a sortie today, but had to taxi back in before getting airborne because his wingman had a large bee buzzing around inside his cockpit and was finding it a massive distraction. 'Steely-eyed Fighter Pilot Grounded by Buzzing Insect' – that's not a heroic sounding headline...

Friday 20 July

More great weather, and I was flying on the first wave trying to conquer air-to-air gunnery. In the movies, it looks so simple, just put the gun sight on the enemy, pull the trigger and the baddie is shot down. I fired 75 bullets at the airborne target and scored no hits.

The airborne target was a large three-metre banner, which was towed behind a Hawk by a long cable and a brave instructor. The banner was flown in a gentle turn to make the gunnery a bit more difficult. It also meant there was less chance of the bullets striking the towing aircraft.

Happy hour in the bar proved a bit of a riot. A bunch of Tornado guys were down with their aircraft for the weekend and they were walking around with jugs of weird cocktails. One of these contained chilli vodka that they had made themselves. The evening started to get out of hand when one of the station admin officers tried to intervene and stop any further drinking. Although he was a squadron leader no one was paying him any attention, until one of our flying instructors nicknamed Welly said, "Enough!"

Welly is a very large man from Newcastle who is usually very mild mannered, but we have found it is in our best interests to take him seriously when he raises his voice.

At this point, Ann and Helen arrived in the bar and became the centre of attention. It was just as well. There were a few people planning a revenge raid on the admin squadron leader as he had continued to insist on proper officer-like behaviour. In happy hour? He is mad. Someone discovered that he lives in the mess during the week and had even gone so far as planning a human pyramid to get to his bedroom window on the first floor when the girls caused the distraction.

Saturday 21 July

A slow morning, but in the afternoon, Bill and I were invited to a party near Andover by Ann and Helen. It was at the house of Ann's parents and was a joint party with her sister. She is a dentist studying to become a doctor, so she can specialise in dental surgery. A super-clever girl and most of her guests were of the same ilk. Bill and I managed to hold our own. I do remember seeing him later on in the evening with Ann holding his arms above his head, while Helen was removing his trousers, and a female medical student was removing his shirt. Strangely, he didn't seem to be struggling.

Monday 23 July

I had only the one trip today, solo air-to-air gunnery with no bullets, just using the camera to record everything and make sure I was using the correct techniques. No real problems with the flying, however, I do need to get closer to the target before opening fire.

The boss is having a contest at the moment to see if anyone can get an erection while flying at low level. The word has gone out throughout the station, and quite a few guys are seeing if it can be done. I certainly will be having a go the next time I am at low level.

The quote of the weekend goes to Dave Wheeler over on 151 squadron. He invited a couple who he had been at school with over for the weekend. The three of them were in the bar on

Friday night and had spent most of Saturday in The Thatch pub where the girl asked, "Do you pilots do anything but drink and talk about flying?"

Dave pondered the question for a few seconds before replying.

"No. Sometimes we just DRINK."

He is right. After all, it was a sunny Saturday afternoon in Croyde, so what else would a tactical weapons pilot be doing?

Tuesday 24 July

I had a rare day off today. There wasn't much flying at the station as tomorrow is the annual station open day and most of the personnel are involved in getting the place tidy for the general public.

Bill Auckland's brother Mike came over from Yeovilton. He is a Royal Navy Sea Harrier pilot, and a qualified test pilot – and we are all a bit in awe of him. We spent most of the afternoon in The Thatch in Croyde, again.

Wednesday 25 July

Today was the station open day and an excuse to pose. We were allowed to wear our flying suits and so stood out among the other uniforms. It was amazing that so many people wanted to get their pictures taken with a pilot and buy the bits of squadron memorabilia that we were selling.

The evening party in the mess was as expected, a mini riot. I have never seen so many women in the place, and there were a lot of badly behaved boys. No memory of getting to bed, the last thing I do remember was being at the bar with Snapper and something to do with tequila.

Thursday 26 July

I don't think I had very much in the way of sleep last night even though I didn't get out of bed until mid-morning. That was for the litter sweep of the runway and taxi areas. Everyone on the station has to participate in this to make sure that there is no debris that can be sucked into an air intake and damage an aircraft engine.

Normally, the fresh air would have cleared my head, but today, there was no improvement and I had to ask Snapper for the afternoon off. He just smiled knowingly and told me to come back to work on Monday.

Saturday 28 July

Shirley and I haven't been dating for a couple of weeks now. There are lots of reasons and it isn't working for us at the moment. She has got a job on a yacht sailing from Plymouth to Spain and then over to the Caribbean. I drove her down to Plymouth, and it was very hard saying goodbye.

Aha

Tuesday 31 July

Another glorious day without a cloud in the sky. In the simulator first thing in the morning, followed by two air-to-air gunnery trips. During the second trip, I fired a total of 75 rounds to achieve five hits. That's not a great percentage, but I tried to convince the rest of the boys that the 30mm rounds are so big that one hit is more than enough to bring down an aircraft.

Gibbo has been struggling with air combat, and I didn't even know. He found the two vs one stuff difficult and needed a few extra trips to pass that phase of the course. It just took him a while to get his head around manoeuvring in three dimensions.

The good news is that Bill Auckland has found a girlfriend. A local girl who I think he met at the open day. She was abusing him on the sand dunes on Saturday night by all accounts.

Wednesday 1 August

Another absolute scorcher of a day and it was very hot in the aircraft even with the air conditioning going. Airborne on another air defence trip flying against John Letton, and I waxed his ass again. It is amazing how much fun air combat is when you are winning.

One of the junior course is currently dating four women. Two of them are in the air force and are based at the same station. How he manages to keep track, I don't know. He is going to be in a whole heap of trouble if they find out about each other.

There still hasn't been anyone on the station who has managed to get aroused at low level. Even the instructors say it is impossible.

Thursday 2 August

I think today was hotter than yesterday. We haven't seen a cloud in days. Perfect weather for air defence, and today it was two aircraft being directed to intercept a singleton and then, once within visual range, into two vs one air combat. Gibbo and I were paired up, and we were very sharp. Snapper was flying the target aircraft and was 'killed' on every engagement without managing to get any shots at either of us.

My instructor was Mike Meredith and on the last engagement, I managed to black him out. Gibbo was valiantly fighting Snapper in the classic high-G circle, and I had managed to get myself several thousand feet above their fight. We are taught on a two vs one that the 'free' aircraft gets into a position so he can rejoin the fight and get an immediate kill. On this occasion, I decided to rejoin the fight from the vertical. I pointed the aircraft straight down towards the middle of the fight, gained lots of speed and then snapped straight to 8G to get the aircraft into position for a quick kill. Mike knew what was coming because I heard him say, "Uh oh!" just before I started the 8G turn.

He next spoke to me half way across the Bristol Channel on the way home. He had tried to brace himself, but because he didn't know exactly when I would start the turn it wasn't enough. He was instantly unconscious. I didn't even grey out.

Gibbo and I were both dripping with sweat when we landed, and we had to go back to the mess and change into fresh flying suits. Air combat is so much fun!

Friday 3 August

I wasn't on the flying programme today, so I gave myself a late start. The weather continues to be clear and hot. In fact, too hot to be sitting around on the squadron, so I wandered up to the air traffic tower to chat to the duty instructor, Richie Thomas.

It was nice and cool up there as they have air conditioning. I was talking to Richie about the recent Iraqi invasion of Kuwait. Neither of us has much of an idea of what will happen next, or if we will get involved.

After that, headed back to the squadron just in time to go flying with Dave Cullen on a flight check of an aircraft on which the engineers have been working. It only took 15 minutes, and most of that time was spent upside down.

One of the instructors is leaving the station for a posting to a front-line Tornado squadron and he had his last flight in the afternoon. It was a formation of four Hawks at low level, attacking a target being defended by two Hawks. No students allowed again, and I have a sneaky suspicion it is because the instructors don't always obeying the rules that we have to stick to so religiously.

Happy hour in the mess started early and the leaving instructor bought a barrel of Guinness. It was free, so that is what I was drinking until it ran out. There is still a lot of rivalry with the boys on 151 squadron, and that manifested itself in drinking competitions. I stayed well out of the way.

Monday 6 August

The weather has started to change for the worse, and I was on the programme to fly air defence. However, we couldn't find a ground control radar station with serviceable radars. Not too sure what would happen if the Soviets decided to pay the UK a visit today. The only working radar was at Benbecula in the Outer Hebrides, so that is where we were sent. A short notice plan with three aircraft for a land-away – 'and by the way Edwards, you can lead us up there'. Great!

I managed a decent job of leading everyone and finding the airfield. It is a very bleak and remote part of the country. My instructor was Dave Cullen, and the other aircraft were crewed by Gibbo with PADS, and Andy Offer with Barry Wright. We just had time to refuel before getting airborne for my instructional sortie. Dave Cullen, The Machine, got me so focused I could do no wrong. Gibbo/PADS were my wingman, and we were fighting against Andy/Barry. It's always good to fly well in front of the boys.

We flew again in the afternoon, and I sat in the back with Dave while Gibbo flew his air defence trip. As always, it was fun flying with no pressure and watching someone else working hard.

After landing, we headed to the small accommodation block on the base and Andy discovered that his bag was packed with some interesting clothing. Because the decision to fly up here was taken at such short notice, he didn't have time to get back to his house for an overnight bag. His wife, Amanda, was at work, so he sent Paul (Rocky) Stone, our junior course navy pilot, to collect some clothes and toiletries for him. That was a big mistake. Rocky had packed brown shoes, white socks, trousers from a suit, a polka dot shirt and a black tie. Not the sort of attire they expect in an officers' mess. Andy decided to stay in his flying suit all evening, although he was grateful that Rocky had packed his toothbrush and wash kit.

Dave Cullen was in full effect in the bar. He was teaching drinking songs and entertaining us with tales of his time in Germany flying a Harrier. He had us in stitches at some of the situations he had found himself in. That got the other two instructors talking, and the evening slowly became a blur.

Tuesday 7 August

I didn't have to fly this morning as it was Andy's turn to fly his air defence trip. Very glad about that since I had a bit of a hangover. Andy had some poor weather to contend with as the cloud base was at 400ft and he had to lead all three aircraft on a close formation instrument recovery to the airfield. Not sure how I would have coped, but Andy took it all in his stride. As soon as the debrief of this sortie was complete, we all got airborne for the flight back to Chivenor.

We hadn't been back on the squadron for very long when Andy received an angry phone call from Amanda. It seems he phoned her last night in a drunken stupor, and she assumed that he was in the mess at Chivenor and would be back home soon. He neglected to tell her he was 500 miles away. Oh dear.

Because Andy was getting a hard time from his wife, John Letton foolishly decided to take advantage and started bantering. Andy simply asked him if his girlfriend, Victoria, had blown him out yet?

"No! Why?" John asked.

"It's only a matter of time!" replied Andy.

That was the end of John's banter. Victoria is a good-looking girl and John is very protective of her with all the predators around here.

Wednesday 8 August

We started a new phase of the course today. It's the final part and the most difficult: simulated attack profiles (SAP). Our first trip of this phase is just an introduction and is not supposed to be too difficult. I'm not too sure who said that, but it didn't apply to me. As soon as I released the brakes at the end of the runway, the goat was out and running and that was the last I saw of it.

I also seemed to have a permanent 'twat' caption illuminated on my forehead and was constantly making little errors. I had hoped to reset the caption on the ground, but it wasn't to be. The afternoon session in the simulator ended in a crash, as I hadn't noticed an altimeter failure.

Pete Lightbody decided I needed some exercise to clear my head and dragged me out for a run. I didn't even fare well with that. Pete is seriously fit and the route he decided to run mainly featured hills. It certainly cleared my head, but I was shattered.

There is a rumour that all the Chivenor Hawks are going to be deployed to Cyprus for local air defence because of a possible Iraqi threat to the air base there. I hope they let us students along if that is the case.

The SAP trips were an amalgamation of all that we had been taught. They became progressively more complex until we were leading a pair of Hawks at low level to drop a practice bomb on a weapons range, followed by a couple of off-range targets. All the time we were being 'bounced' by another Hawk simulating an enemy aircraft.

The bounce aircraft had maps of our route and flew various interception profiles to make our life difficult. If we saw him early enough, we could go around and avoid him, otherwise we turned towards him threateningly and hopefully, drove him away. If he persisted, we fought.

We had to be airborne within 90 minutes of being told our targets, so our planning needed to be fast as well as accurate.

Thursday 9 August

All the good weather has disappeared, but I was still flying a simulated attack profile this morning. My navigation was fine for a change, but it took me a couple of attempts to get used to the off-range dive bomb attacks. The trip in the afternoon concentrated on evasion and countering interceptions at low level. That was a lot of fun, and I was surprisingly good at it.

I tried the low-level erotic erection challenge on both trips, and didn't even get close. I certainly don't have anywhere near the spare mental capacity. There was no chance of maintaining low-level, navigating, keeping a good look out and holding the mental image of the female form for more than a few milliseconds. Certainly not long enough to get aroused. The boys on 151 squadron were trying to be vocal in the bar this evening and not impressing anyone. Pete Lightbody and I decided they were a bunch of girls and therefore should be treated as such. Pete managed to acquire a pot of pink paint and we headed off to their squadron building. We then proceeded to paint their squadron flagpole and all their external doors and windows in this girlie colour. Their flagpole was painted to within one foot of the top and the effect is very feminine. It suits them.

Friday 10 August

We haven't heard a word about 151 squadron's pink windows and doors, but then the entire station has been very busy preparing the jets to go away. No one is sure where to – it could be Scotland or Saudi or Cyprus. There was no flying for any students, so we were all stacked early.

I drove over to the other tactical weapons school at RAF Brawdy in Pembrokeshire for an end of course party. Ian Reid and Andy Pomeroy (the navy guys from my Valley course) have passed, as well as my old creamy instructor Stu Atha. They are all off to fly the Harrier, the lucky bastards. Adrian Bonwitt was on good form and is only a little way behind me on his course.

Monday 13 August

A bunch of our instructors have disappeared up to RAF Leuchars in Scotland to play at being Iraqis with the big Tornado F3 boys. There are only three instructors left on 63 squadron, so we have been sent over to 151 squadron to fly with them. Our junior course has been given a week off.

There is no atmosphere and no banter in the crew room of 151 squadron. We are not sure if it is because of the flagpole incident or if they are always like this.

Flew a dual low-level formation and evasion trip with PADS. Great fun, roaring around Wales at low level in high G turns at almost 500 mph evading or fighting the bounce. Another trip passed with a good score.

Roger was thrown off the range this afternoon for firing his gun outside limits and dropping a bomb way outside the designated zone. I told him not to worry as RBS had recently been thrown off as well and was heard to say on the radio, as he departed, "I've been thrown off far better ranges than this one in my time."

Wednesday 15 August

A hard-working day. It started with an instrument refresher trip in the morning and then my second SAP trip in the afternoon. It was my last dual SAP: from now on, I will fly them solo, leading an instructor as my wingman. I am enjoying these trips even though they are demanding.

My instructor was one of the station wing commanders, and he was saying that until only a few months ago the bounce aircraft would attack as soon the SAP pair had wheels up from the runway. They had to put a stop to that after one bounce developed into a massive free-for-all dogfight. Aircraft in the circuit were powering up and joining the melee. There was even a radio call of, "The fight's on in the overhead."

Anyone airborne in the local area was also joining. Air traffic were not best pleased to have so many aircraft overhead not in their control, so now the bounce has to wait until we are five miles away from the airfield before the fun can start.

Thursday 16 August

I certainly earned my money again today. Spent a few hours in the morning planning, and then flew SAP Three. I missed one of the off-range targets, but that didn't detract from a good trip.

This afternoon was all about SAP Four. It was absolutely the business: down at low level, leading two Hawks; roaring around with your hair on fire; hit the targets; fight the bounce and get the hell out. What could be better on this planet? I am having so much fun. The instructors are back from Leuchars, and they say that the Tornado F3s have had all sorts of fancy modifications and extra equipment bolted on and are being sent out to Saudi to support the coalition forces. The returning instructors have all been given a long weekend so we will still be flying from 151 squadron tomorrow. We still haven't had any banter about the pink doors and flagpole. It is very disappointing.

Friday 17 August

Another early start today and I was a demon in flight planning and in the air. The trip was SAP Five, and I managed to hit the range target within three seconds of the allocated time and the bomb I dropped was a good one, within a few feet of the target.

I was glad I wasn't flying in the afternoon, as I was exhausted. The SAPs are becoming hard, both physically and mentally. They last only 50 minutes as we use fuel at a huge rate, but they need intense concentration for every second.

Finally, some spirit on 151 squadron. One of their junior course has drawn a cartoon of an instructor debriefing his student's camera film after a solo range trip. The best scene featured an angry, red-faced instructor with his eyes on stalks screaming, "YOU DIDN'T PICKLE," at a student, who is saying, "Oh God!" as he cowered in terror in a corner of a debriefing room. They are both looking at a gun camera film of an aircraft in a steep turn with the bombsight slashing across a target. Not the smooth wings level techniques we have been taught. The bomb could have gone anywhere. Sometimes you get caught up in the moment and press the release. I've been there, and so have most other people, including the instructors.

Tuesday 20 August

We are finally back in our own squadron building and everyone is pleased to be rid of 151 squadron. The weather today was mainly low cloud and rain, but that didn't slow us down: we pressed on regardless.

Rocky Stone has got himself a small model of a goat and is now carrying it around as his mascot.

The whole course has had to give Snapper the number of Hawk hours they had flown. We are all around 150 hours except for John Letton who has 250 hours. He was getting a lot of banter for that. Andy wanted to know why, with all those hours on the jet, he was still so useless.

I flew just the once, an SAP Six with Dave Cullen as my wingman. He really is The Machine. We were so fired up that we managed to plan the whole thing in 50 minutes. One of the off range targets was an electrical substation on an active airfield, which added the complication of having to talk to their air traffic control at the busy time at the start of the attack run. The bounce, as expected, attacked us in the middle of all of that, but I had so much adrenalin in my system that I wasn't perturbed.

Wednesday 22 August

We arrived for work this morning to find that 151 squadron had cut our squadron flagpole down to 5ft. It is an amazing piece of work as it is fully functional but just tiny. The boss is not happy and declared, "They have cut my flagpole down, this is f***ing war!"

We were glad that the weather was so bad today, as we could spend the whole day preparing our retaliation. Our instructor Richie Thomas is renting a house on a farm and has persuaded the farmer to loan us two sheep. We had to have two of the creatures, as it seems the animals get lonely by themselves overnight. We equipped ourselves with plastic sheeting and several yards of turf and somehow, Pete (light-fingered) Lightbody has managed to get hold of the keys to the offices of 151 squadron.

As soon as it got dark, we swung into action. We got into their squadron building and took out all the furniture from their boss's office. The plastic sheeting was put down and turf laid on the floor. We then returned the furniture and herded the sheep into the office, before tidying up and leaving. It was a very good job with no external evidence, but the sheep do smell.

While that was going on, another group switched around the flagpoles with the added bonus that we painted the short one, which was now outside 151 squadron in 63 squadron colours.

I thought that was that, until awoken at midnight by one of the guys from our junior course. He told me that the sheep had been discovered, so we got the rest of the squadron out of bed and covertly drove over to surprise Roger Colquhoun and Mike Leckey in the midst of undoing all our good work. They had managed to get the sheep out of the building and were dismantling the turf.

As they were so badly outnumbered they decided not to fight the inevitable and agreed we could leave the sheep where they were, outside their squadron on the grass. As soon as Roger and Mike had left, Rocky Stone did a great job of persuading everyone it would be much more fun to put them back in the office.

Thursday 23 August

Pete Lightbody and I were sat outside our squadron before met brief, talking over the night's events, when we saw the station commander's car drive past on the way over to 151 squadron. Pete turned to me and said, "Trev, that could be really good or really bad!" I couldn't have agreed more.

The met man set the tone for the briefing by saying there were a lot of sheepish faces this morning. The air traffic man said good morning gentlemen and sheep and there were a lot of *baaaa* sounds throughout the recce brief. The station commander thought it was brilliant, and all the senior station officers were heading on down to have a look. The boss of 151 squadron was so impressed he got hold of a small model woolly sheep to pin to his flying suit.

While the rest of the boys went over to rebuild 151's bosses' office, I had my last course trip – SAP Seven – to plan and fly. Dave Cullen was my trusty wingman, and he had Andy Offer in his back seat. Andy finished the course last week, so this was just fun for him. The bounce was PADS, the air defence guru, so we were bound to get a hard time from him. Dave, as usual, managed to up the tempo from the start so we finished planning and briefing in good time. The weather wasn't great and we went into cloud at 500ft on the departure before letting down to low level over the Bristol Channel. Even with that, I was only 20 seconds late over the range target and the bomb I dropped was another good score. Low level was a hoot and a roar. We steamed around the route like mad men being bounced all the time. Dave got shot once when I didn't notice PADS sneaking into his six o'clock from below. That's not easy as we were at 250ft and I'm sure it could be described as cheating.

We hit both off-range targets and Dave got involved in a one vs one with PADS after the second target. We lost sight of each other while that was going on, but managed to get back together to complete the route, and landed with the bare minimum fuel on board. Only 45 minutes airborne but every second was busy. It was the hardest trip I have ever flown and by far the most satisfying.

I was the last man on the course to finish, and today we had our role disposal where we are told which front-line aircraft we have been selected to fly. To celebrate this occasion, the course had decided to build a cannon. It is in reality closer to a mortar than a cannon. It consisted of 10 industrial-sized baked bean tins made into a tube with aviation speed tape. The bottom three cans had baffles cut into them, and the bottom can had a small opening for the lighter fluid we are using as propellant with a bootlace fuse. The projectile was a cabbage, wrapped in tape to ensure a tight fit. After a few teething problems, the cannon was firing cabbages a good 300 metres. It even sounded like a mortar when it went off. The role disposal event was held outside the squadron and attended by most pilots and quite a few of the station personnel. Each graduating pilot had to drink a vile concoction the junior course had created and then run through an obstacle course while being sprayed with water. There was a drink for each aircraft type and after each drink, the obstacle course had to be completed.

I have been selected to fly the Jaguar and by the time, I found that out I was just happy not to have to drink any more cocktails and face the obstacle course again. I still don't believe they have selected me to fly one of the single-seat fighters…

We were given our end-of-course certificates – and even more amazingly, I have won the best student prize. I wasn't sure how that could be, until it was explained that Andy Offer was not eligible as he is a creamy. He is by far the best pilot on the course. Bill Auckland and Andy are both off to fly the Harrier, and John Letton and Gibbo are off to the Tornado GR1.

The party continued into the bar, and the cannon was much in demand. At one stage, Snapper was firing it from his hip at a moving target which was an innocent air traffic girl driving her car to the mess. God knows what would have happened if he had hit her. The cabbage projectile is quite heavy. No memory of the end of the evening, and my last conscious thought was of tequila. Again.

Friday 24 August

I woke up just before lunchtime with a very bad head and dragged myself off to get coffee from the mess ante-room. Dave Cullen and Bill came in shortly afterwards and we headed to the Thatch for a debrief on the night's events.

Dave says he wasn't surprised that I couldn't remember anything as I was drinking whole glasses of tequila while challenging anyone to say that the Jaguar wasn't the best aircraft in the RAF. He and Gibbo had to put me to bed, as I had fallen over and was out of it in the bar. We spent the rest of the afternoon in the Thatch drinking orange juice until Bill and I were sober enough to drive. Then I headed down to London for a long weekend break.

Thursday 30 August

I didn't have to turn up for work until yesterday, and that was a very slow day, mainly filled with listening to all the banter from last weekend. Today, I managed to sit in the back seat of a two vs one. It wasn't a student trip, just three instructors sharpening their skills. Snapper invited a group of us over to his house in the evening. We were discussing how much trouble we could have got into with the sheep incident last week. Snapper and Richie then told a story of getting arrested by the RAF police in Germany after setting alight to an abandoned car. It sounded like similar inter-squadron rivalries getting out of hand after a big happy hour. The car unbeknown to them had a full tank of petrol and after a few minutes, it exploded into a large mushroom cloud. The local emergency services had to be called to put out the subsequent fire. Snapper and Richie both have formal warnings on their files. Who would have thought that of our instructors?

Friday 31 August

I have been given three weeks leave, and they want me back here at Chivenor on 1 October to complete some refresher flying before my Jaguar course starts at the end of October.

The end of my tactical weapons course, and I added an extra 30 hours solo and 35 hours dual flying on the Hawk. I won the top student prize. Most of my scores were above average and overall I have been assessed as PROFICIENT.

Operational Conversion Unit

226 OCU
RAF Lossiemouth,
Elgin,
Northern Scotland,
1990–91

For anyone connected to the RAF, 1990 and 1991 were dominated by the Gulf War and hostilities over Kuwait. The air war over Iraq involved many RAF Tornado and Jaguar aircraft. It started in January 1991 and a few weeks later, on 26 February, Saddam Hussein ordered the Iraqi withdrawal from Kuwait. That was shortly after the ground war started. Meanwhile Britain continued to cope with hostilities from the IRA, who wreaked havoc with a bomb at both Paddington and Victoria stations in London on 18 February 1991.

About five months long, operational conversion courses teach pilots to operate front-line fighter aircraft. Pilots are given instructions on the techniques that aircraft use in combat.

Monday 29 October

Yesterday, I had a marathon 11-hour drive from Devon to RAF Lossiemouth in northern Scotland. It wasn't far short of driving the entire length of the country. Today though, involved nothing more onerous than being shown around the base and getting some paperwork completed. There are just four members of the course, Shaun Wildey, Simon Stocker, David Fellows and myself. I have run into all of them before at various times during flying training. We are what they call ab initio pilots, who have come straight through the training system. Simon is the only married man and has got a married officer's house while the rest of us are living in the officers' mess.

RAF Lossiemouth is situated on the Moray Firth, east of Inverness. It is a very big airbase and in 1990, it was the home of the Jaguar Operational Conversion Unit (OCU) and two squadrons of Buccaneer Fighter Bombers as well as the Buccaneer OCU. There was a search-and-rescue flight of Sea King helicopters, as well as a squadron of the very old and soon-to-be-retired Shackleton maritime patrol aircraft.

The Buccaneers were housed in individual hardened shelters scattered throughout the base, but the Jaguars operated from a traditional hangar away from the main hustle and bustle.

The Jaguar is a single-seat fighter-bomber. The Buccaneer was used mainly for maritime attack and is a surprisingly large aircraft. It had a crew of two and could carry its bombs in an internal weapons bay.

Tuesday 30 October

Ground school has begun and we have had lectures all day. For once, I am ahead of the game as I have read up on most of the systems already. The Jaguar is a very complicated machine compared to the Hawk. I spent a few hours in the afternoon trying to get to grips with some of the checks. That wasn't easy: the cockpit has got switches everywhere. This afternoon, I ran into Dave Morris and Gary Stingmore who were both on my initial officers' training course at RAF Cranwell. They are a Tornado crew on 13 squadron. I was amazed: they were two of the biggest hooligans on the officers' course and someone has let them loose in a multi-million pound Tornado…

Friday 2 November

The base has an old telephone exchange run by some very nice Scottish ladies. We have to speak to them to get an outside line and they route any incoming calls to us in the mess. The telephone exchange lady I spoke to today refused to believe that I am tall and dark. I will have to pay them a visit – she is in for a big surprise.

RAF Lossiemouth used to be a Royal Navy air station and the rooms in the mess are tiny. We have been told that it is because the navy officers had to get used to the small spaces on a ship. To compensate for this, we have each been given two adjacent rooms: one in which to store all our kit, the other in which to sleep. Even so, the sleeping room only has enough space for a single bed and a desk. I'm so glad I didn't join the navy.

By tradition, the Jaguar courses are all accommodated along the same corridor. We also have a common room. This is another tiny ex-navy cabin and is known as the Jaguar office. The Jag office contains a television, a video, a kettle, a toaster and a fridge which, according to some random rules created by who knows who, can only contain one type of beer – Becks. And only the bottled variety. The Jag office is lined with empty Becks bottles and over the years, this has resulted in most of the wall space looking like an Andy Warhol exhibition. The entire week has consisted of lectures and visits to the simulator. I have worked so hard that I have given myself the weekend off and I am heading down to London on a flight from Inverness airport.

Wednesday 7 December

Ground school has come to an end already. It has been hard work for the last nine days. We had a final exam today. It wasn't difficult; it just took a long time to complete. As an added incentive for speed, the person who finished last has to run the tea bar on the squadron for the duration of the course. Thankfully, that wasn't me.

I had my first assessed simulator trip in the afternoon. It was preceded by a lengthy brief and as always there was a thorough debrief. The trip itself was great fun. The take-off happened very rapidly, and I had one flap over speed warning before I could get the flaps retracted. The aircraft is very, very sensitive.

Flaps are devices used to alter the shape of the wing to enable an aircraft to get airborne and land at much lower speeds. Flaps are mounted on the trailing edge of the wing.

Today the station was full of Tornado and Phantom aircraft that are here for a week's exercise. It is all to do with getting everyone up to speed for a possible conflict in Iraq.

The Jaguar simulator was the height of 1970s technology. The visual system was a room-sized model of an airfield and its surrounding areas, and a second room containing another less detailed model to enable some low-level flying. A complicated system of pulleys drove a small camera whose images were projected on to the front of the simulator's canopy.

The simulator was used mainly to learn emergency procedures, but could be used for short low-level routes. It wasn't unknown to be at low level in the simulator, fly around a corner of a valley and come face to face with a 100ft tall toy dinosaur. Jaguar simulator instructors were a warped breed.

Friday 9 November

I had two simulator trips today. The first one was poor, and the second was worse. I am over-controlling the aircraft and my flying is not good. During the second session, I was concentrating so hard on the flying that I missed a fire alarm, and crashed. This didn't endear me with the instructor as it took quite a bit of time to reset the machine.

After work, we all headed over to the squadron for drinks with the ground crew. Those guys can certainly drink. They finished two barrels of beer in a very short time before starting on spirits. I was invited to drink a glass of Wild Turkey American whiskey, which was almost rejected by my stomach. It is nearly impossible to turn down a drink from the ground crew.

They expect a lot from their pilots.

One of our instructors, Sqn Ldr Tim Kerss, insisted that we practise the full repertoire of squadron songs in case happy hour in the bar turned rowdy. The Tornados and Phantoms had finished their exercise and were expected to be in full effect.

Happy hour didn't disappoint, but there was no singing. I discovered that you can order take-away chips and ribs from a local chip shop, and they have got clearance to deliver to the mess. Not only this, but the standard order is called Total Only, and a large is Total Plus, corresponding to the fuel loads on the Jaguar. Total Only is full internal fuel whereas Total Plus is internal fuel and full drop tanks. The chip shop owner is a big Jaguar fan.

Monday 12 November

This morning, I had to head over to the local hospital to get my jaw x-rayed: something to do with wisdom teeth and high-G flying. The doctors have decided that it wasn't a problem, thankfully. I then had a simulator trip that was much better than the last two, but I still can't seem to fly the thing very well.

A group of us from the Jaguar OCU were out for a curry in the local town of Elgin with John Green (or JG) and Jim Frampton from the Buccaneer OCU. I seem to have followed JG through most of my flying training. Jim was discussing the fact that he had to get to Edinburgh this weekend and when asked why, he said, "To get laid!"

There was a bit of chuckling at this, but he then looked down sorrowfully at his plate and said, "I cannot see for tadpoles." We all fell about laughing.

Tuesday 13 November

I was up early today to get myself into the squadron for the met brief. The rest of the day was spent with my head in books and then on a simulator ride.

The Jaguars from RAF Coltishall were deployed out to the Gulf a couple of weeks ago and have been busy preparing for the war that we all know is coming. Today, tragically they had a casualty. One of their pilots hit the ground during some low-level evasion training and was killed. It has made me realise how serious this job is.

RAF Coltishall, in Norfolk, was the main Jaguar base in 1990 and contained the only three operational Jaguar squadrons in the RAF. It was a small base, less than half the size of Lossiemouth.

Wednesday 14 November

I had my first-ever flight in a Jaguar today. Pete Livesey (Livo) was my instructor and he gave me a very thorough brief beforehand. I did have a bit of a sweat on getting kitted out. We are wearing immersion suits again, and I am not used to them after the sweltering summer in Devon. In the north of Scotland no one would survive very long if they had to eject into the North Sea without an immersion suit.

The trip was in the T2 Jaguar, and I hadn't even looked at its cockpit layout. There are some significant differences to the GR1 Jaguar, which is the standard version and the version the simulator is modelled on. Anyway, I coped with it all, completed my checks correctly and managed to get the thing airborne unaided.

I have been told by many an envious pilot (mostly non-fast jet ones) about how underpowered the Jaguar is, but I saw no evidence of this today. The jet leapt off the runway and was a bit of a beast in the circuit. It was a proper grown-up's first flight consisting of a bit of general handling, a look around the local area (the north of Scotland) and a few circuits. Thankfully, I seem to be able to fly the real thing much better than the simulator. Shaun and Dave also had their first trips.

The T2 is the two-seat training Jaguar. It has the same tandem layout as the Hawk, with the student pilot in the front seat. The cockpit has a few differences to a single-seat GR1. These differences stem from the fact that it is a training aircraft and is missing some of the fighting equipment of its single seat stable mate. Jaguars do not have autopilots or even auto throttles. They have to be manually flown at all times.

Friday 16 November

No flying for any of the course today. The majority of the instructors are off to RAF Coltishall for a Jaguar reunion and to have a beer for the lad who was killed earlier in the week. We had our first secret briefing today. It was all about the Jaguar's role out in the Gulf and the new equipment and weapons that will be used. There is even talk that we could get involved if we finish our course early. Not sure what I think about that...excited and scared at the same time; weird.

Happy hour in the mess was mixed, so there were lots of wives and girlfriends around for a change. The Buccaneer boys heavily outnumbered the Jaguar pilots as we had a large contingent down at Coltishall.

Later in the evening, Shaun, JG and I took a taxi into town. JG is on the Buccaneer conversion course and has been living in the mess up here for a couple of months. He introduced us to the taxi driver he uses all the time, a local man called Eric. Although I couldn't guess his age, Eric says he retired 10 years ago, so he must be at least 70 years old.

He really was a poacher who became a gamekeeper, and has had numerous other jobs including being a fisherman. He gave the impression of infinite calm and always had a considered pause before he answered any questions. We managed to get Eric to collect us from Elgin much later in the evening after we had a close encounter with a group of very forward middle-aged ladies. Eric explained that these were fishermen's wives from the town of Buckie, and that as the fleet had been out for a while the girls were getting 'frisky'. There is no way I am touching the woman of a Scottish fisherman.

Saturday 17 November

Unsurprisingly, I had a heavy head this morning, so I did very little all day. I managed to get myself over to the station telephone exchange to talk to some of the ladies who work there.

They aren't fishermen's wives, thank God.

Shaun heard a good story last night. A young pilot from a base down south was in a ground floor room of an officers' mess during a happy hour and needed to get to the toilet. As he wasn't familiar with the layout of this particular mess, he decided that it would be quicker and easier simply to climb out of the window and find a bush in the darkness. Unbeknown to him, the window he chose to leap out of had a 12ft drop to the basement level. As he reached the point of no return and the size of the drop became apparent, he was heard to say, "Uh oh, Kryptonite."

He survived with no broken bones.

Monday 19 November

I had a simulator ride first thing this morning, and it was shockingly bad. A general lack of awareness added up to a very poor session. As the simulator instructor said, "Not really up to speed."

I thought that the day couldn't get worse, but I was wrong again. I had my second trip in the T2 Jaguar and that wasn't great. I struggled to cope with the single engine flying in the circuit and now I can understand why they say this machine is underpowered. You have to be very accurate when flying with a single engine, as there isn't enough thrust to power yourself out of any difficulties. At least my flying instructor, Livo, isn't going to make me fly the trip it again.

Tuesday 20 November

Just the one trip again today and I am improving – I was hopeless for only half the time. The single engine stuff is getting better. We did a full reheat climb from low level. It was amazing, and we were up at 20,000ft in what seemed like seconds.

The report of yesterday's bad simulator trip has arrived on the squadron, and the word on the street is that I will have to do it again. It is all practice, I suppose.

Wednesday 21 November

Today was another bad day for Trevor Edwards. I spent the morning waiting around for the simulator trip, and when I eventually got into the box, I was useless. Not sure what the problem is, so it is difficult to work out a solution.

Shaun flew his first solo this afternoon and has been doing well on the course so far. It has made me more determined to be as sharp as I can be tomorrow. I am on the programme for a pre-ride in the morning and solo in the afternoon.

Thursday 22 November

I was airborne first thing in the morning with Livo on my pre-solo trip. As this is the big boys' course, the trip consisted of a full instrument flying workout and then some circuit work at the end. The instrument flying was good and back in the base I flew a few good circuits, but as I touched down on my last approach, the right undercarriage leg collapsed.

The aircraft was instantly sliding along the runway on its side, at high speed in a shower of sparks. I could hear Livo uttering a constant stream of expletives from the back seat. The aircraft slowly drifted to the right side of the runway, and there was nothing either of us could do to alter that, as the nose wheel wasn't responding to inputs. Eventually, we slid on to the grass. That is when things got interesting.

While on the runway the aircraft was surprisingly stable, but on the grass it was all over the place and violently so. I had a firm grip of the ejection handle and the only reason I didn't pull it was because I knew there was an angle of bank limit on the ground to ensure the parachute opened properly. From where I was sat, I felt as though we were far outside that limit, so I stayed with the aircraft.

Microseconds after we went on to the grass, the stump of the undercarriage must have got stuck in the ground as we were suddenly spun around by 360 degrees and came to an abrupt stop. At no stage did Livo stop the expletives.

I dragged the emergency shutdown drills out of my memory and by the time I had switched everything off and started to open the canopy, there was a fireman trying to drag me out of the aircraft. Livo had left me to it and was 100 metres away from the now steaming wreck.

Those shutdown drills had taken much longer than I thought.

The wreckage was a good mile away from the squadron building, and a firemen kindly offered to give me a lift back, but I decided to walk and get my head sorted. I was convinced that somehow, it must have been my fault, and I was trying to work out if they would let me fly transport aircraft or if they would just sack me.

The first person I saw back at the squadron was one of our senior instructors, Sqn Ldr Wilcox. He just smiled as I walked in and said, "That is the worst piece of parking I have ever seen."

No one was concerned about the wrecked multi-million pound machine. They all wanted to make sure Livo and I were all right. It didn't stop the banter though.

Livo has said it was definitely a structural failure, and it won't reflect badly on me. The whole course, Livo and JG, had a few Becks in the Jag office in the evening. Livo has decided that life is too short, and he is going to be buying the Porsche he always wanted…

Friday 23 November

They tried to get me airborne today, but there was no joy. The wind was out of limits all day and that did not disappoint me as I was still trying to stop shaking.

We all finished work early for the ground crew Christmas drinks. Livo and I bought a crate of beer for the engineers who had worked all night recovering our aircraft. They say that the damage isn't as bad as it looks and that they should be able to repair it. It is going to take longer than the course is scheduled to last, so with any luck, I won't ever have to fly the machine again. The engineers presented me with a map of the airfield, so I would know where to park in future, and they gave Livo a potty so he wouldn't wet himself.

The bar was very busy as there has been a bunch of RAF and Sea Harriers up here on an exercise all week. To add to the spice of the evening, Dave Cullen, my old instructor from Chivenor, also turned up. Oh no! There were a lot of single-seat pilots versus the Buccaneer boys singing and drinking. JG was doing a very good job of keeping everyone in order, but it still degenerated into a minor brawl. I think I ended up in a local nightclub with Shaun, Dave and the Buccaneer boys, JG and John Sullivan (JS). I did my initial officer training with JS all those years ago. He has been on one of the Buccaneer squadrons up here for a couple of years.

Saturday 24 November

A board of inquiry was convened yesterday to establish the facts about the crash. There are a couple of senior Jaguar officers running it, and they wanted to see me today. Fortunately, it wasn't first thing this morning, as I had a very sore head. They eventually called me in the afternoon, asking me to give my account of the accident. I got the feeling they were just ticking boxes as they had already given Livo a good grilling.

I spent the afternoon and evening at a castle that JS and a few of the Buccaneer boys have rented near Elgin. It is beautiful, has got huge rooms with big fireplaces and seems to be stuffed full of antiques. They are even managing to keep it relatively tidy. The only drawback is that it is cold, but they say that is what whisky is for.

As well as everything that has occurred this week, today I was told that Miriam Williams, my old instructor from Linton-on-Ouse, has died. He had failed his A2 instructor grading and because of that, they sacked him from his job as a flight commander. He also had a big argument with his girlfriend. It all seems to have become too much for him and he stuck a hosepipe into his car exhaust.

I know he wasn't the most popular instructor at Linton, but it is still very sad to think he didn't feel he could talk to anyone and get help.

Monday 26 November

There was no avoiding flying today. I got airborne this morning with Livo, for my second attempt at pre-solo. I was a bit tense on the first approach, and I couldn't bring myself to fly any firm landings. However, my overall flying was good enough to be cleared for solo. First solos in the Jaguar are always in the GR1. My first time flying a single-seat fighter aircraft and even with the tension it was a great feeling.

"Seat check? One."

"Crew check? Me."

As I have been told several times, it's the most fun you can have outside of the bedroom. I took my time, and managed to get everything correct and blasted off for a good hour. A bit of low level, a bit of general handling and a few gentle circuits.

I was the last member of the course to go solo, and we had a mini ceremony in the bar in the afternoon where we were presented with our Jaguar badges. We are all now officially Jaguar pilots.

Tuesday 27 November

A busy day today with a simulator first thing, which overran as there were a few technical problems getting the machine up and running. Because of this, I was late for the brief for my first Jaguar formation trip. It was a three-ship formation, and I settled into it quite quickly. I wasn't even hyperventilating in the close, which is unusual for me. We had a look at all the formation positions including the low-level battle, which will be our bread and butter. I managed to surge the engine just after take-off, but that worried me more than my instructor.

When you see a big flame coming out of the back of a military aircraft that's usually because its engine is in reheat. The engine is injecting extra fuel into the airflow just before the exhaust. This provides a big boost in thrust but with very high fuel consumption. In the Jaguar, which had 1960s engine technology, you had to be wary. If mishandled, the engine could surge with some startling results. The airflow in the engine could reverse and in some cases, a large flame could come out of the front of the air intake, accompanied by some very loud noises. Not good for the engine or the pilot's health.

Livo is getting a lot of flak about our crash from the board of inquiry, none of it deserved in my opinion. It is mainly about his decision-making process and whether or not we should have ejected.

Thursday 29 November

The pace of the course has started to pick up. Today, there was a late change to the programme and I was airborne on an instrument trip instead of more formation. I flew an instrument approach to the civilian airfield at Aberdeen and then some self-positioned approaches back at Lossiemouth.

The boys are all working hard, and both Shaun and Simon tried to fly pairs take-offs on their solo formations today when they should have flown 10-second stream. Shaun had to change jets as his first one had a technical problem. He was so rushed that he taxied out with his navigation computer still not having completed its start-up cycle. That isn't good for the computer, and it is just as well he wasn't flying any low level or he would have had to rely on the old map and stopwatch.

Dave had a moment as well today. He had been briefed for his formation and seemed to think that he had 30 minutes to kill before take-off, so he made himself a coffee. His timing was out by 30 minutes, and he was still drinking his coffee when Sqn Ldr Wilcox came into the crew room and politely asked him if he would like to join the rest of the formation who were waiting in their jets for him. I have never seen him move so quickly. Sqn Ldr Wilcox is also giving Shaun banter about his formation flying. He says that his close formation is more like a very loose arrow.

Close formation is exactly as it says: the aircraft are within a few metres of each other. In arrow formation, the aircraft are much further apart – up to about 50 metres.

Friday 30 November

I was supposed to have a solo flight this morning, but there wasn't an aircraft for me.

Instead, I sat in the back of an aircraft flown by our boss, Wg Cmdr Rusling, on a four-ship low-level sortie complete with a bounce organised by the instructors. It is amazing what you can do with this aircraft thanks to all the technology in the cockpit. We were never more than a few seconds early or late, even after being forced off route by the bounce. Happy hour in the mess was immediately followed by a squadron Dining In night.

Saturday 1 December

I woke up this morning and tried to work out whom I had to apologise to. Shaun and I convened in the Jag office and pieced together the night's events.

It seems that Liz, our administration officer, was doing her best to look after us early in the evening but we were quickly beyond help. I had to go to the toilet half way through the meal and returned to find that my chair had been placed in front of the top table, and I had 'earned' a fine of a bottle of port for general consumption. (No one is supposed to leave the table before the Queen's toast.) I also interrupted the boss's speech, as I decided he needed to be an honouree brother on account of his very glittery dinner jacket.

No idea why no one tried to stop me, but that cost me another bottle of port. My memory gets very hazy after that, but Shaun remembers going to the bar and totally disrupting an engineer's party – and a lot of swearing on my part.

The afternoon was spent in the Jag office watching videos until JG insisted that we accompany him to a party being thrown by one of the Buccaneer navigators. We arrived in full effect with a two-litre bottle of tequila, a couple of lemons and a jar of salt. Strangely all the couples left shortly afterwards, but I like to think that we got the party going.

Sunday 2 December

I felt like this yesterday morning. Simon Stocker invited us poor single boys over to his house for Sunday lunch, and it was just what the doctor ordered. We ran into the boss later in the afternoon and Shaun and I both started to apologise for Friday night, but he would have none of it. He said it was what he expected, as we are fighter pilots.

Monday 3 December

There was more formation flying for me this morning and only my third solo in the Jaguar. I led a two-ship formation on a low-level route down to the base at Leuchars, near Edinburgh. Flew an instrument approach and then more low-level back to base. The formation was good, and the low level was fun.

Sqn Ldr Wilcox was in full banter mode again today. He is not giving me too hard a time about Friday night, although he has stated that swearing just displays a lack of vocabulary. I think I have to agree with him on that one. I will have to cut it out. He has also described the met brief I gave this morning as an 'art form'. He is of the opinion that anything with more than seven variables cannot be scientific and therefore must be art. This morning, my met brief had quite a few variables.

Wednesday 5 December

I spent this morning planning like mad for my first pure low-level trip. I like the rapid planning as it gets me concentrating at an early stage and my trips all seem to be better for it. The sortie was semi-decent although we only used the most basic functions of the navigation and weapon-aiming computer. It was a sortie lasting one hour and 30 minutes, and we flew around the whole of the north of Scotland. I was very tired when we landed. I'm not used to concentrating that hard for that long.

There is a hot rumour that the whole OCU is going to move down to RAF Coltishall in Norfolk. The air force has deployed so many aircraft and personnel to the Gulf they need the extra efficiency that having all the Jaguars at one base will bring. The training won't be as good for us, as there isn't the same access to the low-level areas and weapons ranges as there are in Scotland, but as a course we don't care – it will be near civilisation.

Friday 7 December

I had a solo navigation sortie today, my first using the navigation computer. There were no problems following the route as the moving map, head-up display and computer make things easy.

A few days ago, the course was tasked by Sqn Ldr Kerss to write some songs for the joint Jaguar and Buccaneer conversion unit's Christmas lunch, which was held today. Over the last few nights, in between all of our course work, Shaun and I managed to compose three new Christmas carols: The First Sonic Boom; I Saw Three Buccs, and Shaun's favourite, F**k The Herald Angels Sing.

Sqn Ldr Kerss was very impressed with our efforts, and we won the singing competition, mainly because we had more songs then Buccaneer boys.

I was wearing a multi-coloured fez to the lunch, much to the consternation of Sqn Ldr Wilcox. He is such a country squire. I have been threatening to take him down to London for a night out, and that is the only time I have seen him flustered. The lunch degenerated into a mass drinking session, and that continued on to happy hour in the mess. Shaun thought it would be a good idea to recite the Christmas carols again, and although the rest of the aircrew in the bar thought they were great, the station padre wasn't too impressed.

Tuesday 11 December

I was in to work early to plan and fly another dual low-level trip using the aircraft navigation systems, and was glad that we could use all those systems, as the weather was appalling. There is no way I could have stayed at low-level flying in a Hawk and using a stopwatch and map. I had to climb over bad weather three times, but the computer enabled me to get back on track as soon as I got back down to low level. I didn't manage to get to any of the targets due to the weather, but the instructor was more than happy with my efforts. The sortie was all about using the aircraft navigation systems and I certainly gave those a full work out. That was all the flying for the day as the weather got worse. Left work early for a bit of studying and to prepare for the evening party in the mess.

All the officers living in the mess have an annual Christmas dinner. It is a parody of the official Dining In nights. This evening, the Jaguar pilots wore bow ties and DJs over flying suits, and the Buccaneer crews were resplendent in beach shorts. One of the Buccaneer navigators was nominated as the officer in charge and he decided that there would be a 'no right hand' rule. Dinner would be eaten with the left hand only, using a spoon. Dave Fellows was seen eating his dessert with no hands at all, just before he started drinking flaming Drambuie. I decided to get to bed at that stage.

Thursday 13 December

The weather has been very poor for the last few days, and there has been no flying. Most people are in Christmas wind down mode anyway. We heard today that the Jaguar conversion unit would be moving down to RAF Coltishall. We will start flying from there after the Christmas break. Hurrah!

Friday 14 December

Stacked, packed and then headed south via Manchester to see a few old university mates. That's all the flying done until after Christmas.

1991 RAF Coltishall

Wednesday 9 January

After a three-week break, I arrived at RAF Coltishall last night – having driven around the local area for an hour getting lost. It isn't very well sign posted, and there is very little evidence of an air base until you arrive at the main gate.

We all had a late start and spent most of the day visiting the various sections on the base and getting ourselves booked in for a few simulator rides. There are only a couple of the instructors down here. The aircraft, with the majority of the instructors, aren't due to arrive until Monday.

Friday 11 January

Up early today, but I stayed in the mess to study and prepare for my simulator rides. We are working from 41 squadron's offices, as they are currently in the Gulf in case it all kicks off over there. The building is shared with 54 squadron, and I wandered over and managed to get myself a trip in a two-seat T2 Jaguar flown by Mewsey. He is the good friend of Cameron Gair from my basic flying course and I first met him during the Jet Provost course at Linton-on-Ouse. I remember saying that I didn't want to fly a Jaguar back then. It looked too complicated.

We had concrete 1000lb bombs on board and dropped them at Sennybridge training area during a big exercise with the army. *More preparation for a war in the Gulf,* I think. There were eight Jaguars involved in the sortie, and it was amazing. I was struggling to follow everything that was going on, but I am seriously keen again.

Instead of dropping live 1000lb bombs, which are expensive and by their design highly dangerous, concrete bombs are sometimes used for realistic training. The high explosives content of the bomb is replaced by an equivalent amount of concrete. These concrete bombs are deployed in the same way as real bombs – but they don't go bang. They are very different from the practice bombs we used on the weapons ranges. The practice bombs are small and cheap, and to aid assessment of bombing accuracy, they give off a flash when they explode.

Monday 14 January

My first real day of work at Coltishall. I went in for the station met brief and then had a simulator ride which wasn't too bad. The simulator's model is of the area around RAF Bruggen. When it was designed in the 1970s there were several Jaguar squadrons based in Germany.

The Lossiemouth Jaguars arrived after lunch so the flying is due to start tomorrow.

Tuesday 15 January

Today is D-day for Saddam Hussein to get out of Kuwait, so we all expect something to happen soon. Had another simulator session this morning and then my local area familiarisation flight in the afternoon. Local area was a very loose description as we went as far north as Yorkshire. I wasn't too shabby and got better as the trip wore on, except for circuits. I think I am subconsciously nervous about landings.

Thursday 16 January

Gulf war starts when he properly concrete bunker

I was out with Shaun and a few others last night, and on the way home, we stopped at a kebab shop where we saw TV news reports about the opening air attacks in Iraq.

Unsurprisingly, Saddam hasn't retreated and has ignored all the United Nations warnings. It was surreal eating kebabs and watching the GR1 Tornado boys getting back after night attacks. If things go badly over there and they start to lose a lot of pilots, we could easily find ourselves out there.

Work today revolved around the television and radio reports. The only flying for me was a range trip with Sqn Ldr Wilcox. It was a great introduction to the weapons ranges around the Lincolnshire coast and the different types of range patterns we fly on the Jaguar. The Jaguar's head-up display makes the accurate dropping of bombs and firing the guns a much more simple process. We landed just in time to get to a brief from a two-star general on the events last night. So far, it has all gone better than they had hoped.

Monday 21 January

Today I was back at low level for the first time in a month: a nice little solo flight to Wales and back. Not a bad trip either, although it took a little bit of time to get back into the groove.

The Gulf air war is now in full swing. The Jaguars have been in action over the weekend and by all reports are doing well. The GR1 Tornados have been flying some hairy low-level night attacks and have lost four aircraft so far. No Jaguar losses, and I am keeping my fingers crossed for the boys. Livo has been sent out to do some planning job. Everyone is a bit subdued for obvious reasons. There aren't as many jokes or silly quips.

Wednesday 23 January

I have flown a low-level trip each day for the last two days. One dual, the other solo and both trips have gone all right. Shaun was nearly in a lot of trouble today. He misread his fuel gauges and landed with just 350kg of fuel. He is a lucky man, as the engine can flame out around that sort of figure. Shaun doesn't dwell on mistakes, and he is his normal confident self.

Thursday 24 January

It was a misty day over most of the country, so no low-level flying. Instead, I sat in the back seat of an instructor's aircraft to experience some air combat. The Jaguar isn't built for a dogfight. The radius of turn is huge in comparison to the Hawk, and the machine loses its energy very quickly. The fight rapidly degenerates to lots of 2G turns. In this machine if you see the opposition first, you normally win. Spot the baddie, quickly get into range, a quick high-G turn if necessary, shoot and run away.

This afternoon, I was given very little notice to plan and fly a land-away up to Lossiemouth. It was a four-ship high to low-level route, flown by the instructors. Do not pass go and do not go to London for the weekend.

Friday 25 January

I am back up at Lossiemouth, and Scotland is the only place in the whole of the country with good weather, so I planned and flew a long solo low-level route using all the magical navigation equipment. Unfortunately, it was cut short halfway through as I had a generator warning that wouldn't reset. The warning and associated noises occurred in the middle of a target run and gave me a massive dose of adrenalin. It was totally unexpected. I headed back to base, got a new jet and was back in the air to finish the route within an hour. The Buccaneers are all preparing to go out to the Gulf as they are fitted with equipment to drop laser-guided bombs. They are the only British aircraft currently to have this capability. John Sullivan (JS) is deploying with them, but John Green (JG) hasn't finished his conversion course, so he will be staying behind. The truth is we would all like to be out there no matter the danger.

Happy hour was by far the quietest I have experienced in Scotland.

Monday 28 January

I have spent the weekend up in Lossiemouth pretty much by myself. I took the advantage of a quiet evening to say hello to a few more of the ladies who run the telephone exchange on the base. It was nice to put faces to the voices.

I flew back down to Coltishall today with the same four instructors who came up on Thursday. Even sat in the back seat, I was still working hard to keep up with them, but I managed. That was the high point of my day.

I am starting to feel that I am the only Jaguar pilot at Coltishall without a wife or girlfriend. Dave has a long-term girlfriend from his hometown and Shaun is in a bit of a purple patch when it comes to women at the moment.

The boss is sending me back up to Lossiemouth next weekend and most annoyingly, the local Welsh council from RAF Valley have sent me a summons for a poll tax bill I have already paid. Not a good day.

Wednesday 30 January

The weather has been rubbish for the last two days, and there has been no flying for us poor students. I managed to creep into the back seat of a T2 on to a four-ship land-away to Prestwick with 54 squadron. It was a proper operational, low-level training trip complete with a first run attack on a range. We had Tornado F3s bouncing the formation and sections of the low level were flown down to 100ft instead of the usual 250ft. It was absolutely brilliant! The visibility was 60km-plus with very few clouds and the seas calm. We did an airfield attack at Benbecula and then landed at Prestwick for a quick lunch. The boys were all within five seconds of their target time. They plan to be within 10 seconds to get the correct spacing for bombs detonating on the targets. It was very impressive.

We were straight into low level on the way home, including more 100ft flying down some tight valleys. The most amazing flying I have ever experienced in my life. We were so close to the ground and the sides of the valleys that at times I dared not blink. We even spotted a nuclear submarine on the surface just off the coast. In this weather, the islands on the west coast of Scotland are beautiful, as are the cliffs and beaches. Could there be any better job?

Thursday 31 January

The weather still wasn't great today, but I flew a dual general handling trip anyway. Nothing sparkling, just going through the motions. The boss, Wg Cdr Rusling, achieved his 2000th hour on Jaguars this morning, so there were drinks at lunchtime. For a change, it was the boss who over-indulged. Shaun had two telephone calls, and the boss answered both of them. The first one was from his dad and the second from his current girlfriend. They were both very amusing to listen to.

"He isn't doing very well at all, we are about to chop him and I don't like the look of the nervous tick he has developed."

"He always seems to have women in the mess, we can't get him out of the bar and he plays his music far too loud."

Shaun is thinking of hiring the boss as his PR agent.

A group went out to a local pub in the evening, but I stayed in to get some work done and I am glad that I did. Sqn Ldr Wilcox fell head first out of the mini-bus on the way home and knocked himself out. He has a big wound on his forehead. They took him to the station doctor, who couldn't decide if the lack of coherence was due to the alcohol or the head wound.

Friday 1 February

Sqn Ldr Wilcox is in hospital and can't fly for a month. He is lucky there are no serious injuries.

The weather in the south has continued to be bad, so I have another trip up north and a weekend in Lossiemouth. At least Shaun is going up north as well, so I will have some company.

Shaun and I have decided that the boss is super randy. At Lossiemouth, it isn't unknown for him to disappear for an hour or two at lunchtime for what he describes as 'leg-over and chips'. When we landed at Lossiemouth last week, his wife came to collect him from the squadron in leather trousers. Woof woof.

We got up to Lossiemouth in plenty of time for happy hour and the evening ended in a Chinese restaurant in Elgin with the usual crowd, and a bunch of guys from the Shackleton

Maritime patrol squadron. One of them is up here awaiting his pilot training course at RAF Swinderby. He decided that it would be good fun to start baiting Jim Frampton, as he was just a 'lowly Buccaneer navigator'. He realised the error of his ways when he was pulled across the table with one hand, with a fist being waved under his nose. He had called Jim 'queer' a few too many times and Jim had decided to stop ignoring him.

Saturday 2 February

I woke up with the standard Lossiemouth weekend headache and memory loss. I managed to convince JG to give me a lift into Elgin to get some beer (Becks) as there were rugby internationals to watch over the afternoon. JG has got a new Danish girlfriend called Lulu. It seems that she was out with us last night although I have no memory of her being there. She arrived at the Jag office to watch the rugby and said that Shaun and I were 'charming'. We both reckon that she has got a problem with translating words into English. 'Charming' and 'drunk' must be very similar in Danish.

A local girl called Victoria also arrived in the middle of the rugby to demonstrate a water filtration system to Shaun. Shaun just wants to sleep with her, but I think he will have to buy one of the water systems first.

We took her out to a party in Elgin along with JG and Lulu and a two-litre bottle of tequila.

Yet again, people started to leave as soon as we arrived, and I hadn't even started dancing. Shaun was drinking tequila shots using Victoria's bare shoulder to lick the line of salt. I thought that this was a great idea and tried to recruit a suitable woman of my own. The only one I could find was a local girl who wouldn't tell me her name, so I decided to call her Salt Lick. Unfortunately, Salt Lick refused to be used as a salt lick and then started to object to me changing her name.

Sunday 3 February

I have very fuzzy memories of last night, but I think JG managed to get me home. I spent most of the day watching MTV and then Shaun and I went around to Simon Stocker's for dinner. His wife is still taking pity on the poor single boys in the mess. I don't think she has any idea of what we get up to on a Friday and Saturday night.

Tuesday 12 February

I have been back down at Coltishall for the last week, but we have been snowed in for most of that time and there is only so much studying and bookwork a man can do. I finally got airborne again today on a dual instrument flying trip and wasn't surprised to find that I wasn't that sharp. It would be nice to get some regular flying and a bit of familiarity with this aircraft.

We were given a very boring lecture on the engine updates that have been incorporated into the jets flying in the Gulf War. The engineer who gave the lecture was very excited by all the technical aspects, but he could have just said '10 per cent more power and longer lasting engines'. That is pretty much all I could glean from being talked at for an hour.

Wednesday 13 February

Shockingly, bad winter weather all over the country today and freezing fog over most of East Anglia, so I was airborne on another dual instrument trip. It was busy, but I coped and I should be flying my instrument-rating test tomorrow.

Dave Fellows was caught in the bar last night buying a cheap bottle of champagne, and he has confessed that he intends to propose to his girlfriend over the weekend. The boss got to hear about it and is not impressed with his meagre efforts. Dave is getting a hard time. Just about everyone is having a go at him. A night at home with dinner for two and cheap champagne! The boss has said he is in Division Three when he needs to be playing in the First Division. By the end of the day Dave had been convinced he needed to book a weekend in Paris and do the business over there.

Thursday 14 February

Dave has booked his weekend to Paris, and it is going to cost him a fair penny.

I spent the day getting into my immersion suit ready to go flying and then having the flight cancelled. Three times.

Tuesday 19 February

Dave has returned from his weekend in Paris having proposed at the top of the Eiffel Tower at sunset. It was all very romantic, and he got a yes. He says he won't be going out for two months, as he is totally broke. The boss can't wait to tell him that the honeymoon has to be better and more expensive than the engagement weekend.

I finally got airborne for my instrument rating this morning after two days of instrument flying practices – and I failed the test. Not a happy boy. Shaun getting a good pass for his test, hasn't helped my mood. He has made me a card with 'PISSED OFF! DO NOT APPROACH OR TALK TO' written on it.

The boss called me into his office to tell me that as far as he is concerned I will get enough hours to pass the course and I shouldn't worry. He thinks the lack of regular flying is affecting my performance. I still have to pass the instrument-rating test and to judge by today's experience, I have a lot more work to achieve the standard required.

Thursday 28 February

Just to add to my lack of regular flying, I have had most of the last week off with a cold. Back into work today to find that the Gulf War is over, with no Jaguars shot down. The boys will be back in the UK next week, and hopefully, we can get back to Lossiemouth and I can get airborne a bit more often.

Today though, I was flying with the boss for another attempt at a weapons sortie and yet again, the weather prevented the full use of the weapons range. We flew a few instrument approaches instead. They were all right, but I am getting a bit of a complex about instrument flying in this machine.

Friday 1 March

For a change, we had good weather today, so I managed to fly my dual weapons sortie with the boss. It wasn't perfect, but the boss seemed happy and that is what matters. There are several ways the aircraft can drop its bombs and today we concentrated on the most basic modes and also the modes we use if the computer fails. We have got 16 weapons sorties to get used to the sophistication of the weapons systems.

Managed to get away from Coltishall early and headed down to London.

Monday 4 March

The entire station had a late start today. Met brief was at 10.30am and although the weather wasn't brilliant it was good enough for me to fly my first solo in five weeks. I went off to the range and dropped some bombs and fired a few bullets with decent results. Then flew a few instrument approaches back at Coltishall and for a change, I was pleased with my performance.

We were supposed to be night flying hence the late met brief, but it was called off as the met men were predicting low clouds and strong winds. They got their predictions totally wrong. The night was relatively calm with very few clouds. Simon heard one of the met men saying that they were getting much better now, and they were accurate 48 per cent of the time. How anyone can be pleased with being wrong most of the time, I don't know.

The Jaguar has five hard points that weapons or extra fuel tanks can be attached to. There is a big one under the fuselage and there are two smaller ones under each wing. The aircraft has two internal 30mm cannons with space for several hundred rounds of ammunition. It can carry a variety of bombs, rockets and missiles on these hard points.

Tuesday 5 March

I was on the range again this morning with Sqn Ldr Kerss in a jet without the external fuel tanks that we seem to carry most of the time. We just had a single practice bomb dispenser along the centre line, and the guns loaded. It was a very slick machine, and I enjoyed myself, tooling about at high speeds feeling sorry for all those poor ground-bound people. I even got some good strafing scores using the reversionary modes.

We used the head-up display for navigation and deployment of our weapons. However, we also had to be able to complete a mission even if we had a main head-up display failure. In its reversionary (degraded) modes, the head-up display is a very basic gun sight that we could use to aim our weapons. It works; however, accuracy is degraded and constant practice is needed to remain proficient.

We had our night flying today as well. I flew a practice diversion over to RAF Marham, which is a GR1 Tornado base only 30 miles away. I think they are more used to the two-seat aircraft over there, with the navigator helping the pilot, because at one stage air traffic instructed me to turn on to a new heading, descend to another level, change my squawk and go to a new frequency all in the same transmission. I would not have been able to deal with any more information, I was working at full capacity and my hands were dancing around the cockpit.

There was a good story in the crew room about a formation of four Jaguars flying down to the south of France. They were given a new frequency to contact French military air traffic. However, air traffic was refusing to talk to the Brits on that frequency, and after several attempts, a French voice was heard to say, "Jaguar formation you are cleared direct to Nice Airport."

That is an almost unheard of clearance in French airspace, but they set course anyway, eventually contacting Nice Tower and landing safely. During the debrief, the formation leader commented how amazing it was to get a direct track from that far away in French airspace. This was when the No 4 man in the formation said in a French accent, *"Qui! eet ezz emazing how eelphful ze air traffick can be."*

There was stunned silence from the leader and much laughter from the other pilots.

Thursday 7 March

The last two days have been very poor weather down here at Coltishall and also up at Lossiemouth, so there has been no flying for anybody. It has given me the opportunity to get some serious studying done and also to get into the simulator to practise my instrument flying. That has finally been improving and, therefore, I have been much happier. This disrupted course has not helped me: I perform to my best when I have continuity, and there is a distinct lack of that at the moment. I am lucky that the boss recognises this or I could be in real trouble. Not that I am going to complain. The Jaguar pilots in the Gulf War suffered extreme stress every combat flight, and I would not consider myself fit to join their ranks if I couldn't cope with the stress of a failed instrument test.

Friday 8 March

At last some good weather, so I was airborne solo and off to the range along with everyone else. I managed to drop some decent bombs, but I wasn't as 'godlike' as Shaun, who scored a very impressive 75 per cent accuracy with his strafe. He is on a bit of a roll at the moment. Happy hour was a quiet one as the fighter controllers from the underground radar centre nearby were using the mess for a dinner night. Bill Auckland from my course at Chivenor came over to join us. He is on a Harrier conversion course at RAF Wittering. He knows Shaun very well, as they completed their basic flying course together. We ended the night at a club in Norwich where two older ladies approached me. They offered me a threesome, but I ran away. A lack of moral fibre, as Shaun calls it.

Monday 11 March

I flew an inverted flight check in a T2 Jaguar with an instructor this morning. We had to find some loose articles that had been seen in the cockpit. Even small bits of debris can get into control runs and have disastrous consequences. That was all the flying for the day as the weather was rubbish again.

A VC10 transport aircraft from the Gulf landed in the afternoon. It was bringing back some of the ground crew and a few of the pilots, one of whom had phoned his wife to warn her that she had better have the bed ready for his return. She replied that he had better be the first one off the transport.

Wednesday 13 March

The boys are back from the Gulf. The last eight jets landed today, and it was great to see all those sand coloured aircraft with mission scores along their cockpits. The atmosphere on the base was amazing. One poor woman was so nervous waiting for her husband that she was visibly shaking.

Livo was flying the last aircraft to land, much to everyone's surprise. He had been sent out to do a ground job, but it seems that they needed a pilot to fly daily reconnaissance missions and as he was already there and was a qualified recce pilot, he volunteered. He hadn't even told his girlfriend that he was flying combat missions. She had turned up at the base expecting him to arrive in a transport plane but instead he climbed out of a fighter. He was typically modest about the whole thing, and I wasn't sure if the look his girlfriend was giving him was good or bad.

Friday 15 March

There was more good weather today, and I launched solo into the range. It took me a while to get settled into the pace of things again, but the bombing and strafing scores were all right.

Happy hour in the mess was a mega one. The bar was packed with pilots, many of them in sand coloured flying suits. There were stories of GR1 Tornado aircrew blowing themselves up with incorrectly fused bombs, messing up low-level delivery profiles and getting themselves shot down. There was also a lot of banter about the fact that our air defence F3 Tornados were so useless that they weren't allowed into enemy territory.

Shaun managed to acquire a bottle of tequila and then proceeded to use a few of the wives' shoulders as salt licks. At one point in the evening, he ate the rank slides from my uniform. Why? I don't know.

RAF Lossiemouth

Tuesday 9 April

I have time-warped to 9 April. I think my hangover from the post Gulf War happy hour was so large that I have been unable to write my diary for the last few weeks. Anyway, the whole OCU is now back up at Lossiemouth with its full complement of instructors and aircraft. We have had a few days leave and for the last week, the weather has finally changed for the better and we are all now getting in a good amount of flying. I have been airborne every day, and on a couple of occasions twice. We have all been working very hard to keep up with this increased pace.

The next station commander for RAF Coltishall, Group Captain (Gp Capt) Dacre, has arrived to start his refresher course along with two other pilots. They are all experienced Jaguar pilots who have been on the ground for a few years and are on a short course to get them back up to speed before going down to Coltishall. Gp Capt Dacre used to be a bare-knuckle boxer before he joined the air force and I get the feeling that he would not be a man to cross.

Saturday 13 April

A nice slow day that started well and then went rapidly downhill. There were cocktails in the mess bar in the afternoon and I was joined by John Green and Shaun. We used the cocktails as a warm up before calling our usual taxi driver, Eric, and heading out to Elgin for the night. As far as I remember, it was a standard excessive Elgin evening. We drank too much in the local bars, where I am sad to say we have become so well known that in one establishment the barman had our drinks ready before we got to the bar. The evening finished in a curry house and then Eric took us home.

Sunday 14 April

I woke up this morning with a massive headache and total memory loss of the last couple of hours of last night. Eventually, Shaun and JG arrived in the Jaguar office, and they were both in an equally unfit state. This afternoon, I got a call from the ladies at the base telephone exchange who wanted to know if I got home all right last night. I thought that was more than a bit strange until they explained that at 2am, they had a call from me and all I said was, "Send Eric!"

What Shaun, JG and I managed to piece together was that at the end of our curry I was told to order a taxi to get us home. The only number I could remember in my drunken stupor was the one for the base, so I rang that. The poor ladies at the telephone exchange recognised my voice, but initially had no idea who Eric was. They thought that it could be one of the local taxi drivers, but did not know where he worked. So, they started ringing the local taxi firms and eventually found one that had a driver called Eric. They then had a three-way conversation with the taxi controller and Eric to ascertain if he knew who I was and then if he had any idea where I would be at that time of the night, as I needed a taxi. Eric, being more than used to our movements over a weekend, realised that we would either be at a nightclub or a curry house. He drove past our usual haunt and saw JG, Shaun and myself waiting for him on the pavement. We just jumped in, and he took us home without us realising all the investigative work that had gone on to get him to pick us up. The boys clubbed together to get the ladies of the telephone exchange a bunch of flowers for their efforts.

Monday 15 April

I had two trips today, a dual in the morning and a solo after lunch. The dual involved using the weapon-aiming computer to attack targets off the range. I didn't realise how hard it would be when you haven't got the nice flat sterile environment of a weapons range to drop your weapons. Undulating terrain and even trees make accurate bombing more difficult. To ensure our weapons are delivered accurately, the aircraft needs to be at a steady height and speed for a few seconds. Just overflying the target as we have been doing to date is no longer good enough and to add to the fun, everything seen through our head-up display will now be recorded via a new video system.

The solo trip was more range work. I was practising a complicated delivery profile where we 'toss' the bombs into the target from a few miles away. We normally let the computer release the bombs in this profile. The pilot just has to follow a guide in the head-up display at the demanded speed. As with everything we do, there is a manual back up for this profile that involves lots of mental gymnastics and ideally an extra pair of hands.

Shaun has discovered a song from a group of lads from a northern industrial town and has spent most of today walking around the squadron singing, "He's a puff, he drinks lemonade. He's a puff, he likes his BUTTOCKS SPLAYED." I think he likes the song because it is crude and it has a good tune. The instructors don't know what to make of it. Fortunately, Sqn Ldr Wilcox hasn't heard him yet, as I am sure he would have some cutting remark.

We were introduced to first-run attacks on the tactical weapons course at Chivenor. As you can't go around dropping practice bombs on the barns and small factories selected as targets, we normally dropped a practice bomb on a weapons range whenever we flew a simulated low-level attack profile. The range visit was planned as part of the low-level route and we got the one pass to drop a bomb – and our accuracy was recorded. These attacks had to be booked in advance, and the formation leader had to get radio contact with the range controller to get clearance before entering. He had to do this while flying at low-level and preparing all the switches that are necessary to release any weapon.

Tuesday 16 April

I was straight into low-level navigation planning this morning to fly a trip with Uncle Livo. It was a navigation trip without using any of the clever electronic aids on the aircraft. Back to the old stopwatch and map techniques and I wasn't too sure if I would remember them. I finished the planning with so much time to spare that Livo brought forward our take-off time. The trip wasn't bad either. No problem with the navigation and hit all my targets and even managed a good score on first-run attacks on two ranges. I enjoyed myself for a change.

My instructor from my sortie yesterday morning was Steve Thomas and today I received his write up of our trip. It read:

1. Don't get changed too early.
2. Always be late for the final brief with the duty pilot.
3. Walk faster. Which he had then amended to say – Swagger to the jet don't walk.
4. Take off on time.

It seems I'm just not cool enough. I've got the right colour, but I'm at the wrong temperature.

Wednesday 17 April

Today was not a good day of flying for me. I had an instrument trip in the morning during which I didn't perform very well. Then I was straight into my last solo weapons sortie, which I really didn't enjoy for several reasons. The first jet I climbed into wouldn't start, and the second had a problem with the main computer, which meant that I couldn't get any weapon aiming information. I had to fly the whole sortie using very basic modes which as well as being hard work weren't very accurate.

Friday 19 April

I had the re-test of my instrument rating today and I managed to get around the whole trip without making any great errors. It was a decent pass. Finally. A big weight off my shoulders, and I can concentrate on getting to a good standard for the rest of the course. That was all my flying for today, and I stacked early to get the civilian flight down to London from Inverness.

Monday 22 April

I was suffering from the Monday blues again this morning. Flew a solo trip, which was a simulated attack profile, and the old Chivenor goat was out and running. I was the number two of a pair of aircraft and was working hard. At no stage did I feel on top of things, but I got away with only a minor telling off for not dropping a bomb on the range.

I did have a second simulated attack profile on the flying programme, but the jet refused to start, so that was scrubbed.

We spent the evening hosting four Spanish pilots who are at Lossiemouth for the week. Livo was out along with a squadron leader from Coltishall. The squadron leader had a big dislike for the RAF Regiment although he didn't hold my previous membership of that branch against me. The Regiment boys in the Gulf War got on the wrong side of him on more than a few occasions. He became so fed up with them that he eventually told their boss, "You are a git, your friend is a git and in fact you are all gits."

As Livo says, the RAF Regiment didn't miss any opportunities to 'fuck up'.

Wednesday 24 April

Another very busy flying day. I had a solo attack profile trip in the morning and then I was straight into more planning for another in the afternoon. They were both a pair of aircraft at low level with two off-range targets and a range target. The afternoon sortie was my first strafe first-run attack on the range, and it wasn't great. It all happened much more quickly than I expected, so my score was nil points! The rest of the flying was good and I am a very tired boy.

Bizarrely, after the conversations of Monday night, there were a lot of RAF Regiment officers wandering around the mess today. I think they have got a big exercise over at RAF Kinloss, which is our sister base up here. Livo doesn't like them either, so we left them in the mess bar and retired for a quiet beer in the Jaguar office. 'Decorational not operational' is how Livo describes them.

Thursday 25 April

Today, I was off on a dual land-away to Coltishall with Steve Thomas. It was a bit of a mad rush to get the planning done, but we managed to launch in good order and I tried my best to swagger out to the jet. The trip down was a good one, and I am getting the hang of this machine in the low-level environment.

Steve Thomas is a much happier man down south that is for sure. He is another one of our instructors who fought in the Gulf War with 41 squadron and I think he would be back down at Coltishall with them in a flash.

Friday 26 April

This morning, I was straight into a rapid plan at Coltishall for my trip back up to Lossiemouth. It was my first time leading an attack profile trip in the Jaguar, and although it was not easy, the sortie went quite well and I even got good bomb scores on my range target. I was very tired when we got back and foolishly thought that would be my lot for the day. How very wrong I was. They had sneaked me on to the programme for a solo general handling trip late in the afternoon. It was a beautiful day for flying in Scotland, but I was still feeling tired, so I spent a lot of time with the engines in full burner and got rid of my fuel very quickly.

We had a squadron Dining In night that started badly and got distinctly hazy. Shaun arrived with the standard bottle of tequila and convinced Gp Capt Dacre's wife to let us use her shoulder for the salt. In retrospect that was not clever. Our senior engineering officer was leaving the station and he sang a farewell song instead of giving a speech. The speeches were not very good, and Gp Capt Dacre fell asleep during the last two.

Saturday 27 April

This morning was very slow which wasn't entirely unexpected, but by the evening, we were all back to our regular selves. The usual team went into town again with our taxi driver Eric, and frequented our usual haunts. We were having our normal late-night curry, and I thought I was dreaming when I looked up to see a fireman walking through the restaurant in full firefighting gear. Shaun was insisting it was because someone had ordered a curry that was too hot, but I think they had had a minor fire in the kitchen. It didn't seem to interrupt the service, or it could just have been that I was so tired and emotional that I didn't notice the blaze.

Monday 29 April

The course is rapidly coming to an end and I flew twice today. This morning, I had a low-level trip where I learnt how to 'guns jink' and make life difficult for any air-to-ground systems defending a target. We are supposed to do this if we get missile or guns warnings on the way into a target as well as dropping accurate bombs within 10 seconds – just as I was thinking I was getting the hang of low-level attacks in this machine.

My afternoon sortie was a dual air combat. I thought I was good at this, but as I have already seen, the Jaguar is a very different beast to the Hawk. The phrase the instructors at Chivenor use to describe air combat in the Hawk is 'a knife fight in a telephone box'. It is true when compared to the Jaguar. The amount of airspace we cover in a fight is huge. I was flying with Sqn Ldr Roche and fighting against Shaun and his instructor Sqn Ldr Mallorie.

We were soundly beaten, twice.

There are a bunch of boys from the Hereford Sports and Social (SAS) staying on the base. They are up here with some of their students doing some laser target marking and forward air control. They are going to spend a week living out in the open and doing some walking. Crazy buggers.

Tuesday 30 April

Another two dual air combat trips today. They were both with Sqn Ldr Roche against Shaun and Sqn Ldr Mallorie, and although I was beaten again in the morning, by the afternoon I had finally got to grips with how to fight in this machine, and Shaun got his just desserts.

Great fun.

After work, Shaun went off to get a haircut which caused Livo to suggest that he was giving up on using pure flying skills to pass the course and had decided to improve his personal appearance to see if that could help. With all the socialising that has occurred up here, he has a long way to go before he can redeem himself. I am going to be sticking to the pure flying skills approach.

Shaun has survived the last four days having a curry for every meal, and as we waited for dinner in the mess, he was complaining that he couldn't face another one. That was a mistake on his part, as Dave Fellows changed Shaun's order to curry. To give the man credit, he ate the meal.

There were a couple of pilots on a land-away from RAF Chivenor staying in the mess, so I caught up on the latest news from that part of the world. My old instructor from Linton-on-Ouse, Andy Arundell, is on the course down there. He has said that he likes the idea of flying the Tornado F3. Everyone is appalled at this, and he isn't even having any counselling for this mental problem.

The F3 was designed specifically to intercept Soviet bombers over the North Sea, a role that no longer existed. It was an air defence fighter, but it wasn't as capable as some of the NATO air defence fighters of the time.

Thursday 2 May

I had only the one trip today, a dual pair tactical evasion trip, which was bounced. Simon Stocker was dual in the other aircraft and was leading the formation. He was working hard controlling everything. I had a bit of spare capacity and knew what was going on for most of the time. We are still getting used evading the bounce and then getting back on to the route at the correct time.

If we saw the bounce, we would warn our wingman and then it would be every man for himself. It wasn't unknown for your wingman to disappear for a few minutes as he took evasive action and then suddenly reappear in perfect battle formation. That was all thanks to the great navigation equipment in the Jaguar.

The boss of the RAF Regiment has told his officers that he doesn't want any of them wearing jeans on the base. He is insisting on 'slacks and flannels' only. I have no idea what flannels are. One of the pilots on the refresher course thinks that they could be a knotted hanky that you place over your head, and Shaun thinks they are similar to a loincloth. If that is the case, I will have to get one. Even his own officers now think that the RAF Regiment boss is a git.

Saturday 3 May

For the first time in ages, we have had bad weather up here. There was no flying yesterday so we were all given a long weekend. Shaun and Dave have driven south, and Simon has flown down to Coltishall with Livo. I am up here as the only Jaguar student and ended up going out with John Green and three ladies from the base telephone exchange.

They had never had tequila before, so we sorted out that problem for them. They later told JG that they were feeding me double shots and waiting for me to fall over, but it never happened. They can't believe that we put our bodies through this every weekend. They don't seem to understand that it has taken more than two years of extensive training to get ourselves into such a peak of fitness. After a week of hard work and stress on the course, we need a bit of a release.

Tuesday 7 May

The rest of the course is back from the long weekend, and they have all sorted out any hormonal imbalances they might have had. Shaun is getting banter on the squadron. He was on the telephone talking to Bill Auckland at RAF Wittering and was overheard by Sqn Ldr Mallorie discussing the possibilities of 'doggie' on a first date. Sqn Ldr Mallorie says he expects more from officers, but I don't for a moment believe it was any different in his day. I flew only the once, on a general handling trip, which wasn't too shabby, but somehow I managed to shut down both engines whilst taxiing back. I was going to shut down one, but mentally I got into the total shutdown routine. The incident happened in sight of our ground engineers and they have been giving me endless banter.

Wednesday 8 May

An outstanding day of 50km visibility and hardly a cloud in sight – the perfect weather for a couple of tactical manoeuvring sorties. I was so busy that my feet barely touched the ground all day and once again, I am worn out.

The banter from yesterday's engine shutdown has continued. The senior engineer's wife has made me a tartan garter to wear on my leg so that I can tell my right from my left, and the boss has ordered me to wear it outside my immersion suit when I go flying. The ground crew haven't stopped laughing at me all day.

Thursday 9 May

I have had another nightmare trip today. They have now added a heavy aircraft with eight concrete 1000lb bombs to the mix. The aircraft was a bit sluggish and I was so conscious of all the extra weight that I was very cautious with my handling. So much so that I was out of position for most of the formation turns. I was rightfully slated in the debrief and I will have to fly the trip again. In the back of my mind, I was very aware that if mishandled at these weights, it is possible to lose control of the Jaguar, leaving a smoking hole in the countryside.

Friday 10 May

I flew the heavy weight trip again this morning with Sqn Ldr Mallorie, and learned a lot. The techniques we have been taught on the course keep us well away from any loss of control and I was surprised by how aggressively I could handle the aircraft. I should have believed what I have been taught. Right now, I just want to get this course over and done with and get down to Coltishall.

Monday 13 May

The met man got it totally wrong today. We followed his advice and went south to find that the low-level weather was unsuitable. I was flying solo as a wingman in a two-ship evasion sortie, which degenerated to an arrow and then a close formation workout in the poor weather. I was working so hard to stay in position that at times, I had sweat running into my eyes. We went north and re-flew the sortie in the afternoon and funnily enough, the weather there was beautiful. I even managed to put together a decent trip. Getting the hang of this again.

Shaun and Simon both finished today, the lucky buggers, and the new Jaguar course has turned up on the base.

Wednesday 15 May

Today was a very busy day for me. This morning, I planned and flew a simulated war trip with the jet loaded up with all our electronic defensive gear, chaff and flare dispensers. I had to lead a pair of aircraft on a high-to-low-level mission with a bounce. The plan included a range target, a couple of off-range targets and a pass through the electronic warfare range to the north of Carlisle. It was the first time I had a chance of using the electronic jamming equipment, the chaff and flare dispenser and to practise my guns jink. It was very hard work, and there were lots of weather decisions for me to make. Still I got around in one piece and it was a good trip.

I debriefed from that and was straight into an instrument flying revision trip which was thankfully with Uncle Livo, who didn't give me too much of a hard time. Our jet had a problem with its air conditioning and no matter what we did, it was blowing out hot air.

There was a very sweaty Trevor by the time we landed.

My experience with failing the first instrument test has definitely caused me to have a bit of an aversion to instrument flying. I wouldn't go so far as to say I hate it. It is more like a necessary evil.

Thursday 16 May

I was up at the crack of dawn to prepare the maps for my last trip. It was another simulated war trip. It was dual this time, with Sqn Ldr Wilcox as my instructor and the station commander as my wingman. It was a very similar trip to yesterday: high level down into the north of England and then low level back to Lossiemouth, while being bounced by another Jaguar. The electronic warfare range also simulates ground-to-air missiles by firing what are essentially big smoky fireworks. One of these went screaming past my left wing missing the aircraft only by a few feet. It got my pulse racing and even Sqn Ldr Wilcox said that it was very 'adjacent'. The trip itself went well, and I was actually enjoying myself and really getting into it. We 'hit' both targets on time and even got a good score on my range target. I am the last man to finish, so we had our course reports in the afternoon. Mine was better than I expected, although Sqn Ldr Roche said that he was worried that I wouldn't make it at times. Just glad to have passed, but I know that I am going to have to work hard to get combat-ready.

Simon Stocker and I have both been posted to 54 squadron, Shaun Wildey is off to 41 squadron and Dave Fellows is going to 6 squadron. There was surprisingly little ceremony. We were all given a certificate, a small briefcase embossed with the Jaguar, ties and other goodies supplied by British Aerospace and then sent on our way. The squadron has another bunch of students to convert to Jaguar pilots. There was no time for parties.

That was the end of my time on the Jaguar operational conversion unit, and I had 50 hours solo and 60 hours dual on the Jaguar. Most of my scores were average and overall I was assessed as PROFICIENT.

Operational

54 Squadron
RAF Coltishall,
Near Norwich,
Norfolk,
1991

Shortly after I joined 54 squadron at RAF Coltishall, the old Soviet Union came to an end: on 10 July 1991 Boris Yeltsin was sworn in as the first president of the Russian Federation. Meanwhile in the Middle East peace was elusive. Although the first Gulf War saw Saddam Hussein thrown out of Kuwait, the situation in Iraq was increasingly turbulent, particularly in the Kurdish populated north of the country. The RAF would become involved in enforcing a no-fly zone over northern Iraq to help protect the Kurds from Iraqi aggression.

New pilots arriving on front-line squadrons still have to learn all the squadron tactics and develop the skills to enable them to fight in their aircraft to a required standard. Once, they do this, they are said to be 'combat-ready'. Normally, this would take around six months to achieve.

Friday 17 May

I was up early at RAF Lossiemouth and managed to pack the car and get on the road by 7am.

Even so, I didn't get down to Coltishall until 6pm. I must have taken a longer route as Shaun Wildey managed the journey 90 minutes quicker, and I am sure he wouldn't have been speeding. I had already arranged to have a room in the mess, and it didn't take very long to unpack, and there was just enough time to get to the bar to meet a few of the boys from my new squadron.

My new boss, Wg Cmdr Tim Hewlett, happened to be there and as soon as he saw me, he placed a two-pint jug of beer in my hand – my arrival jug. "Great! Thanks, Boss!" I said. I was very thirsty, so it only took about 30 seconds to finish, which I was told wasn't a bad time. Simon Stocker had his jug a bit earlier and took three minutes, but as a married man, he has not had the intensive weekend bar training.

There were lots of familiar faces around and although I wanted to have an early night, every time I made a move for the door, Mewsey kept putting more beer into my hand.

Monday 20 May

My first day on a front-line RAF squadron, and it wasn't too much of a shock. This was because I was already familiar with the base and most of the guys. Still, it was a busy day of form filling and trying to get to grips with what I need to study.

I have been allocated Ted Stringer as my mentor. He is a senior flight lieutenant and is a Gulf War veteran. As a mentor, he is a friendly face who can answer any of my stupid questions and guide me, as I work towards getting combat-ready. There is much more to learn than I realised. The Jaguar operational conversion unit has only scratched the surface.

A Jaguar combat-ready pilot in the RAF is one who is a capable wingman and able to lead a pair of aircraft if required. While there is no fixed syllabus, there are certain skills that the pilot must gain proficiency. These include simulated attack profiles, low-level evasion, electronic warfare, accuracy in deploying weapons, close air support, air-to-air combat and air-to-air refuelling. A combat-ready pilot is declared operational by the RAF and is officially added to the pilot strength of NATO.

Today was my first trip on 54 squadron. It was a squadron acceptance trip with the deputy boss, Sqn Ldr Mike McDonald. I flew the two-seat Jaguar T2 on a low-level route into Wales, and then a few instrument approaches into one of the nearby Tornado bases followed by circuits back at Coltishall. All good stuff and I will now be allowed to fly solo, which is great as the squadron only has two of the T2 two-seat jets. My office from now on will be the single-seat Jaguar GR1.

Thursday 23 May

Unexpectedly, this morning I was again airborne in another T2 aircraft and this time for a weapons check with the squadron weapons instructor, Nick Connor. It was just a standard range trip, a bit of strafing followed by various bombing profiles. It did take a while to get back into the groove, but there were no big errors, so now I am also cleared to visit any range solo.

In the evening, Shaun and I were taken into Norwich by a couple of the other single pilots on the station, Nick Collins and Mal Rainier who are both Gulf War veterans. There are three squadrons at Coltishall: 54 where I have been posted with Simon Stocker; 6 where Dave Fellows now dwells, and 41 where Shaun is now in residence. Mal is on 54 squadron with me, and Nick is on 41 squadron with Shaun.

We were sitting in a pub when John Letton, from my Hawk course at Chivenor, walked in with his girlfriend, Victoria. He has just started flying the Tornado at a nearby base. John made the error of joining us for the evening, and didn't realise that Shaun spent most of the time distracting him so that Nick could chat to Victoria. His sharpness hasn't improved from Chivenor.

Friday 24 May

I finally got my hands on a single-seat GR1 aircraft today, and was sent off to practise my low-level flying on another route into Wales. I was at high level, transiting across the civilian airways in the middle of the country, when air traffic informed me that I had been recalled. The weather in Wales had deteriorated and was unsuitable for any low-level flights. That was all my flying for the day.

I spent the afternoon reading a large file about electronic warfare and the electronic counter-measures pod that we use on the Jaguar. One of the squadron leaders saw me resting my chin on the file and questioned whether that was an effective method of learning. I responded by saying, "I'm learning by absorption and I am currently increasing my knowledge by osmosis."

Score one to me, I thought. Later as I walked along a corridor holding the file behind me, the same squadron leader passed and casually said, "So you can absorb information through your arse as well?" I am going to have to improve my banter around here.

The squadron had only 13 pilots. The boss was a wing commander; there were three squadron leaders, including the deputy boss; the rest of us were flight lieutenants. We had eight GR1s and two T2 aircraft, and about 100 ground crew to look after them.

Wednesday 29 May

The weather over the past few days has been very poor, so there has been no flying. I have been working hard trying to improve my knowledge of the aircraft electronic warfare systems. I have even spent hours listening to recordings of the noises the various Soviet radars make in our warning systems and I am getting to the stage of being able to recognise most of them.

Got airborne today, on a dual trip with one of our flight commanders, Sqn Ldr Sudlow, to demonstrate my skills in air combat against my mentor Ted Stringer. They said I was 'okay' but I am not convinced, as I managed to get myself shot down twice, with an interesting head-up display video from Ted to prove it. During the second engagement, I'm still not too sure what manoeuvre Ted flew to force me out in front of him and shoot me.

I have taken advantage of the lack of flying this week to get certified to carry out the basic maintenance actions on the jet. It was good to spend some time with the engineers and it also means that I can now fly solo land-aways.

The GR1 Jaguar is equipped with a radar-warning receiver (RWR), which has a large aerial located high on the tailfin. The RWR detects any radar emission, and a display in the cockpit shows which direction that emission is coming from. At the same time, the equipment generates a tone unique to that radar signature into the pilot's headphones. I have become very good at listening to the bleeps and squeaks and knowing which radar systems they are – especially the ones controlling ground-to-air missile systems. These missiles will be our main threat in any conflict.

Monday 3 June

I had my station commander's interview this morning with Gp Capt Dacre. It wasn't as scary as it could be, as we were both students up at the Jaguar conversion unit at Lossiemouth. He gave me the standard welcome to RAF Coltishall chat.

"Don't get cocky in the aircraft, or you will die. Do your secondary duties well. And make sure you enjoy yourself."

The station commander was one of the very first Jaguar pilots in the mid-1970s and has buried too many pilots in his time.

Back on the squadron, I had my final dual check flight. Strangely, it was the flying instructor's check. I had expected this to be my first dual check, but it just reinforces the fact that I am out of the flying training system. The first thing the squadron wanted to know was how good I was with the weapons system – not whether I could fly a nice accurate circuit. Anyway, the trip was a good one, flown with one of the senior flight lieutenants, Peter Warren, in the back seat. We just took ourselves on another low-level route into Wales, followed by general handling, aerobatics, circuits and a bit of instrument flying.

Friday 7 June

I have flown six times this week and the flights have mostly been as a pair on simulated attack profiles without any airborne threatening aircraft (so they were unbounced). I am slowly getting used to the way the squadron flies. The low-level formation dimensions are even bigger than at the conversion unit. It isn't unusual for your wingman to be in the correct position but not visible due to the terrain. We just trust that he will be in the correct position. We can still look into each other's six o'clock for any baddies or missiles. Some of the radio calls are different as well. We use standard NATO terminology on the radio, and that is a whole new mini-language for me to learn.

Today though, I was allowed to take one of Her Majesty's aircraft to an air show all by myself. As it was my first solo land-away in a Jaguar, I was given a very thorough briefing from Pete Warren, who was running the desk and authorising flights today.

Got airborne in the afternoon in some very poor weather, completed a solo low-level route and landed at RAF Church Fenton, a Jet Provost training base near York. The weather was appalling, a constant deluge of rain. Not that it made much difference to me, I am now very used to flying in marginal conditions. The hosting by the student pilots was very enthusiastic and they whisked me off to the mess and tried to feed me alcohol.

Sunday 9 June

The air show itself was yesterday, and unfortunately, the rain did not let up. As a consequence, there weren't very many visitors, but my old university friend, Gary Fisher, came over from Manchester. It was good to be able to show him around the Jaguar although we were both disappointed by the lack of any flying display.

Today has been a complete wash out, but I spent most of it visiting old haunts in York. It's been a while since I was last in this town.

Tuesday 11 June

I arrived at work early this morning, and was immediately given a late notice simulated attack profile to plan and fly with Pete Warren as my wingman. I was leading and was working very hard as the weather throughout the route was marginal. I had to call Pete into a closer formation for quite a long time as we were forced far off the planned route. In the debrief Pete said that he had wanted to see how big my balls were and he was more than happy with my performance, but to be honest from where I was sitting, my balls were shrinking not growing. It was busy navigating around the weather and I was a bit daunted with the responsibility of not flying Pete and myself into a hillside.

After lunch, I departed to Denmark with Mike Sears for a two-day NATO exercise. Mike is another Gulf War veteran and has been flying the Jaguar for several years. We flew into the Danish air base at Karup, where they fly the old Draken fighter. As well as our two Jaguars there were also two RAF Tornados GR1s participating in the exercise, which will be simulating a Soviet attack of Denmark from East Germany.

The base wasn't very big, and they are obviously struggling for accommodation as they gave us rooms in a building called 'Dog Handlers Quarters'. The Tornado boys were very upset, as the rooms are tiny. They have the smallest beds I have ever seen, and the whole place has a very strange smell. Mike and I were not bothered by the state of the rooms as we only intend to sleep in them. We dropped our kit and headed out to the local town to explore.

Wednesday 12 June

It has rained torrentially all night and the met men are predicting more of the same over the next few days. The exercise has been cancelled. Only the Tornados can fly in this weather as they have terrain-following radar systems, but they aren't going to get much value as they will be flying all by themselves. Even the Danish air defence F-16 fighters are grounded. We phoned Coltishall to tell them the bad news and the boss wanted us back straight away, but both our aircraft had developed faults. Mike's jet had a head-up display failure, and his navigation computer won't align. My jet had some very strange electrical problems, with both of the alternators refusing to work. We handed both jets over to the engineers, who said they would take at least 12 hours to fix. That was it for the day, so Mike and I headed off to the town of Aalborg for the evening.

In the RAF, this place has near-mythical status, and it didn't disappoint. The main party street is known throughout NATO as John Wayne Strasse after its most famous bar, the John Wayne. Every building is either a bar or nightclub.

Aalborg is a university town and this, combined with the very social nature of the Danes, means that every night of the week tends to be fun.

The first bar we went into had a hen party in full swing. The bride-to-be was charging five kroner for a look under her skirt, and there were more than a few takers. She had some very nice underwear it seems. The rest of the girls in her group were partying like there was no tomorrow. Mike and I didn't get back to Karup until the early hours of the morning – and we didn't pay to look under any skirts. Honest!

Thursday 13 June

We managed to get on to the base for the morning met brief and unfortunately discovered that the engineers had fixed most of the problems on our jets. They had succeeded in getting my aircraft working properly, and that was enough to get us back to Coltishall. I had to lead, as Mike still had no head-up display and no navigation computer. We had a 50-minute low-level trip across the North Sea, avoiding oilrigs and finally some very shabby circuits back at Coltishall. Fortunately, neither of us featured on the flying programme, so I went back to my room for some sleep.

Tuesday 18 June

Until today, all my low-level simulated attack profile flights on the squadron have been straightforward unbounced pairs. This morning, I flew dual in the T2 with Pete Warren, for my bounce qualification. Mike Sears was in the other jet and the boss, Wg Cdr Hewlett, was the bounce. As expected, this was again different from what I was taught at RAF Lossiemouth. The conversion unit is mainly concerned with teaching pilots how to fly the aircraft safely, and they give an introduction to the squadron tactics. The operational squadrons are all about getting the mission successfully completed.

On the way to a target, you are expected to deal with any attack by yourself. Your wingman, as always, will tell you of any threat he sees, but we assume that everyone is laden with bombs and not very manoeuvrable. It is stressed at the start of every mission brief that your task is to get to and destroy the target. Individual aircraft might have to dump their bombs to survive an attack by an enemy aircraft or missiles, but the rest of the boys will probably be flying even lower and faster to get away from any threat area.

We planned and got airborne for a land-away down to RAF Brawdy in south Wales, and although the weather was again very poor we managed to get there and back. I hadn't forgotten all the evasion stuff I had been taught at Chivenor and Lossiemouth, so both trips were good, and Pete has signed me off as fit for bounced trips. I have got a feeling that my workload for getting combat-ready has just increased.

Back at Coltishall, Shaun and the boys on 41 squadron had returned from their two-week detachment to Bardufoss in northern Norway. This is one of the Jaguar wartime forward operating bases. Should things turn nasty, Jaguars would be sent there in support of the Royal Marines who are deployed to protect that area of Norway from the Soviets. It's a tradition of 41 squadron to play hoaxes on the most junior pilots during their visits to Bardufoss; on this occasion, it was Shaun.

He told me that the Norwegian station commander had interrupted a morning-met brief last week to inform the assembled pilots that the Russians at their naval base in Murmansk had gone into high alert. They had sent several groups of warships around the North Cape and out into the North Sea. NATO headquarters had sent a flash message to Bardufoss requiring the Jaguars to provide reconnaissance photos of these ships so they could be accurately identified. As a precaution, all the aircraft were to be armed.

Shaun says he was very worried at this point and that his tension increased when his boss, Wg Cdr Bill Pixton, said that the two of them were going to fly a mission to locate a battle cruiser and its escort destroyers, and they needed to be airborne in 90 minutes. Shaun was left to do most of the planning as his boss kept on being called away for 'important meetings' and the rest of the pilots all seemed to be extremely busy planning their own missions. He completed a plan and loaded it on to the data transfer units to input into the aircraft. The boss arrived back for the pre-flight briefing and they hurriedly got dressed and headed off to their machines.

The jets at Bardufoss are kept in individual hardened aircraft shelters and the first aircraft Shaun got into wouldn't start. He had to race to the spare aircraft in another shelter only to find that the engineers weren't quite ready and were still loading the guns with ammunition. Shaun was extremely stressed at this point and was screaming obscenities at the poor engineers. He says he set a record for getting the aircraft started, but when he signalled for the door to the shelter to be opened so he could taxi out, he was faced with the whole squadron laughing and waving at him on the taxiway, with the boss directly in front of him. He says he was so full of adrenaline that it took his brain a while to comprehend what he was seeing.

As a hoax, it really doesn't get much better than that, but Wg Cdr Pixton doesn't think it will work again as the Soviet threat is rapidly diminishing.

Wednesday 19 June

Today was amazingly busy. I was due my monthly simulator check, but the simulator at Coltishall was broken. Whoever wrote the programme last night came up with an elegant solution:

"Let us send Trevor on a pair low-level land-away to Lossiemouth to practise his newly acquired evasion skills. He could then have an hour in the simulator up there and then another pair's evasion on the way home."

The trip on the way up was high to low level, with the low level starting in North Yorkshire. The weather was great, and I worked hard and did well. We landed and debriefed and I was straight into the simulator and then back to complete the plan for the low-level trip back to Coltishall. The trip home was just as busy, and I used up so much fuel evading the bounce, that I had to pull out of low level before the end of the route, as I was 'chicken' on fuel. By the time we had debriefed that trip, it was well past 6pm and I was worn out.

Thursday 20 June

Compared to the last few days, today was very slow. I planned a pair's trip with Ted Stringer in the morning, but it was cancelled because all the aircraft on the base have been grounded with suspected fuel contamination. I'm not going to call these trips simulated attack profiles any more since they are all along the same theme. From now on, it is going to be rare to get airborne without some simulated threat from the air or ground. That is what training is all about, and I do seem to be getting better at everything.

This afternoon, I discovered that a lot of the work I have completed over the last month is no longer necessary. All the Coltishall jets are being modified with a small monitor to display radar-warning receiver alerts. The equipment will then tell us the exact direction of the threat and which radar system it is. There is no longer a need to listen to all the bleeps and squeaks. Technology is great, but I have spent hours learning what all the Soviet radar systems sound like.

Wednesday 26 June

Another hard-working day, and it included a couple of firsts. The first time I had actually flown myself in a four-ship low-level trip and the first time I had experienced Tornado F3s as the aggressor aircraft instead of another Jaguar.

I was number four in the formation, and today number four did bugger all in the planning phase, just made the coffee and ran errands. Anyway, we planned, briefed and walked to the jets in good time. I started up the first jet to discover the radios weren't working, so I had to shut down and race to the spare aircraft. There is nothing like getting a bit of sweat on before a difficult sortie.

The F3s aren't given our exact routing, as a Jaguar bounce would be. They use their radars to try to find us. This is where the radar-warning receiver comes into its own. It gives an indication when the F3's radar is searching, and that indication changes when it finds you. The most disturbing sound is when there is an incoming guided missile. Even though the missile is simulated, the radar-warning receiver emits a high-pitched wail that gets the adrenaline flowing. There is a set of manoeuvres and tactics that comes into play against these threats, and it was the first time I have had a chance to practise all the theory I have been absorbing over the last month. The F3 and its missiles can shoot at us from more than 20 miles away.

The four Jaguars did very well against the pair of F3 Tornados and managed to defeat all but one of the radar missile shots. However, the F3s closed to within visual range on two of the engagements and got some heat-seeker missile shots against us. The speed of these close-range engagements was a big surprise. I am used to the Jaguar's closing speeds, but the F3 is about 150mph faster, and they get into range, shoot and pull out in mere seconds. They don't mess around at low level.

When the debrief was finished, I was told that the boss wanted to see me in his office. I instantly racked my brains as to what I could have done wrong in the last few days. The boss only tends to get people into his office to dispense a bollocking. Once, in his office, the boss told me to take a seat, which is always a good start. Bollockings are always delivered standing.

"Trevor, how was the trip this morning?"

"Oh, it was good, Boss, lots of new stuff but I coped fine."

"Very good. I did notice that you were a bit rushed at the start."

The boss has an office that overlooks the flight line so he can see what all the jets are doing. "Yes, Boss, my first jet was unserviceable, so I had to get to the spare, and I was rushing to make the take-off time."

"That is all very well Trevor, but you were RUNNING between the aircraft!"

"Uh! Yes, Boss, I was."

"Trevor, an officer NEVER runs, it makes the men nervous. Do you understand what I am saying?"

"Yes, Boss, sorry, Boss."

"Okay then, off you go."

The boss is a proper old-school English gentleman, and he has just told me, a black man from London, that my street cred is suffering by running in front of the boys. I am a fighter pilot and should always look cool…

Friday 28 June

I was in the squadron crew room this morning chatting to Mal Rainer, when the station commander, Gp Capt Dacre, walked in and asked where he could find Tim. I was busy trying to work out who Tim was, when Mal replied that he was in his office. Mal then explained to me that he was referring to Tim Hewlett, our boss. I had only ever heard anyone refer to him as Boss and had forgotten that his first name was Tim.

Five minutes later, the station commander walked back into the crew room with our boss 'Tim' and the boss of 41 squadron, Wg Cdr Bill Pixton. The two bosses started making coffee and the station commander calmly walked up to Mal and said, "Congratulations Flying Officer Mal Rainer DFC."

It is the first time I have ever seen Mal stuck for a reply. He was doing a good fish impersonation as everyone was shaking his hand.

Mal isn't the only one getting an award. Wg Cdr Pixton and Sqn Ldr Mike Gordon over on 41 squadron are also getting the DFC. They were all heavily involved in the fighting in the Gulf War.

The Distinguished Flying Cross (DFC) is awarded to pilots for 'an act or acts of valour or devotion to duty whilst flying in active operations against the enemy'.

Monday 1 July

I was down in London for the weekend and arrived back at Coltishall for my annual medical, during which the doctor discovered that I have a hernia. Great!

Another operation. As if I haven't had enough of those. I've got to get down to the RAF hospital at Ely in Cambridgeshire tomorrow to get assessed. The doctor believes all the high-G flying during the course at Chivenor initially caused the hernia.

Tuesday 2 July

I spent the morning swimming with Mal, Andy Sudlow and Mewsey and then drove down to Ely to have my balls groped by a surgeon. I have managed to delay the operation until February next year and have been told that I can continue flying until then.

Wednesday 3 July

I was programmed to fly a one vs one against my mighty mentor Ted Stringer this morning, but the weather wasn't good so it was cancelled. I sat in the crew room brushing up my warship recognition when Sqn Ldr Andy Sudlow walked in looking for a volunteer to fly a two-seat T2 down to the navy air base at Yeovilton, with an engineer in the back seat. Mewsey was stuck there with a broken jet. Flying beats studying every time, and I soon found myself airborne heading south to Yeovilton.

The flight was a relatively short one, and the jet was still a bit heavy, so I thought I would dump some fuel. I have never done this procedure before and after today, I won't be in a hurry to do it again. The dump valve in the aircraft got stuck open, and I dumped fuel throughout the approach and on to the runway before the valve would reset. All the houses under the approach path to Yeovilton were covered in aviation fuel, and the station had a few complaints. Luckily, the locals would automatically have thought it was a navy aircraft, or so I thought.

The engineer told us that Mewsey's aircraft couldn't be fixed until the morning, so we stayed the night, and went out for a curry with Ian Reid and Andy Pomeroy from my Linton-on-Ouse course.

Thursday 4 July

A late start and a bad head this morning. I am sure those navy guys feel that it is their duty to try and take advantage of us poor air force boys. I won't be surprised if they have been given the day off today. Anyway, after Mewsey's jet was fixed, I managed to stagger airborne and stayed on 100 per cent oxygen for most of the way back. It certainly cleared my head.

Another range trip in the afternoon, which was my first attempt at medium-level dive attacks. These are 30-degree dives from 10,000 ft. Great fun, although with our 'dumb' bombs, not as accurate as the low-level techniques we normally use.

On landing, I had to go and see Sqn Ldr Sudlow, as the navy had forwarded some complaints about my fuel-dumping incident. Suds is not happy with me. It seems I should have told the navy that I had a problem with the aircraft, and that would have negated all the extra paperwork he now has to deal with.

Wednesday 10 July

This morning's trip was a four-ship low-level sortie, against a pair of Tornado F3s, and although I am learning fast I still managed to get well and truly shot. The F3 drivers were on the ball today. Another was planned for the afternoon, but I couldn't get the second engine started and there wasn't a spare aircraft. The rest of the formation went without me, which was a real shame since we were playing against F3s again, and I could do with as much exposure to that environment as I can get.

I heard a great story about a pilot called Dim Jones, who is an ex-boss of 54 squadron. He was in his Jaguar at low level over the sea and had a mid-air collision with a Tornado. Both aircraft crashed, but Dim and the Tornado crew managed to eject safely. A search-and-rescue helicopter eventually picked up all three. The helicopter plucked Dim out of the water first and then flew the couple of miles to pick up the Tornado pilot and his navigator. As the Tornado pilot was winched into the hovering helicopter, he recognised Dim, who was sitting in the cabin (they had worked together a few years before) and said, "Dim Jones, hello mate. How long have you been on helicopters?"

"Oh! Only about five minutes, you idiot. It was me that you hit!"

Thursday 11 July

More four-ship low level again this morning. I will eventually get good at this stuff. We went north on this one. Our opposition was a solo Jaguar and he made us earn our money. The afternoon saw me aloft trying to fight Mike Sears in a one vs one. I seemed to spend most of my time trying to avoid him or just plain running away. At no point was I even remotely threatening his aircraft and eventually, I got shot. Not very good fighter pilot stuff. I must have looked a bit down in the dumps, because when I got back to the mess I was dragged off to the bar by Andy Cubin, who has just arrived on 54 squadron, having been away on secondment flying Jaguars for the Sultan of Oman. They have no low-level height rules over there and Andy says the pilots get quite comfortable flying down to about 10 feet – he has got video to back up the claim. How anyone can be 'comfortable' at 10 feet and 450kts I really don't know.

Sunday 14 July

Shaun Wildey and I have to attend an air-to-air refuelling course at RAF Brize Norton in Oxfordshire on Monday morning, so we have taken advantage of the timings to visit his parents, Brian and Anne, in Wiltshire. They organised a big barbeque for the weekend, and a few pilots from Shaun's old basic flying course turned up.

I found myself doing the cooking on the barbeque, which was a very good way of meeting people. There was one chap called John who is an inventor and was very interested to see the mess cannon that we had built while at Chivenor in action. I could now understand why Shaun had persuaded me to bring the thing all the way down to Wiltshire. We dragged the cannon out and had six or seven very successful firings of a cabbage projectile, until a very angry Anne Wildey confiscated the weapon. We hadn't noticed that her dogs had hidden in the house, and her horses in a nearby field were running around with their tails in the air shitting themselves.

Monday 15 July

Shaun and I left his parents' house at the crack of dawn to get to RAF Brize Norton for the air-to-air refuelling course. It wasn't the most intensive day's work, and the whole thing could have been done through a video. We managed to get away early for the drive back to Coltishall. All in all most of the day was spent in the car.

The RAF uses the probe and drogue method of air-to-air refuelling. The tanker, which is usually a converted airliner or ex-bomber aircraft, trails a hose with a basket, or drogue, at the end. The receiver aircraft is equipped with a probe, which is flown into the basket and connects with the tanker. Fuel can now be transferred. The Jaguar GR1 has a probe that is stowed inside the aircraft and deploys on the right-hand side of the nose. Only the GR1 has a probe – the training T2 aircraft doesn't have one.

Tuesday 16 July

Today was another good learning day with only one sortie, which was a two-ship close air support sortie into Wales. Although I had learnt all the theory, putting this discipline into practice used all my capacity in the air.

The army was having a big exercise, including the training of several new forward air controllers, and we flew three different attacks with three different controllers. One of the attacks was from medium level where the controller talked our eyes on to the target. He started with big, easily identified features, moving to smaller and more precise features until we could identify the vehicles on to which we simulated a dive attack.

The other two attacks involved the controllers giving us very precise coordinates and attack directions. These two attacks were performed from low level after we had programmed our computers with the necessary information and worked out how best to approach the target. That one trip exhausted me. The concentration needed to keep the aircraft flying in a holding pattern at low level while listening to the army guys, inputting information into the computer and plotting coordinates on a map tested my abilities. It was the first time I wished the Jaguar had an autopilot.

Close air support involves providing direct support to ground forces. You get airborne with no specific targets. The formation flies to an initial contact point and gets an update on the battle situation before being handed to a forward air controller who passes on details of specific targets.

Wednesday 17 July

I thought yesterday was a hard day with my one close air support trip, but that was put into the shade today, with two close air support trips into Wales and a weapons sortie on the range in between them.

After just three close air support trips, I have improved immeasurably and wasn't just following my leader around today. I was planning ahead and even giving suggestions of attack directions which is a sure sign of excess capacity. I was so tired that I didn't even bother going to dinner in the mess, just had a shower and went straight to bed.

Thursday 18 July

The amount of work I am putting in seems to be very high at the moment. I no longer worry about planning, as I have become very good at working out low-level routes and attack directions. My flight briefings are good, but I know my debriefings need work. The Jaguar force has a no rank policy during the debrief. The formation leader always runs it, even if the station commander is in the formation. I have been in debriefs where the boss has had to explain why he missed a target or didn't see the bounce closing in on a wingman. The important thing is that everyone learns from any mistakes. There is no room for egos in a debrief. The guys seem to have more respect for the senior officers who admit their mistakes. After all, we all make them.

My problem is that I still don't think I am any good. I am surrounded by veteran pilots, who make everything look easy and I hang out with Shaun Wildey, who always gives the appearance of supreme confidence even when he is struggling to cope.

Monday 22 July

For the last few days, the squadron has been preparing to deploy out to Gibraltar. Six aircraft are flying out to spend two weeks working with the navy and honing our air combat skills. The whole thing has been organised by Sqn Ldr Andy Sudlow. As with all these deployments, there is much more to it than meets the eye and there is a shocking amount of paperwork.

A couple of Hercules transporter aircraft arrived on the base today to take our engineers and their equipment off to Gibraltar. The engineers will be ready for the jets' arrival down there tomorrow.

Today, I was given the task of flying a young pilot who has been holding with the squadron before his course at RAF Linton-on-Ouse starts. He has been helping to organise the Gibraltar deployment, and this flight was his reward. He was strapped into the back of a T2 and we flew a low-level route that included RAF Swinderby where he had recently completed the elementary flying course.

He thoroughly enjoyed himself, and so did I. It was just nice to get airborne with no pressure.

Tuesday 23 July

An early start today for the flight down to Gibraltar. Our take-off was delayed by an hour as French air traffic control were not happy with our flight plan. The six aircraft eventually got airborne as two three-ship formations separated by 10 minutes. We are taking five single seat GR1s and a dual-seat T2. I have been given a GR1 and I flew in the front three with a massive smile over my face. We stopped at the French air base of Istres near Marseille for quick refuelling and proceeded onward to Gibraltar.

Since the Spanish don't recognise Gibraltar as British, we flew down the middle of the Mediterranean along the edge of Spanish airspace. We tried to converse with them, but they refused to talk to us. It was a very boring flight: a long way over the sea with nothing to do. I was very glad to see Gibraltar emerge from the horizon.

It is a very big rock with a very small runway which can have massive up-and-down air draughts. We flew in formation at low height and high speed over the runway to announce our arrival, followed by a circuit around The Rock to land. The airfield has no taxiway, and there is the sea at both ends. Aircraft have to turn around and taxi back along the runway to the parking areas. Strangely, the main road in and out of Gibraltar crosses the middle of the runway and they have a level crossing system – a barrier comes down and stops pedestrians and traffic so that aircraft can land.

I was the last of the front three aircraft to land, and the other two were waiting for me in the turnaround area at the end of the runway, so we could taxi back together to park. I couldn't understand why the other pilots had their canopies open and sunglasses on until we taxied across the main road. There were hordes of people/girls madly waving to us from the other side of the level crossing barriers. Note to self: always have sunglasses in a pocket.

I put down the dark visor on my helmet and tried to look cool, but it wasn't the same. The Gibraltar officers' mess is amazing. It has a patio overlooking the sea, a swimming pool, its own beach, and the staff wear white uniforms. I have never experienced anything like it. The squadron was hosting an evening meet-and-greet for all the Gibraltar military officers and local dignitaries. There are lots of navy personnel on The Rock as well as a sizeable army contingent.

I managed to stagger into town with Mal Rainier and Simon Stocker. We visited two bars before I gave up and went back to the mess after discovering that the girl I was trying to chat up, was a medic from Coltishall and had flown in on the Hercules yesterday. No wonder she was looking at me as if I was slightly crazy.

Wednesday 24 July

This morning, I was on the programme for two trips. The engineers have worked hard overnight and have removed the external fuel tanks from the aircraft so we are flying them 'clean'. They are different beasts like this, much more responsive and just right for air-to-air combat. However, without the extra fuel, and because a lot of time is spent with the engines in reheat, the trips don't last long.

I fought the two flight commanders today, Sqn Ldr Dick Midwinter in the morning and Sqn Ldr Andy Sudlow in the afternoon. I didn't embarrass myself and even managed to shoot down Suds on one engagement, although he says that was only because he had lost sight of me. Both trips were only 30 minutes long but were still tiring. I haven't had to fly continuous high-G manoeuvres like that since being in the Hawk at Chivenor.

Simon Stocker has now acquired a nickname. He is being called Gull, as in seagull. He briefed and walked out to his aircraft for two trips today, but had two broken jets. The poor man has had several incidents like this back at Coltishall, so now the banter is that he is very much like a seagull, as you have to throw stones at him to get him airborne. Nicknames have a habit of sticking, and I don't think he will get rid of this one for a while.

Mal and I crawled over to the gym for a workout before an evening drinking cocktails on the mess patio.

Thursday 25 July

Another clear and cloudless day and another two trips for me, this time against Nick Connor and Simon Young, both very experienced Jaguar pilots. And that is the excuse I am giving for getting soundly beaten. The fight against Nick Connor was a real learning one. I am going to have to refresh my knowledge of air-to-air combat tactics. Nick and Simon were both giving Suds a lot of banter for losing a fight to me yesterday.

We tended to fight over the Mediterranean about 20 miles to the east of The Rock, so it didn't take us long to get to the play area. It has become standard on our return to fly low and fast over the runway, followed by a circuit of The Rock before landing. These fly-bys are getting lower and faster, and air traffic is now closing the road to allow them. Otherwise, there would be injuries especially amongst the pedestrians.

Simon Stocker's nickname of Gull is going to stick. He still didn't manage to get airborne again today. He is missing great opportunities to improve his skills – and a lot of good fun besides.

Friday 26 July

No flying today as we had low cloud, and we need enough visibility to complete a visual approach to the runway, as there are no radar approaches here. Mal and I spent most of the morning in the gym.

The evening started with happy hour in the mess bar and then we progressed across the border to the Spanish town of La Linea. We had a Chinese meal, and I think the food was good, although my memory is hazy. Simon Young (not Gull), Suds and myself decided to head back into Gibraltar and ended up in a nightclub with a group of our engineers. As is always the danger when socialising with engineers, I was encouraged to drink too much and somehow ended up back across the border in the villa of a Scottish woman, with a couple of her friends. I woke up in the morning on the sofa (honest) and then had to find a taxi back into Gibraltar.

Saturday 27 July

There was a visit to a Royal Navy nuclear submarine this morning, which I missed and that caused a lot of banter when I eventually surfaced in the afternoon. Suds and Simon Young were a little bit upset, since I had disappeared with the cash we had clubbed together to buy drinks. They didn't like the idea that they financed my night, but the rules are quite clear on the matter. Once, a cash kitty is formed, it is up to the contributors to make sure they stay with the holder of the kitty. I was holding the kitty and went back to Spain, so according to the rules, they should have followed.

We had just started a barbeque on the mess beach when Sqn Ldr Dick Midwinter's pager went off. The subsequent telephone call informed us that there was a major alert and the whole squadron was on standby to deploy out to Turkey: something to do with a situation developing in north Iraq. The boss wants his aircraft back at Coltishall immediately. The engineering officer has had to send his sergeants out to the bars in Gibraltar to find the rest of his boys, and all the pilots have headed over to planning to work out how we are going to get to the UK on a Sunday.

Sunday 28 July

The engineers were up most of the night preparing the jets. They had to re-attach all the external fuel tanks and test them to make sure they were functioning correctly as well as ensuring the jets are fully serviceable. We launched all six jets together, and I was in the back seat of the T2 with Suds driving.

We were the last aircraft airborne, and it was weird. There wasn't very much wind and the other jets had heated up the local air to such an extent that we used the whole runway to get airborne. We were just skimming across the sea until we could get some clear air and a bit more power from the engines.

Our refuelling stop this time was at Nice International airport since all the military airfields in the south of France were closed on a Sunday. Nice airport is dripping in money. We parked among the private jets, and our £20m fighters were very much the poor neighbours. I was just glad that none of the owners were around to see the seven scruffy, sweaty, fighter pilots cluttering the planning area.

Coltishall was opened especially for our arrival and Suds and Dick Midwinter disappeared off with the boss to discuss events. I decamped to Mal's house for pizza.

Monday 29 July

The squadron is on 72-hour alert to deploy to Turkey. We are going to be part of a policing force in north Iraq. Mewsey wants to get a flashing blue light to put on the top of the aircraft. I can just imagine his idea of policing:

"I was proceeding down a valley in an easterly direction when I encountered two Iraqi Sukhoi SU-22 Fitters, who I suspected had concealed weapons. I instructed them to land which they did by descending vertically into the ground after deliberately running into my 'AIM 9L sidewinder missiles'.

As I have said before, Mewsey doesn't do subtle.

Tuesday 30 July

I didn't fly until this afternoon. The trip was a four-ship with high-angle bombing practice on a weapons range, followed by close air support practice over in the north of England. The boss has told me that I won't be going with the squadron to Turkey if they deploy. I'm not combat-ready, and they won't be able to fly any training trips out there. He wants me to stay in the UK, fly with 41 squadron and work towards getting combat-ready with them. I'm not happy about it, but he is right. I haven't even flown an air-to-air refuelling sortie yet, and they will have to do that every day out there.

Simon Stocker is going to help out with ground duties out in Turkey. He is also not combat ready, but I would rather stay at Coltishall and get a consistent amount of flying until I am more familiar with the Jaguar. I don't want to fail with the end in sight.

Thursday 1 August

Today, I flew as the formation leader of an unbounced pair. We had a first run attack on Holbeach range, followed by a low-level route and then some forward air control up in the north of England. It was by no means my best trip but I got Ted Stringer around in one piece, and I suppose that was the overall aim of the sortie.

The station had happy hour this evening instead of Friday as there is going to be a standdown from flying tomorrow. It is to give the engineers a chance to get a few more jets up to full-combat specification for the Turkey deployment. It looks as though it is only a matter of time before the guys head east.

Happy hour seemed to follow the usual format. Somehow, I ended up at a village not far from the base, at the house of Mike Sears and his wife, Mel. I was in the company of Andy Cubes and Mewsey, who managed to fall asleep while eating a takeaway Chinese meal. We could not wake him so Cubes and I had to carry him to the taxi and eventually into his house. I left Cubes to explain to

Mewsey's wife, Jenny, what had happened to him. She can be as formidable as Mewsey.

Friday 2 August

I was up early today to drive to Beverley in Yorkshire for the wedding of Dave Fellows. It wasn't a big affair as I think Dave is still recovering from spending a small fortune on his engagement in Paris.

It was a typical air force wedding in that the serving officers were kitted out in no. 1 uniforms with swords and gloves. We made an arch of crossed swords for the couple as they left the church. I was on best behaviour, partly as a result of the excesses of last night and also because I had planned to head over to York for the weekend to meet up with a few guys from my old Linton-on-Ouse course.

Saturday 3 August

Today was spent in York, mainly catching up with Cameron Gair from my basic flying course at Linton-on-Ouse. He has recovered from his bout of salmonella poisoning and is finishing a multi-engine pilot course, although he still isn't well. He walks with a limp and has been told that his spinal cord is fusing together, which has big implications for his later life. All of this due to not keeping our tea bar and snack preparation area clean while we were on the course at Linton. Mark Harris from that course was also out and about in the evening. He is on the F3 Tornado, and I have discovered that his squadron colleagues have started calling him Bart Harris – the Underachiever. He obviously hasn't improved very much – still only putting in as much work as is required and not a drop more. Bart left the pub early in the company of two very good-looking women, so in that respect he hasn't changed either.

Tuesday 6 August

I strolled into work today to be told that I could go home, as I would not be flying, somehow I ended up staying the whole day. I got my monthly simulator check out of the way, completed a load of trivial jobs that had been slowly accumulating, organised to take an aircraft to a static display at a USAF base in Germany in two weekends' time and then finished with a workout in the gym.

I moved out of the mess today and into the house of a squadron leader who is retiring from the air force and has got a job flying for Cathay Pacific in Hong Kong. I'm renting his house for six months, as he is taking his family out with him. It is a luxury pad, very modern, five bedrooms and just me to look after it.

Wednesday 7 August

Another low-level lead today with my steely mentor Ted Stringer. We were bounced on this one by the boss of 41 squadron, Wg Cdr Pixton. In the debrief, he said that because the weather and visibility were so good he could keep track of us while orbiting at 16,000ft. He could then descend, barely keeping subsonic, to threaten us. With his high-speed advantage, we had very little time to react when we spotted him. The result of this was I got shot twice! Anyway, I must have impressed him, as he has invited me on his squadron detachment to Portugal in September. I can't wait.

Ted has been trying to improve my swimming over the last few weeks, and I had another session at the station pool this afternoon. I still can't say I enjoy it, but it is good for my fitness and I need to get better – there is a lot of water around Great Britain.

Thursday 8 August

There is a good story doing the rounds at the moment about a student pilot from Linton-on-Ouse crashing his car. The road from the base into York has a T-junction that as the driver, is hard to see along until your car has stopped. It's a tradition that if you are driving, your car with another pilot in the passenger seat, your co-pilot will check the road on his side and if there is no traffic call; 'Clear left'.

This usually means that you don't have to stop at the junction.

This lad was dating a local girl who had been in the back seat of several cars that had approached this junction and had heard the call of 'clear left' numerous times. On this occasion, the girlfriend was in the front passenger seat and as he approached the junction, she said 'clear left'. He made the big mistake of trusting her, pulled out into the road and was hit by a car moving at speed from the left. There were no serious injuries but his car was written off. When he asked his girlfriend why she had said 'clear left' when there was a car in the road, she replied that she thought it was just what everyone said when they got to that junction.

Friday 9 August

I woke up early and headed to the station pool before work to swim a few lengths. Ted's wife, Louise, was the only other person there, so my little swim turned into a mini-coaching session. As we were finishing, what seemed like the majority of 6 squadron's pilots entered for their dinghy drills and started giving us a lot of banter as Louise and I were the only people in the pool. Like the true gentleman I am, I denied nothing. After all, Louise is one of the station doctors and very pretty. It all adds to my street cred.

My only trip today was also the most fun I have ever had in an aircraft. It was an eight-ship Jaguar low-level mission with two Jaguars and four F4 Phantoms as the bounce. Our new squadron weapons instructor Pete Tholen was the leader, and I was completely at a loss during the planning. We were hitting multiple targets simultaneously on the electronic warfare range in the north of England, and I had never seen such a complicated plan before.

Once airborne, I was working at maximum capacity from start to finish. Unlike the F3 Tornados I have flown against, the Phantoms had a habit of intercepting from low level without using their radars. Most of the time, we had no warning of their arrival. A couple of them would suddenly appear at low level in the middle of the formation and chaos would ensue: aircraft all over the sky and Jaguars splitting to the four winds to get away from them. I was working so hard that I missed my target and had to pull out of low level early, as I was 'chicken' on fuel. There must have been four or five occasions when I didn't have a clue as to what was going on, but I didn't care. It was BRILLIANT.

Thursday 15 August

Although 54 squadron is primarily a ground attack squadron, the Jaguar does have a low-level reconnaissance capability. The boys over on 41 squadron are the specialists in this discipline, but it has been deemed by the higher echelons that all pilots must now have a basic knowledge of the operation of the reconnaissance equipment.

So today, I had my first taste of flying with a recce pod, which contains cameras to record targets for reconnaissance purposes. I have spent the last couple of days on 41 squadron getting up to speed on its operation and picking Shaun Wildey's brain as to how to best employ the cameras. I launched as a singleton and managed to get decent photographs of all five of my recce targets.

The afternoon was spent sorting out the details of a trip over to the USAF base at Spangdahlem in Germany tomorrow. The weekend sounds as though it will be fun. There is an open day on Saturday, and they are expecting a big turnout. I even had a phone call from one of the event organisers explaining all the entertainment planned.

Recce pods are fitted under the fuselage of the Jaguar. They contain a nose camera and four other cameras that enable horizon-to-horizon photos in a swathe from under the aircraft. The pod is linked to the navigation computer to adjust shutter speed and exposure times according to the aircraft's speed and height. On landing, films are processed and analysed by experts whose life is made much easier if the pilot knows on which camera they can expect the target and can give an accurate description of that target. There is yet another panel in the cockpit to control these cameras.

Friday 16 August

Self-solo, with no wingman, and off to Spangdahlem for the weekend. The flight was my first experience of European airspace, and I have to admit that I had a five-minute period when I had no idea as to which navigation point German military air traffic wanted me to fly towards. I just couldn't understand what they were saying – a combination of bad English and an incredible accent. Anyway, I got down safely after a minor altercation with the American air traffic controllers on the base. They thought my approach speed was very high.

They just aren't used to the Jaguar aircraft.

The American military is great. Lots of 'yes, Sir! No, Sir', and saluting. The engineers at Coltishall only do that if they have messed up. The black American engineers especially seemed amazed to find that there were black pilots in the RAF. No one seemed ever to have seen a Jaguar before, or should I say 'Jag War', as they pronounced it? I gave up trying to correct them by the end of the weekend.

A F4 weapons systems officer hosted me, and he kept on apologising for not having a beer for me when I landed, but he made up for that when we got back to his squadron. They were a friendly bunch of guys and I teamed up with them and an EC-135 crew for the entire weekend. The EC-135 is a big American electronic signals gathering aircraft, which is also equipped with some fancy ground scanning radars.

Saturday 17 August

Got myself out of bed in good time to meet the public. Most of the day was spent in my flying suit next to the aircraft explaining its role and getting my picture taken. It's amazing the number of people who wanted their picture taken with me. The nicest was a black grandmother from somewhere in the south of the States who didn't believe a black person could ever be a pilot in the Royal Air Force. I tried to explain that we weren't all white guys with handlebar moustaches, but the slightly suspicious look never left her face.

The Hungarians pilots however, stole the show. Although the Berlin Wall has been down for a year, it is very rare to see Warsaw Pact military equipment at NATO bases. The Hungarians arrived in four MIG 21s. They are truly tiny machines, but everyone wanted to see them, and when the pilots started letting people sit in the cockpits, there was a constant crowd around their aircraft.

The RAF has a long history of black pilots – I wasn't even the first black Jaguar pilot. There were many black pilots in the Second World War, including black Spitfire pilots. The numbers haven't been great, but we have almost always been there.

The show organisers provided a bus to take all the crews to a local beer/wine festival in the evening. There was a big funfair and lots of stalls offering wine tasting as well as German food and beer. It was a nice, civilised way to start the evening although the Hungarians managed to over-indulge and were in fine vocal form on the way back to the base. I'm not sure what they were singing, but it sounded very good. The officers' club had an outdoor party going on when we got back, so I joined in and eventually went to bed in the early hours.

Monday 19 August

Up early to file the flight plan back to Coltishall, prep the jet and fling myself back into the sky. My first experience of the USAF has been a good one and I have been most impressed by their base. It is very big and seems to be small-town America transported to Germany. There were no problems getting back, and I landed to find that next week the squadron is going to deploy out to Incirlik, which is an American base in Turkey. I am not on the flying programme, and realistically, I won't be for the rest of the week. The boys are using the time to hone their skills before their deployment.

I have jumped the gun and have started prostituting myself over on 41 squadron. I've let it be known that I am willing to do any flying. Almost immediately, I have been invited on a 'shopping trip' later in the week with their German exchange officer Lieutenant Dieter Knorr. Shaun just laughed at me when I said I was going with him. Dieter has already asked everyone on 41 squadron and no one wants to go. Shaun says everyone is afraid of spending a night at his hometown in Germany and then having to fly the next day. I'm beginning to wonder what I have wished on myself.

Tuesday 20 August

I was airborne at lunchtime today in a 41 squadron jet for the trip with Dieter to Husum in northern Germany. Husum is an Alpha Jet base – the Alpha Jet is equivalent to the RAF Hawk but the Germans also use it in a light ground attack role. Dieter was based here before he started his exchange tour with 41 squadron. The town isn't very big, but I am convinced we visited every bar in the place. The night culminated in Dieter asking, "Hey Trevor! Have you ever visited a whore house?"

"No! I can't say I have Dieter."

"Okay then, I will take you to the squadron whore house."

He wasn't kidding either, but thankfully he did brief me not to buy the girls any drinks, as it would be extremely expensive. The place was like a bar, but with hardcore pornography showing on the televisions instead of sport. The girls were friendly enough when they realised that we were only there to have a drink. It was a very weird experience.

Wednesday 21 August

I woke up this morning not knowing where I was for a few minutes, before getting ready and staggering over to breakfast in the officers' mess to meet Dieter, who naturally was suffering no ill effects. We then went shopping.

As well as an overseas training flight, the second reason for Dieter making this trip was to buy wine and beer for a German party he was hosting at Coltishall. We bought 50 five-litre barrels of beer and 96 bottles of wine, and I was wondering where it was all going to go when Dieter showed me his cunning plan. The two aircraft we had flown over had had their 30mm cannons removed. These vacant spaces and their ammunition storage areas are perfect for stacking beer and wine. There are also numerous empty areas on the aircraft if you know which panels to remove. We managed to pack everything into the jets and, best of all, externally they looked no different from any other Jaguar. There were no external baggage pods to hint of our illicit cargo to any customs officers who might be lurking when we arrived back at Coltishall. Obviously, Dieter has done this before.

Our arrival at Coltishall was another great piece of planning by Dieter. Shortly after shutting down, the engineers pulled both jets into a hangar to start the process of emptying them of alcohol.

Tuesday 27 August

I invited the mentor and mentoress, Ted and Louise Stringer, over to dinner at my new pad, along with Mewsey, his wife Jenny and Adrian Bonwitt, who was on my basic and advanced flying courses. Adrian is visiting for a couple of days. It was a lot of fun and I think they were all surprised that I can cook. I didn't confess that I had been dating a chef for three years and was her kitchen slave whenever she cooked.

Wednesday 28 August

The first elements of 54 squadron are heading out to Turkey, and I am now a permanent fixture on 41 squadron. They sent me off to the range today, and it was a crazy sortie. The local farmers have been burning stubble in their fields, and the entire range was smothered in smog. I had to use 'The Force' to find the bombing target, and strafe was a complete giggle. I fired 120 rounds and hit the target once.

Because I had a little extra fuel when I got back to the base, I flew a couple of instrument approaches, voluntarily! I still have an aversion to flying instruments in this machine, but I have to practise. We are tested once a year, but I could be called upon to lead a formation instrument approach at any time. If the boys on your wing don't trust you to do a good job, then you will not last very long on the squadron. Most of the pilots tend to fly an instrument approach or two at the end of the low-level sorties, but Mr Ham Fisted Trevor Edwards doesn't normally have any spare fuel. I am told this will get better but we will see.

Thursday 29 August

Today, I was on a European delivery tour. I was sent to Denmark to deliver a part for a jet that had broken down. From there it was on to Florennes air base in Belgium to exchange aircraft – there are two Jaguar pilots in Florennes taking part in a NATO tactical leadership course and they were having problems with the attack systems of one of their aircraft. I got back to Coltishall to find no other jets in the air or on the ground. The engineers informed me that Bill Pixton had been flying Wg Cdr John Mardon in a two-seat T2 when they had a mid-air collision with a light aircraft. Bill ejected safely, but John was killed. The mess bar had been opened early so everyone was down there, and there were a lot of very subdued people.

It all seems so unfair. John had been diagnosed with a serious heart condition a couple of years ago and had survived a heart and lung transplant. His recovery had been so good that he had gone back to work in the office, had been promoted, and was about to leave the station. The medics had given him clearance for a single trip as a passenger before he left the base.

Traditionally, if someone is killed in a flying accident, a tab is opened at the mess bar in his name and any drinks bought that evening are put on it. This encourages everyone to get together and talk about the person and the accident. It is a surprisingly effective way of dealing with loss. All the officers on the base share the cost of the bar bill.

Friday 30 August

The morning after the night before and it showed. I stumbled into work on 41 squadron to find a very jaded bunch (not that I was much better). The deputy boss, Sqn Ldr Froggart, looked as though he was going to be sick and Nick Collins just took himself off the flying programme.

Tuesday 3 September

The boss of 41 squadron has kept his promise to allow me to join the detachment out to Montijo in Portugal. Montijo lies across the River Tagus from Lisbon, and the air base is home to a Fiat G-91 reconnaissance squadron that is affiliated with 41 squadron.

We have taken four jets, and I was given the T2 to fly down, although I was flying it solo. We refuelled at St Mawgan in Cornwall and then crossed the Bay of Biscay to Portugal. The support staff, engineers and all the equipment were flown out yesterday in two Hercules transports.

On our arrival, the G-91 squadron pilots greeted us with a little trolley containing a barrel of port and then we were taken straight to a barbeque. It was very sociable and I made a complete pig of myself. Unfortunately, we couldn't stay very long as our hotel was an hour's drive away.

The long drive caused a lot of complaints until we pulled up at the hotel. It is in a town called Estoril, and it is the most luxurious place I have ever set foot in. I couldn't believe that I wasn't sharing my room – it is huge. The bathroom is twice the size of the rooms I was given at the mess at RAF Lossiemouth.

Thursday 5 September

Today, there was a mini reconnaissance competition with the G-91 boys. Sqn Ldr Froggart and I were representing the RAF, and we got soundly beaten. It was a bit embarrassing as the Jaguar is two decades more advanced than the G-91. The Portuguese were using underhand tactics though. The maps we were given for our planning dated back to the Middle Ages. They were like parchment, and we subsequently discovered they were as inaccurate as they were old. They were missing a massive dam and lake that had been built since they were drawn, and this feature was nicely placed five miles from an almost identical dam and lake. It caused huge confusion for us Brits who didn't have local knowledge. The G-91 guys had a good laugh over that.

We had a night out with the Portuguese pilots and events rapidly spiralled downwards. I was pleased to see that the Portuguese have their own version of Mewsey. He was insisting that everyone drink something called aqua ardenis. This was very dangerous stuff, a sort of high-octane tequila. The Portuguese Mewsey spent the later part of the evening chasing our rotund female admin officer.

Friday 6 September

It was a struggle to get out of bed this morning, and there weren't many G-91 pilots at work.

We only flew the once, and it was a mixed low-level sortie with four Jaguars and two G-91s. The Portuguese guys planned it, and I think there was more local knowledge being put to use again as our target was what I can only describe as a plank over a stream. Quite why that deserved six aircraft and a simulated load of 24 tons of bombs, I really don't know.

The boys went off to play golf in the afternoon and I went to the gym.

After the excesses of last night, I didn't think I would be up to much, but I ended up in a nightclub and was still there when the club closed at 4.30am.

Monday 9 September

Today was our last day of flying with the G-91 boys, and it was a memorable one. We planned a 10-ship attack on an airfield in the south of Portugal. Sqn Ldr Froggart came up with a great plan that had the Jaguars simultaneously targeting the airfield's radar and surface-to-air missile sites. It must have been great to watch from the ground: four jets at high speed over different parts of the airfield.

I had the added delight of having a large blue whale painted on to the side of my aircraft. There is a rumour doing the rounds that I have carnal knowledge of the rotund female admin officer. Typically, the engineers know all the dirt on everyone, but in this case, it just isn't true. Not that the truth ever stops them.

Tuesday 10 September

I have had a day of minor faults, which meant that getting back to the UK was a real struggle. I was scheduled to fly as the wingman of Sqn Ldr Froggart, but his jet had a defect that took a few hours to repair. One of the other Jaguars also developed a fuel leak when it started its engines, so the pilot took my jet since I was stuck waiting for Sqn Ldr Froggart anyway. Then the engineers discovered that the fuel leak was a punctured external tank that they could not repair and would limit our range. This meant that we had to have an extra refuelling stop in Porto. On landing in Porto, I had another problem, this time with the aircraft's oxygen system, which limited our cruise height. Then as we got airborne, my navigation computer failed and shortly after that, so did my head-up display. Great. I had to follow Dave Froggart back to Coltishall and use the secondary instruments to fly the aircraft. Not a problem, just lots more hassle.

Wednesday 11 September

This morning, I was an errand boy. Did the shopping for the tea bar and got some flowers for the grave of the pilot who died during the work up to the Gulf War. He is buried in a small cemetery at the end of the main runway at RAF Coltishall, and he is the second pilot to be buried there in the last two years. Very sad and very sobering, as there are only about 50 pilots on the base at any one time.

I got back on the squadron just in time to be included in a bounced four-ship trip, which was being led by Andy Cubin as part of his combat-ready work up. He is already an experienced Jaguar pilot, so it was really a formality for him.

At the end of the working day, there was a mad rush to get some clothes packed, as I was being sent on a weapons employment course at the RAF College Cranwell with Ted Stringer and Stu Richardson. Stu is another experienced pilot from 41 squadron.

We travelled down to RAF Cranwell in flying suits and went straight to the bar where we were almost immediately told that we were incorrectly dressed. Cranwell is where all RAF officers are trained and I had forgotten how much etiquette matters here.

Ted and Stu merely ignored our first warning and stayed in the bar. As a junior officer, I followed their lead. We didn't leave the bar until a senior officer with wings on his chest suggested that to stop any further trouble we had better get changed out of flying suits. We did get changed, but headed out to a local pub for the evening instead. Whilst there we met a very interesting man called Nev.

Nev is in the process of transferring into the Royal Air Force from the old Rhodesian Air Force. He has been in the country only a few months having spent the last two years in solitary confinement. He was accused of blowing up several jet aircraft by the Zimbabwean government. He was the prime suspect, having spent several years as a Rhodesian SAS trooper before becoming a fighter pilot.

Saturday 14 September

I finished the weapon employment course yesterday and learnt a lot about effective targeting. I consider myself very lucky to have been sent on the course given that most of the other participants had flown on the front line for at least three years.

Today, though, I spent most of my time trying to weld my car, the trusty Alpha Romeo Sud, back together so it had a chance of passing its annual roadworthiness test. One of the sergeant engineers is helping me. My car is great mechanically, but it is an Italian design and the body is rusting away rapidly.

Tuesday 17 September

I got into work this morning to be told I was being sent to Denmark to work with 6 squadron for the rest of the week. They are taking part in a big exercise and a couple of their pilots have fallen sick. I had to rush home to get some clothes, then a quick flight plan to get into Danish airspace and off I launched.

On landing, I was told that I had just missed the weekend of a lifetime. 6 squadron is working from an airfield called Tirstrup, which is a Danish base with hardened aircraft shelters to protect any jets based there. There wasn't enough accommodation for the pilots on the base and they were accommodated at a nearby holiday camp – because it is off-season the rates there are very low. Last week, they had the place all to themselves, but at the weekend the holiday camp held a female softball competition. The place was full of tall, young, athletic Scandinavian women. The married men on 6 squadron were afraid to leave their rooms, and a few of the single guys were dragged off and abused. I can't believe I spent the weekend welding my car. Things like this only happen once in a blue moon.

Friday 20 September

The rest of the week has been very busy. I flew some forward close air support trips for the Danish army and a few low-level attack missions with Danish F-16s attacking and defending us. It is the first time I have encountered the F-16 operationally, and I have to say I am jealous. They can do everything a Jaguar can, and a whole lot more. Their performance is just awesome, and I have learnt never to get into a turning fight with them.

Working from a hardened aircraft shelter site has been a new experience. We had the use of an underground operations and planning building and would only leave it to go straight to our aircraft in their individual shelters. All our targets and tasking for the exercise were sent over a secure telex printer from headquarters somewhere else in Europe.

Thursday 3 October

I have been a bit tardy writing my diary for the last week, but nothing unusual has happened. I spent some time at RAF Coningsby flying air-to-air combat with the Tornado F3s. That has been very useful as I now have a greater understanding of how radar-equipped aircraft go about their business. The F3 is difficult to fight against in air-to-air combat, but it isn't a patch on the F-16s that I fought against a few weeks ago.

Anyway, today I had another emergency in the Jaguar. I was fighting one vs one against the boss of 41 squadron and was in a T2 aircraft with a young pilot, who is waiting for his basic flying course, sitting in the back. During the last engagement, I was flying the jet at the edge of its performance to try to get a missile shot, and I lost control. The aircraft flicked into the vertical, and I found myself pointing straight up with a rapidly reducing airspeed and both engines surging. As I was taught on the conversion course, I closed the throttles to stop the surges and centralised the controls to stop any further loss of control. However, now the jet had no thrust and was pointing straight up. The airspeed reduced rapidly and then, unbelievably, we started to fall backwards. Like most jets, the Jaguar isn't designed to fly backwards, and it was making some very disturbing noises as it fell. Fortunately, it quickly fell on to its back from where I could get it back under control, only to find that one of the engines had temperature readings that were off the scale. It was cooking, so I had to shut it down. At that point, Wg Cmdr Pixton, as cool as you like, asked over the radio, "Are you having fun down there?"

I told him I had lost an engine and he just said, "Okay, I'll see you back at base."

He left me to get on with it. I have had lots of practice flying single-engine approaches and dealing with emergencies and didn't need my hand to be held. The young lad in the back seat thought the whole thing was great, and had no idea how close we had come to not being able to recover the aircraft and ejecting. He said that at no time did I sound stressed and that was why he wasn't worried.

When I got back on to the ground, I had to explain what had happened to Wg Cmdr Pixton and the squadron duty pilot, Flt Lt Rob Last. Rob is the weapons instructor on 41 squadron and one of the senior flight lieutenants. He summed up the events as 'growing pains' and Bill Pixton just smiled. I seemed to be the only person to be at all disturbed by how close I had come to losing one of Her Majesty's aircraft.

Even with the emergency today, I am getting more confident with the machine. The exposure to all the different situations over the last few months has been very good. I don't have any doubts that I will achieve combat-ready status. What I doubt, is that I will ever get to the stage that I land after an hour and half of low-level and think that was effortless. I enjoy my flying, but most of the time I am working hard and almost at full capacity. I am no longer afraid of failing, but I am terrified of letting any of the boys down.

Friday 11 October

During the last week, I have flown one trip every day and these have been a mix of range trips and paired low-level trips, and I am getting the hang of leading and controlling a pair of aircraft.

I haven't been writing my diary very much as nothing of note has happened, and I have been working on a speech. Adrian Bonwitt, from my old basic flying course, is getting married this weekend and I am going to be his best man. He is flying the Tornado GR1 and is based 30 miles away at RAF Marham.

Today, as part of my best man duties, I had to collect and take him to his parents' house north of London, with the intention of delivering him to the wedding tomorrow. I got away from work at lunchtime changed into jeans and a shirt, and made my way over to Marham. Adrian is still living at the officers' mess and when I arrived, it was obvious that the mess staff were busy preparing for some special occasion. I used the internal phone to tell Adrian I had arrived and was waiting for him in a corner of the reception. I had been there only for a minute when a harassed looking young corporal came up to me and said, "Deliveries round the back, mate."

It took me a second to realise what he was implying, so I smiled at him and replied, "I think you will find it is, Deliveries Round the Back, Sir!"

The poor lad looked shocked and then did a very good impression of a fish before scuttling off without another word. They obviously don't have any black officers at RAF Marham. Adrian and I both thought that the whole thing was comical. Marham is very close to one of the Queen's main residences, and they were expecting a royal visit over the weekend, hence the hassled and confused corporal. Maybe I should dress in a jacket and tie every time I visit an officers' mess, just to be taken seriously. Then again, maybe not.

At Adrian's parents, we discovered that Verity, his bride to be, had left us two beers in the fridge. I think she expected us to have a quiet night in, so naturally, I dragged Adrian down into the local town, poured lots of beer down his neck and tried to get him to change his mind.

Saturday 12 October

I failed to get Adrian to reconsider, and I had to go through with all the best man's duties. All the military men were in no. 1 uniforms with gloves and swords and we composed the traditional archway of swords for the newlyweds as they left the church.

I managed not to drop the rings despite all the banter from several of my old course mates. It was then very busy organising people for the wedding photos and getting the military boys out of the local pub for the evening events. The speech went surprisingly well and it was a great day. Nevertheless, it is the sort of event that would have been better with a girlfriend in tow.

Wednesday 16 October

I was programmed to be flying a low-level trip today, but the weather was shockingly bad. I eventually got airborne by myself to practise my instrument flying and a bit of general handling.

Shaun and Dieter have been on an exercise over in Germany and have had fun over there.

Last week, Shaun somehow managed to shut down both engines while still on the taxiway. As he was restarting them, he had flames shooting from the exhaust of his number two engine. On the radio, he heard Dieter saying, "Hey, Shaun! You are on fire, fire in your number two! Hit that fire extinguisher, I want to see that baby go!"

Mad, Mad German!

Tuesday 22 October

Wg Cmdr Pixton discovered today that the reason his leg has been hurting for the last month is because it is broken. Not sure how the doctors could have missed that. They were supposed to have given him a full medical after his ejection.

I had another hard-working day including a four-ship range trip in the morning. Dieter Knorr is definitely mad, and I am sure of that now. I am going to be very circumspect in following him anywhere from now on. He almost flew into me today and then said over the radio, "Hey, Trevor! I bet that scared you. Yah!" Crazy German.

The afternoon had me airborne again as part of another one of those big multi-aircraft missions: Jaguars from RAF Coltishall accompanied by F4 Phantoms from RAF Wattisham. Our target was RAF Coningsby, which is a Tornado F3 base – and the F3s were doing their best to protect their home base.

I managed to follow most of the radio calls and keep a mental model of what was going on, as well as doing my job to a reasonable standard. It is mightily impressive how the formation leader manages to keep track and direct the various elements at low level. It is going to take me years to get to that standard.

During the debrief, it became apparent that we had some excellent results. The Phantoms had managed to keep the Tornados occupied long enough for the Jaguars to get some very good hits on their base. If it were a real operation, the Tornado F3s would have landed to find most of the base infrastructure seriously damaged.

I am going to try to get on a few more of these complex multi-formation sorties, because that is how real-world operations are carried out. 54 squadron is flying similar multi-aircraft missions into north Iraq, involving 60-plus aircraft. They are still enforcing the no-fly zone that has been created to protect the Iraqi Kurds from Saddam Hussein.

November 1991

I managed to convince Sqn Ldr Froggart to give me the whole of November off, and went to Australia via Los Angeles. My university friend, Louise, had married an American actor and was living in Santa Monica, and another university couple, Cathy and Greg, were out in Brisbane. I needed the break.

Tuesday 3 December

It is my second day back from holiday and my first day flying. I am finally back with 54 squadron, as they have returned from Turkey with lots of tales of derring-do. After such a long break, I needed a flying instructor's check, so I launched in the morning with Andy Cubin to demonstrate my proficiency. He was happy with my efforts, so I was given a jet to play with by myself in the afternoon. It is great to get back flying again, and I don't seem to have lost my ability.

Friday 6 December

I have done so well this week that the boss has put me up for my combat-ready check. The planning went well, but we got out to the runway and found that the bounce aircraft was broken, with no spare available. I took off anyway to lead an un-bounced pair around the low-level route. No challenge and no combat-ready.

Unfortunately, that was most of the flying for December. The whole station was on a wind down to Christmas and the boys on 54 were also on a wind down after all the operational flying they had done in north Iraq. My combat-ready check had to wait until January.

1992 54 Squadron

Monday 6 January

Back after an extended Christmas break, my lack of flying over the last two months showed. I was a little rusty this morning on a solo general handling trip and this afternoon, I planned to lead a low-level trip, but unfortunately, one of my engines had a surge on the runway, so I aborted the take-off and taxied back to the squadron. Headed off to the gym to work off some of the Christmas excesses instead.

Tuesday 7 January

Today was a surprisingly busy day. I was in early to plan a two-ship low-level trip against two F3s. The trip went well although the weather was very poor at low level. So poor that we never even saw the F3s, but from our radar warning receivers we knew they were looking and shooting at us. It was a good refresher for all my radar missile evasion techniques. I have noticed that I no longer have to think about flying the aircraft. By that, I mean the actual go up or down, left or right and fast or slow bits. It all seems to happen at a subconscious level. All my capacity is taken up spotting the bounce or any ground threats, keeping track of my wingman or leader, moving switches to get bombs off the aircraft or fire missiles and numerous other bits of management.

Spent the afternoon revising air-to-air refuelling, as I have my first attempt at that tomorrow.

Wednesday 8 January

Leaving flying training and joining 54 squadron has been very much like leaving university and starting out at work for the first time. There are only a few young guys around. The majority of the pilots are married with children and there is very little unrestrained student type behaviour.

I have been getting more comfortable in the low-level environment in small increments day by day and so far, I haven't encountered any flying techniques dramatically different to what I had been taught in flying training. Today, was very different, as I have been air-to-air tanking for the first time, a controlled collision with another aircraft at 300mph.

This morning, I was airborne in a T2 with Steve Shutt in the back seat. Steve and David Foote are the other qualified flying instructors on 54 squadron and they are both Gulf War veterans. We went out over the North Sea and rendezvoused with a VC10 tanker. Steve talked me through the airborne procedures and showed me the visual picture I needed to get a successful contact. Only the single seat Jaguar GR1 has a refuelling probe, so this trip was very much a 'look see'. I can understand why they call this stuff 'jousting'.

Airborne again in the afternoon for the real thing, and again over the North Sea and flying up to a VC10, but this time I had Dave Foote accompanying me in another Jaguar. He was there to offer advice in case I struggled. Slowly, slowly is the name of the game. I got my fuel and then watched Dave Foote cruise up to the basket, connect and get his fuel without any fuss. On my attempts, I had been jousting with the basket for a good 10 minutes before I managed to make a good contact.

We then left the tanker and headed off for someone vs one combat. I must be getting better, as I wasn't beaten on any of the engagements.

I had forgotten how much concentration is required when learning a new skill, and was very weary by the time we landed.

Monday 13 January

It has been a week of tanking, and I was up again this morning as part of a three-ship with Nick Connor and our Danish exchange officer Ole Nygaard. We were tanking from a Victor, and it is the first time I have seen one of these in the air. They are 30 years old, but still look amazingly futuristic. I have been getting better and my first three practice contacts were faultless, then I started to get cocky and had a good five minutes jousting before the fourth contact. That wasn't good, with two colleagues watching.

I heard a scary tanking story this afternoon. One of the rules we are taught is that when using one of the wing pods on the tanker aircraft, we should never get high enough to see the top of the wing, as it would put the jet into the wake vortex of the tanker – the tankers are invariably large transport aircraft that have a very strong wake vortex. A member of 6 squadron discovered this fact last month. He got himself high on the wing of a VC10 and into the wake vortex. This vortex was so powerful that it tossed his Jaguar right over the tail of the tanker. He says that he was upside down out of control, looking on to the top of the VC10's tail and was so close that he could clearly read NO STEP in red letters. When he got control of his aircraft he immediately headed home, and I don't think the VC10 boys have got any idea how close they came to a mid-air collision – from which they would not have survived.

The RAF employed three types of aircraft in the tanking role in the 1990s. The VC10, which is a converted 1960s passenger aircraft; the Victor, which is a converted nuclear bomber and the Tristar, which is a big, modern converted passenger aircraft.

Wednesday 15 January

I was late into work this morning, and I missed met brief. My day didn't improve after that. I launched to the tanker with one of the station wing commanders leading. The tanker today was the Tristar, and I had real problems getting into the basket initially, but eventually managed to figure out what was wrong.

When the probe is deployed, it causes the aircraft to fly a little bit sideways, and I had forgotten to correct for this. If I had taken my time and done everything nice and slowly, I have no doubt there would not have been a problem.

Later in the afternoon, I had to go and see the wing commander, who accused me of destroying the basket on the tanker. The Tristar crew had discovered some damage when they landed and were telling everyone who had made contact with that basket, in case their aircraft had any damage. The wing commander was convinced that I was the cause, although another six aircraft used the same basket after us. I didn't argue, but I think he is a GIT.

Tried to tell my sad tale to Andy Cubin, but got no sympathy. Cubes is distracted as he has got a new girlfriend and is smitten at the moment. She is a model and Cubes says he was having phone sex with her for a month before they met. He won't say how he got hold of her telephone number.

Tuesday 21 January

I was in early for another one of those mega, multi-aircraft, low-level attack formations. It contained only four Jaguars but was also joined by four Tornado GR1s, with our defence provided by four Phantom F4s. All these aircraft were attacking RAF Leuchars, which is a Tornado F3 base in the south east of Scotland, and they were hoping to have 20 F3s in the air defending their base.

The plan was very complicated, requiring a lot of co-ordination from all the attacking aircraft, as they were getting airborne from different airfields, flying up the North Sea to attack Leuchars and then landing at RAF Lossiemouth. The afternoon saw the route in reverse, south from Lossiemouth and again attacking Leuchars. For the first time in one of these complicated missions, I was given the number two position, which meant I was involved in all the aspects of the plan.

As we got airborne, the Jaguar formation leader Andy Sudlow had a problem with his aircraft and had to return to base. I was now the Jaguar leader in charge of controlling the co-ordination between the Tornado GR1s and the F4 Phantoms. Uh oh!

The route north went very well, helped by the majority of the F3s not being in a position to threaten the ground-attack aircraft. Our F4 Phantom protectors kept the few F3s that were airborne and in a good position very busy.

The trip south was much better in that respect. I don't think we would have come anywhere near Leuchars in real life. The attacking aircraft spent a lot of time trying to break missile lock from some very valid F3 shots. A senior officer at Leuchars had made some very unflattering comments about their performance in the morning.

To my surprise, I didn't have any difficulty in leading the Jaguars and even had enough capacity to follow most of the engagements. I might be better at this fighter pilot stuff than I thought. But I still find it difficult debriefing the trips.

During flying training, the debrief would consist of the instructor telling the student where they went wrong and what they needed to improve on the next flight. Today, I had to stand up in front of an Iraq war veteran and the squadron's weapons instructor and confess to my mistakes and then ask them to explain their failings. I still find doing this a bit intimidating with the senior pilots. I work hard to lead formations and minimise my errors and I know they are operating with lots of spare capacity and will have spotted many of my mistakes. It is another reason to be totally honest in the debrief.

Fell into bed mentally and physically exhausted.

Wednesday 22 January

There was another first for me today, firing at a target being dragged at high speed by a Royal Navy warship. This is known as splash firing for obvious reasons. Four aircraft headed to the south coast and the English Channel where we found HMS Norfolk towing the splash target. We simulated a few high-speed low-level bombing attacks, so they could practise using their defensive missile and gun systems and then we had fun trying to destroy the splash target with high explosive bullets. It wasn't as easy as I expected, mainly because the target was moving at 30mph. All the strafe targets we practise against are stationary. Still great fun.

On our weapons ranges we used ball ammunition. This is a solid bullet, which passes through the canvas targets and is scored acoustically. We could not use high explosive ammunition on ranges, as the targets would be destroyed after just a few hits.

What wasn't as much fun was my second near-death experience in two days. Yesterday, on the way back from RAF Lossiemouth, I nearly collided with another Jaguar while trying to evade a missile shot from a Tornado F3. That was debriefed as being just unlucky. The other Jaguar was being flown by the boss of 6 squadron and was on a totally separate low-level flight.

Today, I nearly collided with a little civilian Cessna aircraft that I didn't spot until very late. I had to push and roll my aircraft to get below and avoid him, and have a very vivid memory of seeing the grooved pattern on his landing gear wheels as they passed over the canopy. Too close…

Tuesday 28 January

I was supposed to have my long overdue combat-ready check this morning, but the met man got his weather prediction totally wrong. Again. There was a thick fog layer over most of the country, so low-level flying was not going to happen.

Instead got airborne on a two vs one air-to-air combat trip with Sqn Ldr McDonald, fighting against Andy Cubin. There were military aircraft everywhere trying to do the same thing, but we eventually found a clear spot for our combat. Sqn Ldr McDonald managed to stay out of the fight for a very long time and then when he did rejoin, he somehow managed to fly nicely into the 12 o'clock position directly ahead of Cubes who promptly shot him. A beautiful manoeuvre and I couldn't stop laughing, especially as he had been giving me a hard time about my positioning shortly before. Cubes had fun in the debrief about that.

Monday 3 February

I was programmed for my combat ready-check again today. So foggy all day and no flying. No! I am lying. It was a beautiful blue-sky day with great visibility. My check was a straightforward low-level pair with a Jaguar bounce. I had to lead the pair with the boss, Wg Cdr Hewlett, on the wing and Sqn Ldr McDonald as the bounce. Before getting into the low-level bit of the sortie, we went to the range to drop a practice bomb. My bomb was a direct hit, which was a great way to start.

The rest of the trip went very well. I got to the target, didn't have any screw ups and kept the boss from getting shot by the bounce. I even managed not to get fazed in the debrief.

The boss then shook my hand and said, "Well done, Trevor, you only have one more thing to pass."

That was the operations pot. I was escorted to the bar after work by all the pilots and presented with the pot. It looked very suspiciously like the arrival jug I had to drink back in May last year. The rules were that once it touched my lips, it wasn't allowed to be removed until all the contents were drunk. There was no way I was going to stumble at the last hurdle.

I haven't stopped smiling since I landed in the morning, and after the drinks in the bar I headed off to Norwich to party seriously. I am a Fully Qualified, Combat-Ready, Fighter Pilot in the Royal Air Force, and the boss has given me tomorrow off.

So after three years of flying training and almost ten months on 54 squadron, I am an operational fast jet pilot in the Royal Air Force. Flying the Jaguar accurately at low level has become as natural as walking. I am qualified to take part in any war mission, can hold my own (against another Jaguar) in air-to-air combat and am even competent at flying reconnaissance missions using the recce pod. I have had my first squadron assessment and have been classified as, AVERAGE. I couldn't be happier.

Thanks to,

Shirley, whose idea it was to write a diary.

Nick and Izzy, for getting me started and all the technical help.

Gary and Sue, for their constant encouragement.

And Katie.